PRAISE FOR *THE ENERGI*

'Perry Timms inspired me again! *The Energized Workplace* challenges the new world of work by proposing non-traditional HR/OD solutions and unconventional models, along with practical case studies. His concepts will definitely support the wellbeing of employees as well as help leaders and colleagues gain a better understanding of how to harness employees' energies in the workplace.'
Marguerite A Ulrich, Founder and Chief Inspiration Officer, Inspire HR Consulting

'I felt thoroughly nourished having read Perry Timms' book. It's thought-provoking, progressive and gives you the space to think about what the future of work has in store for us and the potential impact that not taking care of our energy will have in this era of "peak work". In his unique style, he talks about how the "dirty energy" will slow us down and how natural energy will lead us to flourish. If you're someone who wants to understand how to better manage your energy in the modern world of work, this book is for you.'
Natasha Wallace, Founder, Conscious Works, and author of *The Conscious Effect*

'At a time when the world is facing unprecedented challenges, Perry Timms brings the strategy and focus to recreate our organizations anew. *The Energized Workplace* offers a blueprint for how the workplace should be – not in the future, but NOW! This is no run-of-the-mill book – it really will leave you energized and ready to bring your full self to work and help those around you achieve the same. A must-read for anyone fed up with the status quo!'
Miranda Ash, Chief of Community and Transformation Expert, WorldBlu

'*The Energized Workplace* is a book the world of work needs more than ever. Through a rich and considered blend of research, case studies and evident soul searching, Perry Timms holds a mirror up to the design flaws and leadership foibles that continue to plague people and organizations, and boldly lays out a blueprint for us to reinvent work with energy, engagement and eudaimonia as a source of superpower.'
Rob Baker, Chief Positive Deviant and Founder of Tailored Thinking, and author of *Personalization at Work*

'Making positive change happens best from a place of understanding. In *The Energized Workplace*, Perry Timms helps us to understand the energy (or lack of!) in organizations, identifying approaches we can all take to design better experiences, raise energy levels and maximize engagement. A stunning read that takes you on a real journey of discovery about organizations, about energy and about yourself.'
Joanna Suvarna, Learning and Development Specialist

The Energized Workplace

Designing organizations where people flourish

Perry Timms

Publisher's note

Every possible effort has been made to ensure that the information contained in this book is accurate at the time of going to press, and the publishers and author cannot accept responsibility for any errors or omissions, however caused. No responsibility for loss or damage occasioned to any person acting, or refraining from action, as a result of the material in this publication can be accepted by the editor, the publisher or the author.

First published in Great Britain and the United States in 2020 by Kogan Page Limited

Apart from any fair dealing for the purposes of research or private study, or criticism or review, as permitted under the Copyright, Designs and Patents Act 1988, this publication may only be reproduced, stored or transmitted, in any form or by any means, with the prior permission in writing of the publishers, or in the case of reprographic reproduction in accordance with the terms and licences issued by the CLA. Enquiries concerning reproduction outside these terms should be sent to the publishers at the undermentioned addresses:

2nd Floor, 45 Gee Street	122 W 27th St, 10th Floor	4737/23 Ansari Road
London	New York, NY 10001	Daryaganj
EC1V 3RS	USA	New Delhi 110002
United Kingdom		India

www.koganpage.com

Kogan Page books are printed on paper from sustainable forests.

© Perry Timms, 2020

The right of Perry Timms to be identified as the author of this work has been asserted by him in accordance with the Copyright, Designs and Patents Act 1988.

ISBNs

Hardback   978 1 78966 107 1
Paperback   978 0 7494 9866 5
Ebook   978 0 7494 9867 2

British Library Cataloguing-in-Publication Data

A CIP record for this book is available from the British Library.

Library of Congress Cataloging-in-Publication Data
Names: Timms, Perry, author.
Title: The energized workplace : designing organizations where people flourish / Perry Timms.
Description: 1 Edition. | New York : Kogan Page Inc, 2020. | Includes bibliographical references and index.
Identifiers: LCCN 2020011649 (print) | LCCN 2020011650 (ebook) | ISBN 9780749498665 (paperback) | ISBN 9781789661071 (hardback) | ISBN 9780749498672 (ebook)
Subjects: LCSH: Organizational change. | Work environment. | Personnel management. | Organizational effectiveness.
Classification: LCC HD58.8 .T56 62020 (print) | LCC HD58.8 (ebook) | DDC 658.3/14–dc23
LC record available at https://lccn.loc.gov/2020011649
LC ebook record available at https://lccn.loc.gov/2020011650

Typeset by Integra Software Services, Pondicherry
Print Managed by Jellyfish Solutions

CONTENTS

Foreword by Trish Uhl ix
Acknowledgments xiii

Introduction 1

01 2050 voyaging 11

    What will work even be in 2050? 12
    Utopian or protopian? 18
    Endnotes 20

02 20th-century design flaws 21

    A psychological theory of human evolution 21
    How we feel about the systems of work 23
    Knowing the history of work – a personal story 25
    Organization development – a discipline most powerful 26
    From flawed design to designing from the 'floor-up' 28
    From mechanics to heuristics 32
    Endnotes 37

03 80/20 variances 39

    We all know Pareto's rule – or do we? 40
    Who am I and what am I here for? 43
    80/20 and the *What's Going On* factor 47
    More than numbers 49
    Values are an energy source and indeed a manifestation of our energies 52
    Endnotes 54

04 1/20 or a 20 per cent probability 55

    Introduction – a stress pandemic 56

Who is to blame? 57
Use of energy/depletion of energy at work 58
Psychological and physiological energy 63
Energy management not time management 66
A safe workplace 67
Endnotes 73

05 The 5 x 20 life and the redesign of age 77

Introduction – happy 200th birthday! 79
The three-stage model of now 80
What is the five-stage model of the future? 81
An additional dimension: eudaimonia as a business model 84
Economics and a regenerative model 88
Conclusion 90
Endnotes 92

06 20:20 vision 95

Overview 96
Work/life balance 97
So what is human energy and its connection to nature? 102
From Eastern wisdom to the Western psychological and physics approach 103
The Jungian opera 104
Modern physics 105
Energy in 'alternative' medicine 106
Spirituality 107
The Chakra System 109
Chakras and HR – a PhD thesis 115
In summary 119
Endnotes 123

07 The 20 misuses of energy in the workplace 127

Misuses #1–5: cult workplaces 128
Misuses #6–10: scare-ups 134
Misuses #11–15: faux trendy 138
Misuses #16–20: living museums 142
Endnotes 147

08 The 2020 list of energized workplaces 151

Self-managed organizations 152
Rewarding organizations 154
Open value organizations 157
Personal growth-focused organizations 159
Well-being organizations 162
In summary 163
Endnotes 164

09 20 minutes per day to energize yourself 167

NQ element 1: SO – source energy 168
NQ element 2: SU – sustainable energy 170
NQ element 3: IN – introspective energy 174
NQ element 4: PL – self-system interplay 175
NQ element 5: PU – purpose: yours and the organization's 176
NQ element 6: PR – the promise (aka the deal) between employee and employer 177
NQ element 7: FL – flow, deep work and understanding your optimized self 178
NQ element 8: VA – variety: the spice of life or a life of space? 181
NQ elements 9–12: The Edge – DI (Discovery), RE (Relationships), LE (Learning), and IN (Innovation) 183
In summary 185
Endnotes 186

10 Tools for the next 20 years 189

What is organization design? 190
The writing on the wall story 194
Your story 196
Our organization design process for a eudaimonic business model 204
In closing 204
Endnotes 208

Index 209

FOREWORD

Please take responsibility for the energy you bring into this space.
JILL BOLTE TAYLOR

Some days it can feel as if we are here to watch the world burn.

This moment in our shared human history, caught up in the volatility of the coronavirus pandemic, isolation, economic crisis, geopolitical uncertainty, social injustice and civil unrest, has shaken some of us to our core, making us feel vulnerable, even helpless, as we re-examine our once-familiar constructs of job, work, home, family, community and relationships.

Take heart!

In this book Perry Timms offers respite, relief and leadership via a framework and toolkit to use this fertile ground as the catalyst for transmutation and positive whole-system change.

As these powerful forces have stripped our organizations out of the status quo, stirred us from our reverie, jolted us awake, displaced our habits and parted us from our automated routines, we have the opportunity to rally, to seize this moment and capitalize on this momentum to transcend what no longer serves and metamorphosize into something new.

What you hold in your hands sets forth a grand vision and a plan.

What might this transmutation and metamorphosis look like?

Who might you become?

How might we, together, create a world that works better?

As we move to reopening and recovery, Perry Timms provides a roadmap, with his signature earnestness and passionate style, for how we can reunite around a shared sense of purpose; reignite our imaginations; realign work and our organizations to more humane and sustainable goals, such as the triple bottom line of harmonizing outcomes across people, planet, profits; and ultimately rebuild so we reemerge better, stronger, happier and healthier.

We are capable. We have it within us.

We can transcend current conditions, make positive impact, extend our reach, make meaningful contributions and create positive change!

Begin by revisiting the basics:

What is the purpose of organizations?

What is the role of organizations in modern society?

What *now* is the meaning of work?

Positive organizations have proved vital to our need for human contact, connection and social interaction, especially during this period of extended separation from friends and family. Our institutions have served in some respects as surrogates, providing us with shared purpose, a place to gather – to get along, belong, congregate, cooperate, collaborate and 'organize' – combining and amplifying our collective efforts, strengths, talents, synergies, energies and contributions towards a common set of goals.

We are also seeing more organizations focusing on positive societal impact. In fact, how organizations have navigated this intense period has greatly influenced our perceptions of and relationships with the brands we interact with, as employees, customers, clients and consumers. I think it is safe to assume we have all taken note of those brands who have (and have not) shown up to authentically serve people, the community and the greater good.

In a post Covid-19 world, trust, transparency and reputation matter more than ever. How does your organization stack up?

How might you draw from your personal experience of various brands to better lead your organization's internal and external positive people impact?

Work itself has shone a hot spotlight on our deep reliance on the work of healthcare and other essential workers to operate the public systems that support our survival. It is the essential workers' work that primarily provides our basic physical needs of shelter, food, clothing and care.

How might these observations change how you restructure work?

Between Zoom Zombies and double shifts, people are burning out.

How will you re-engineer their work beyond a means of survival to something more meaningful?

What if that became standard post-pandemic practice – if we took our and others' work beyond survival and reached for more?

What if we leveraged these challenging times to co-create organizations and work for inspiration and aspiration?

What kind of world would it be?

This gets to the heart of Perry Timms' work in guiding HR professionals in exploring, experimenting with and applying real-world practices and principles, drawn from positive psychology, to elevate the nature of work, accelerate organizational agility and effectiveness and improve the health and well-being of people.

Imagine – our and others' work lives contributing to a 'meaningful life'; lives made richer, more robust and vibrant infused with positive emotion by, as pioneer Dr Martin Seligman said of the meaningful life, 'belonging and contributing to something greater than ourselves'.

What could our world be with whole humans contributing wholeheartedly?

> *Your work is to discover your work, and then with all your heart give yourself to it.*   BUDDHA

How about you? Are you ready to engage wholeheartedly?

Facilitating these seismic and systemic shifts takes courage, commitment and coherence.

How will you commit your head, hands and heart to your work and your practice?

If you're curious and eager, you're in the right place as you prepare to journey with Perry in the following pages!

That said, I'd like to equip you with a brief activity to help you get underway.

It's an exercise practiced by Olympic athletes from all over the world. This exercise helps these high-calibre athletes to clear their minds, get present, raise their energy, improve their coherence and their mood as they prepare to perform at their highest.

You too might find this exercise helpful in enhancing your own performance.

Ready?

Here's what to do:

Be seated. Check in with yourself – how do you feel?

Rate your emotional state on a scale from 1 (overwhelmed, anxious) to 10 (joyful, exhilarated).

Place your right hand over your heart. Bring to mind someone or something you are most grateful for.

Got it? Feel the flood of gratitude and positive emotion paired with the sensation of the beating of your heart.

Now modify your breathing. Slowly inhale for a count of 4. Gradually exhale for a count of 5. Repeat.

Maintain that rhythmic breathing for a full 60 seconds while keeping your feeling of gratitude top of mind and staying attuned to your heart beating under the palm of your hand.

Close your eyes.

After a minute, as you breathe out for your last long exhale, picture pushing gratitude with your breath straight through your hand and into your heart.

Stay still for a moment, then open your eyes.

Check in with yourself – how do you feel? Has your emotional state moved higher up the scale?

Keep experimenting – with energy!

From my heart, home, family – to you and yours,
Stay safe. Be well. Remember – we are #InThisTogether
Trish Uhl
President, Owl's Lodge LLC
@trishuhl

ACKNOWLEDGEMENTS

This book is dedicated to my Mum, Rita June Timms, who sadly and peacefully passed away on 23 April 2020, as this book was in its final stages of printing and production.

All the energy for all I have in the world came about because of her tireless dedication to me as her son, and the guidance and care bestowed upon me throughout her life and with that of my Dad, Terry. I am who I am because of them both.

I would also like to thank with all my heart my wife Teresa. For over 30 years we've been through the ups and downs of life together. In 2006, she was diagnosed with multiple sclerosis, an energy-zapping condition that impairs abilities through a misfiring of the central nervous and immune systems. That she is dedicated to supporting me in my endeavours in life, despite this terrible condition, is a testament to her energy, determination and love for the life we've created together.

I would also like to thank the team of people who have come together under the PTHR banner for creating our purpose in work, *Better business, for a better world*: Broch Cleminson, Catalina Contoloru, Crystal Castillo, Jessica Bailey, Emily Woolgar, and Kirsten Buck.

Broch, in particular, helped me craft the TEDx talk – The Edge – which gave life to this book, and Kirsten with her input to various chapters throughout this book. And thank you to Kogan Page for again believing in me and the team of committed people who made this idea into the book you have in front of you.

I would like to thank Laura La Barbera for her work in shaping particularly Chapter 6 and her extensive knowledge of the human energy map that is the Chakras. Laura was vital in helping me shape the later chapters and whilst our collaboration was a brief one, it was a monumentally helpful one and your mark in the world will always be within this work.

ACKNOWLEDGEMENTS

I thanked a cast of many in my previous book, *Transformational HR*, and there are still lots of generous, supportive and smart people who deserve a mention:

C-J Green, Barbara Thompson, Damiana Casile, Garry Dickson, Neil Usher, Su Sehmer, Katie Marlow, Shakil Butt, Gethin Nadin, Garry Turner, Natasha Wallace, Rob Baker, Miranda Ash, Aimee Cassidy, Erik Korsvik Ostergaard, Barry Flack, Frank Douglas, Tim Littlehales, Louise Ash, Nilofer Merchant, Trish Uhl, Robert Ordever, Samantha Betts, Emma Browes, Chris Wade, Peter Reeve, Alison Williams, Shaun Rickard, Lynn Demeda, Kim Atherton, Martin Baker, Matt Manners, Matteo Violi, Alessia Mivoli, Massimilano Riccardi, Ana Gabrscek, Natasa Tovornik, Laura Smrekar, Matic Vosnjak, Tina Novak Kac, Meg Peppin, Louisa Scanlan, Joanna Suvarna, Jenny Streeter, Siobhan Sheridan, Tim Pointer, Julian Summerhayes, Dr Steve Marshall, Chris Furnell, David James, Rowena James, Gaylin Jee, Nathan Ott, Jaana Nyford, Traci Fenton, Mervyn Dinnen, Angela O'Connor, Katharine Gourley, Dr Judy Lundy, Jacqui Findlay, Joanna Bojarska-Buchic, Selena Govier, Denise Sanderson-Estcourt, Rob Neil OBE, Peter Cheese, Andy Lancaster, Michelle Parry-Slater, Steve George, Simon Lancaster, Ian Pettigrew, Julie Griggs, Lynne Booth, Paul Taylor-Pitt, Matt Ash, Duncan Ledger, Lesley Giles, Rebecca Webber, Naeema Pasha, Maddy Woodman, Jenny Andersson, Henry Stewart, Annette Jensen, Matthew Gonnering, Matt Perez, Tamasin Sutton, Lucy Dodd, Niall Gavin, Michelle Harte, Lara Plaxton, Helena Clayton, Ed Griffin, Kev Wyke, Jayne Harrison, Steve Browne, Paul Duxbury, Tony Jackson, Jacqueline Davies, Nicole Ferguson, Karen Beaven, Nebel Crowhurst, Ben Gledhill, Jeff Phipps, Frank O'Sullivan, Mat Davies, Margaret Burnside, Andy Campbell, Wilson Wong, Cheryl Allen, Lorna Leeson, Mark Hendy, Colin Newlyn, Anna Hobson, Gareth Jones, Trudy Wonder, Gail Hatfield, Heather Hanson Wickman, Boris Diekmann, Klaus Kammermaier, Bruce McTague, Zach Mercurio, Jon Husband, Stelio Verzera, Paul Tolchinsky, Sharon Clews, Kevin Green, Sharon Senior, Chris Nicholls, Trish McFarlane, Mohammed Hosny, Giles O'Halloran, An Coppens, Ruth Sharpe, Cathryn Newbury, Sarah Potter, Andy Swann, Jos de Blok, Nathalie Nahai, Frank Lekanne Deprez, Angela

Newman, Sandy Wilkie, Lori Niles-Hoffman, Jane Watson, Dan Pontefract, Amanda Nolen, Ainsley McLeod, Hung Lee, Laura Weis, Brennan Jacoby, Roxana Mocanu, Haider Imam, Jonathan Richards, Ted Hewitt, Francois du Plessis, Stephen Bevan, Vicky Carruthers, Lisa Hamill, Jane Barry, Alexandra Enke, Marie Ballesty, Giulia Moretto, Julia Flower, Marian Bloodworth, Marguerite Ulrich, Matt Pitt, Porteur Keene, Sue Yell, Eugenio Pirri, Charlotte Sweeney OBE, Luca Solari, Nick Court, Alexandra Delott, Steve Toft, Tamar Hughes, Jenny Roper, Tania Atallah, Marta Machalska, Emma Parry, Valentina Battista, Sharon Davies, Gemma Dentith-Jones, Tonja Blatnik, Christen Bavero, Aimee Mensch, Katrina Collier, Tom Paisley, Julie Bishop, Helen Sanderson, Teresa Wilkins, Deb Pellen, Liz Lempke, Nadia Moeil, Ciprian Arhire, Matt Partovi, Rob Ashcroft, Katie Slogett, Sharron Ford, Jemma O'Reilly, Mariska Van Ijzerloo, Lee Avery, Jason Yeomanson, Lee Bryant, Pete Russian, Sharon Green, Amanda Munday, Michelle Clark, Karin Tenelius, Carl-Erik Herlitz and Lisa Gill.

You all bring the energy game and I'm charged by you all.

As I wrote this book, the world was gripped by the Covid-19 pandemic. I'll confess, I wondered how relevant this book would be during and post-pandemic. My sense is that as we reshape from our lock-downed status work – where, and how in particular – will be very different.

We've seen parents grappling with home-schooling and work, taking a huge amount of energy. And we're already seeing things like 'Zoom-fatigue' for video calls and tiring schedules as people either attempt to adapt to home-working or still turn up as key workers.

These people – health and social care; delivery and utility work, grocery and medical support and justice and journalism – have proven something: people have the energy for their work and in the limelight of a pandemic response when everyone stood still, they kept the world moving.

We owe them a debt of gratitude we can never probably repay. Because of their energy, many of us stayed safe and experienced inconvenience rather than illness and, in so many sad cases, death.

An energized workplace is a dream but also something that should be a reality. Whatever work we do, in the great words of philosopher Howard Thurman, should *bring us to life*.

We can all reinvent work, our lives and society in response to this pandemic because when we have the energy for our life's work, we can do amazing things. **Human energy is the world's most powerful force. It's time we used it for the good of us all.**

Introduction

We have a quiet crisis in society.

One that's been building up for quite some time, probably since the 1970s/'80s:

- It isn't political – although we can see how much of the political world of late is in meltdown let alone crisis.
- It isn't (totally) in economics – though we have wealth inequality Mahatma Gandhi might have called call a social sin.
- It isn't in ecology – yet we know the sea temperature continues to rise, freak weather continues to become a norm and the polar icecap continues to melt.
- It isn't in science – yet we know that as we make huge strides in science and health, rare and deadly diseases such as Ebola or Covid-19 occur to remind us of our vulnerability.
- This crisis is in *workplaces across the globe*, right before our eyes. The crisis even has a name (something I've created, admittedly): **Peak Work.**

By *Peak Work* I mean an intolerable excess of demand, pace, complexity, commitment, time, effort, frustration, anger and energy that we experience in our jobs, doing our work. A 2019 survey undertaken by H&H Comms[1] of over 500 people in communication roles revealed that almost half the respondents felt negative pressures and even burnout-like conditions. As a norm. Not in exceptional circumstances but every day.

So how did we get to this state where it is normal that we experience such pressures in our jobs? Well this is perhaps part of the problem: the construct of jobs. Cut-and-paste approaches to how we recruit, develop and deploy people have fallen out of step with the flexible approaches we now need to cope with 21st-century demands of a digital world and the high expectations of customers and, yes, we as job holders.

A brief history of the job

Work has, since the beginning of recorded time, been a key feature of human existence. We've worked to protect ourselves, to eat, to procreate, to survive. Upon forming into early societal units, we've worked in cooperative bands – first as foragers, then as tribes, and then into institutions like monarchies, religious groups and military units. Work was done by us as serfs, missionaries, warriors. Or, as Joshua Cooper Ramo describes in his book *The Seventh Sense*, **Sages, Merchants and Soldiers**.[2]

In the industrial era, we continued to act as sages, merchants and soldiers via a new construct: paid work and the advent of the **job**.

The job has been our economic engine for over 200 years: in factories, mills, dockyards, tanneries, warehouses, fields, houses of worship, classrooms, theatres, barracks, and of course offices.

Since we headed into the information age, offices have become the predominant place of work for many of us. So much so that when we think of a workplace we tend to instantly think of offices. Governments, financiers, lawyers and more – all located in places where clerical, administration and knowledge work is done through the construct of jobs.

And with this work came more processes and thinking into how work gets done. The factories gave us commoditized efforts packaged into efficient lines of assembly and managed time-based activities to incentivize us to perform to standards. So it was that this approach from the early 20th century became the norm and followed through from manual to cognitive labour. Taylorism is the name given to the well-known time-and-motion study of human effort.[3]

And this thing we call a job (and refer to as work) has, for some time now, been the subject of studies, hopeful proclamations of change and cynical disbelief that there could ever be another way to do it.

In constructing the technology of the job, we have adopted the long-standing hierarchical set-up, of layers of leaders, managers and 'subordinates' doing the bidding of governmental, shareholder or non-profit aspirations and expectations, in return for some form of compensation package – salary, benefits like pensions and child care – and of course professional development. And let's not forget stock options, shares and profit-related bonuses.

This state of affairs has been the case – maybe even more intensely fine-tuned – in the increasing spread of a capitalist model (with exceptions being dictatorships, extreme forms of religious power and those war-torn and often poorer nation states).

And yet, we're seeing productivity stubbornly flatlining in most countries (the Organization for Economic Co-operation and Development (OECD) researches and publishes data in this area[4]) and sharp growth inclines becoming more and more enigmatic – even in emerging states who have discovered oil, minerals and more agricultural utilization. All of this whilst the individual value of some of the *Titans of Technology* (aka GAFA – Google, Apple, Facebook, Amazon) has breached the $1 trillion mark. But still productivity remains a major issue across all economic spheres.[5]

This has also come at a cost for ecological impact, wildlife, oceans, forests and water supplies. We're overspending and effectively bankrupting our futures – we're overdrawn on our *Earth Bank* account.

There's a further cost of this **Peak Work**. And a detrimental impact on the human spirit.

We're now literally working ourselves to death. *Karoshi*[6] – the Japanese term for this – and recent work by Stanford Professor Jeffrey Pfeffer (in his book *Dying for a Paycheck*[7]) show us that we are being put into a position normally associated with forms of forced labour like slavery, the middle-ages' *serfdom* or a conscripted form of working from the early Industrial era.

It can be seen in algorithm-based gig working using technology as an overlord; long-hours cultures in professional services firms where the macho approach is creating extreme schedules and demands on our mental processing; repetitive and highly challenging work in call centres; demanding schedules in warehousing tuned to the nanosecond; or healthcare under constant funding cuts with overworked practitioners doing their best.

As recently as December 2019 there was a court case that revealed the tragedy of a telecommunications giant in France, where 35 employees took their own lives due to an 'atmosphere of fear'. The court proceedings resulted in three senior officials (including the CEO and former HR Director) receiving jail sentences and fines.[8] The court found that the executives perpetrated 'a conscious scheme to worsen the work conditions of the employees in order to speed up departures', and their policies ultimately 'created a climate of anxiety' that led to the suicides. The duty of care to employees was abandoned with the direst consequences, causing people to end their own lives.

What are we doing to people?

With the bizarre realization that this is also an era of the highest spread of a standard of living the world has ever seen, with people lifted from extreme poverty across the globe, we surely have a paradox to settle. We have more but we live less well?

We've designed into our jobs this affliction I've called **Peak Work**. We have hit a peak of working time, effort and mental processing, and simply cannot conjure up any more time, energy or headspace to deal with it. What time/effort/thinking we do spend appears to be no more effective, productive or efficient, for a range of factors this book will explore.

People are taking their work home with them (ie via their phones or laptops), working over the weekends and when on vacation, and generally are NOT switching off. Weeks of 60, 70 and 80 hours are considered valiant, even normalized. A YouGov survey in 2013 revealed that 20 per cent of us had put in 'all-nighters' to get the job done.[9]

We hear of new graduates being given huge responsibility, having to work on client briefs they're simply not equipped for or trained to deal with. So they put in hours and hours of additional research, work and rework and generally find themselves claiming for a set number of hours from the client but probably working double (so all of that extra work in their – so-called – own time).

We probably haven't been this 'time poor' since wartime efforts and this is now compounded by having to tackle our lack of time alongside our responses to the coronoavirus outbreak.

Indeed, so bad is our mental health crisis that Zen Buddhist Master Nan Huai-Chin was quoted in Joshua Cooper Ramo's aforementioned *Seventh Sense* describing mental ill-health as 'the likely greatest cause of people's premature death in the 21st century: eclipsing cancer and pneumonia in previous centuries'.

This is backed up by the UK's own Health & Safety Executive statistical analysis from 2017/18.[10] According to this research and analysis, *595,000 of us were absent from work due to work-related stress,*[11] equating to *15.4 million working days lost, totalling around £15bn of losses to the business world.*

How has this sorry state of affairs come to be for 87 per cent[12] of our working population?

On a more hopeful note, not everyone has this issue with their job or their work – plenty of people report a strong connection to the purpose of their organization. Record numbers of start-ups[13] show us that people are taking matters into their own hands; rapid scale-ups and a bigger pool of freelancers are showing us there are alternatives to a job working for 'the man'[14] (as the saying goes).

In a study in Sweden of healthcare workers, a six-hour working day (but still paid as if working eight hours) revealed an increase in productivity and a sharp decrease in employee absences.[15]

The norm, though, appears to be represented through surveys from workplaces which reveal that when it comes to the way people feel about their job, they're either disengaged or borderline saboteurs.[16]

In the simplest of terms, the problem of **Peak Work** lies in the **design of jobs**. Poor, accidental, naive, deliberate and just downright bad design. So if we've designed it this way, I'm certain we can design it into a *better way*.

Whilst years of entrenched and normalized behaviours and methods aren't easy to decouple or overwrite, we have to try and reboot, upgrade or even hack into the system we have and design, deploy and deliver a working proposition fit for human beings in the 21st century.

And with all this in mind we turn to an even bigger issue to tackle in workplaces and society at large – the looming spectre (to many) of automation, with advances in digital, machine and synthetic replacement of human effort via simulated artificial intelligence (AI).

Taking stock then, our jobs are:

a Unfulfilling for 87 per cent of us; AND

b about to be dismantled and done by robots (with a variety of projections – some suggest around 50 per cent of work currently done by people being done by machines[17]); SO

c we will be displaced, under-engaged and experience lower esteem that could lead to the foul stench of a decaying society pressuring already stressed socio-political systems and governments.

Even more reason to design something better for work.

So it is the lofty ambition of this book – whilst recognizing its limitations on authority – to help us understand what we can do to design better work, to build better businesses for a better world.

And with this aim, this book is targeted at Human Resource Management professionals, those who work in leadership, management, change and organization design. Academics, researchers and teachers of workplace models and methodologies. Agencies who recruit, select and help people get to the right place of work for them and their clients. And mostly, you, me and everyone else trying to find their best working environment to be economically sound, psychologically stimulating and emotionally rewarding.

We should at least set out to explore how we can start the design process from the perspective of regenerating – not simply depleting – human energy at work.

How can we design for better?

In this book we will look at the what and the how (the why is clear from this introduction) and take some very specific angles on things like:

1 How we are energized by the work we do. Of course, not everyone is energized by the same things but then not all work is of the same nature anyway.
2 The sciences behind our creation and use of energy, and how we can bring more balance and regenerative ways to our energy source/supply.
3 Workplaces where there is an abundance of energy and what has been designed to make this so. We will look at the stories of people and their work that is fulfilling, energy creating and above all, psychologically safe for them to give their best to the work they do.
4 Approaches we can all take to design for better experiences of work, reinventing the thing we call work and/or jobs.

With so many things to consider in how to redesign work, and the part a job has to play in that, this book will provide a stimulus and suggestions that could be applied by individuals, teams and at organization level (with the appropriate adaptations for context and scale).

I return to my opening point about a 'quiet crisis', and apologize to the many people where it is far from a quiet experience. If their job and their work may be making them ill, that's going to a rather loud part of their life, occupying a lot of their energy.

And alongside such terrible personal consequences being suffered by so many people there is an economic cost and a loss to entire nations and regions.

That amount of human suffering and economic haemorrhage amounts to a crisis in most people's definition of the term. It is therefore time to do something about this, and no longer accept this design failure and loss of compassion for our fellow humans.

As Dr Martin Luther King Junior said, 'The time is always right, to do what is right'.[18]

What (in my opinion) is undisputedly right, is that we pay heed to the subtitle of this book and *design organizations where people flourish*.

Endnotes

1. H&H Communications (nd) Wellbeing at work: the surprising activity that improves employee wellbeing. Available from: https://handhcomms.co.uk/internal-communications/employee-wellbeing-the-surprising-activity-that-improves-wellbeing-at-work/ (archived at https://perma.cc/4YAV-TCDT)
2. Ramo, J C (2016) *The Seventh Sense: Power, fortune, and survival in the age of networks*, Little, Brown & Company. http://joshuacooperramo.com/ (archived at https://perma.cc/LP4T-F3XM)
3. https://www.britannica.com/science/Taylorism (archived at https://perma.cc/N27W-JSJ4)
4. OECD (nd) Labour productivity and utilisation. Available from: https://data.oecd.org/lprdty/labour-productivity-and-utilisation.htm#indicator-chart (archived at https://perma.cc/S7WQ-83KV)
5. Focus Economics (nd) 23 economic experts weigh in: Why is productivity growth so low? [blog] Available from: www.focus-economics.com/blog/why-is-productivity-growth-so-low-23-economic-experts-weigh-in (archived at https://perma.cc/L3JP-574F)
6. https://en.oxforddictionaries.com/definition/karoshi (archived at https://perma.cc/S6VM-JWZP)
7. Pfeffer, J (2018) *Dying for a Paycheck*, HarperBusiness. https://jeffreypfeffer.com/books/dying-for-a-paycheck/ (archived at https://perma.cc/R4UH-7F94)
8. Kelly, J (2019) French CEO sent to prison after his policies resulted in the suicides of 35 employees, *Forbes*. Available from: www.forbes.com/sites/jackkelly/2019/12/23/french-ceo-sent-to-prison-after-his-policies-resulted-in-the-suicides-of-35-employees/?utm_source=FBPAGE&utm_medium=social&utm_content=2988894567&utm_campaign=sprinklrForbesMainFB#24ae45364192 (archived at https://perma.cc/558X-TGGA)
9. Dahlgreen, W (2013) Working sixty hours a week is dangerous, *YouGov*. Available from: https://yougov.co.uk/topics/politics/articles-reports/2013/08/23/working-sixty-hours-week-dangerous (archived at https://perma.cc/KU8H-RMQR)
10. HSE (2019) Work-related stress, anxiety or depression statistics in Great Britain, 2019. Available from: www.hse.gov.uk/statistics/causdis/stress.pdf (archived at https://perma.cc/6677-4DRV)
11. Work-related stress, depression or anxiety is defined as a harmful reaction people have to undue pressures and demands placed on them at work.
12. Gallup (nd) Engage Your employees to see high performance and innovation. Available from: www.gallup.com/services/190118/engaged-workplace.aspx (archived at https://perma.cc/D6RS-95LG)

13 Dutovic, G (2019) The 20 most important startup statistics (2020 update), *Fortunly*. Available from: https://fortunly.com/statistics/startup-statistics/ (archived at https://perma.cc/E9A4-XRQL)

14 www.urbandictionary.com/define.php?term=working%20for%20the%20man (archived at https://perma.cc/8XQ5-X3HZ)

15 Greenfield, R (2016) The six-hour workday works in Europe. What about America? *Bloomberg*. Available from: www.bloomberg.com/news/articles/2016-05-10/the-six-hour-workday-works-in-europe-what-about-america?utm_source=feedly&utm_medium=webfeeds (archived at https://perma.cc/QMY4-DAYT)

16 Gallup (2017) State of the global workplace. Available from: www.gallup.com/services/178517/state-global-workplace.aspx?g_source=ServiceLandingPage&g_medium=copy&g_campaign=tabs (archived at https://perma.cc/WQZ2-ZTR2)

17 Osborne, M and Frey, C (2018) Automation and the future of work – understanding the numbers, *Oxford University*. Available from: www.oxfordmartin.ox.ac.uk/opinion/view/404 (archived at https://perma.cc/778U-KPDM)

18 www2.oberlin.edu/external/EOG/BlackHistoryMonth/MLK/MLKmainpage.html (archived at https://perma.cc/U3QS-L99M)

01

2050 voyaging

A glimpse into the future design of work

> In this chapter we will explore the possibilities being afforded to us by digital and sociological advances, to build a narrative of what the future might be like where we are supported and enabled by such technologies. We will create an optimistic view of the future whilst accepting there will be aspirations in this chapter that may only be realized through the choices we make as a society and as individuals.
>
> Nevertheless, with a look at developments over the last 30 years, and awareness of what is potentially arriving in the next 30, we can see the possibilities and boldly attempt to envision a future with much-improved ways of being, living and, of course, working.
>
> In the following chapters, we will take this futuristic look ahead and review the past and present circumstances that have created our crisis of compassion, and consider the potential models, theories and practices that will rescue our fellow humans from a degenerative working experience and bring our collective efforts to the forefront of progressive organization and job design as we face a digital technology-fuelled version of work and life.

If we were to project ourselves to a far-off version of life – 2050 – then we should have a generational timespan to look back on and explore what it might be like once we have experimented more, learned more and adapted more to a world very different from now.

Making predictions is both easy and hard. Easy because they can be based on hopes, trends and interpretations. Hard because human history is littered with self-destructive qualities, unforeseen circumstances and the variable nature of what motivates us, with power, greed and envy all playing their part in disrupting our attempts to become better versions of ourselves.

And yet we can see beyond our current situation with modelling, scenarios and analysed patterns of data so this chapter paints a view that is (in my opinion) as realistic as possible.

What will work even be in 2050?

The world of work in 2050 will be different in three key ways:

1. the automation of around 17–35 per cent of all the work we do in 2020;[1]
2. the rise of new and adapted jobs, roles and work as a result of the challenges we face in 2050; and
3. the emergence of adapted socio-political ideologies and applications.

In 2050, we find ourselves in partnership with machines more than ever. In 2020 we saw this through the dependence on and use of smart devices. Our smartphones and computational equipment were already becoming our instruments of life and work. We were already doing our banking, purchasing, working and entertaining through the screens of laptops, tablets and phones.

What's different in 2050 is that we now have **personal robotic concierges**; programmes and algorithms that are accessible through a range of connected technologies providing automated, learning-based and co-created **digital scripts** that run our lives.

Education

Whilst at school in 2050, we learn with our robot partner. This is not a physical cyborg assistant but a combination of a series of implanted, wearable and portable devices connected to (what we once called) the **Internet of Things**. We combine our robots to research differing perspectives and hypotheses around learning subjects like:

- looking after our planet;
- looking after our society; and
- looking after each other.

Subject-matter learning was phased out five years earlier and it is now all about topical areas of global and local interest (pioneered in Finnish schools[2]).

We learn quickly about the skills and behaviours we need to understand each other as human beings with different interests, ideologies and perspectives on life.

Whilst we still earn academic attainment through our schooling, we qualify with different grading systems built around what were once known as *life skills*. Where there were interests in science, medicine and art, these became optional as younger children started to develop their personalities and preferences and could see through discovery where their interests – and therefore skills – lay. We can study to be a medical professional knowing that our robotic assistant will be at our side for technical insight, so we can show our compassion, inclusivity and focus on patients, while our robot assistant helps us with up-to-the-second medical knowledge to help us with physical and mental medical support.

Working

We will have seen the move from five-day working weeks, to variable three to four days as the norm. We might choose the portfolio approach and spread our time between more than one 'employer', with the nature of what we work on changing according to our circumstances.

Traditional career structures have been struggling for some time and broader, more discovery-based careers now allow us to mix something humanitarian and communal with something like legal advocacy or creative marketing.

Because machines are making so much more, the costs of production have plummeted. Green, clean and renewable energy powers the planet whilst use of fossils fuels is a tiny fraction of what it was even in 2020.

What is occupying us economically is planetary and wildlife conservation and regeneration.

We're at the start of the repair to the planet but it's already neutral in terms of consumption and extraction, with places like India, Brazil and parts of Africa learning from the developed West's pillaging of natural resources and reclaiming space and land for the reforestation and refertilization of much of the land we stripped in the recent past. Indeed, desalinated parts of once-barren desert are now flourishing microcosms of wildlife reserves, agricultural engineering and habitation to account for the 10 billion people now living on planet Earth.

So our work has found itself less in search of personal gain or purely about wealth, and more about restorative, community-based action. The Climate Change strikes by school children in 2019 showed an activist streak in those under 16 who are now in their prime and largely occupied as bio-engineers, social scientists and life-long educators.

With three- to four-day working weeks the norm, and entertainment now fused with education, we see more learning about the world, ourselves and the arts than ever before.

Society

Electrified travel and the early stages of the metamorphosis of the car industry into shared transport vehicles have seen a reduction in ownership but a rise in utility models. Not many people own a car now; they merely lease as they need from a pool of vehicles provided by a range of manufacturers. If you want a Tesla or an electric Jaguar, you can have one for the lease period you wish to pay for, but it'll cost you more than an electric Toyota or Skoda.

The beginning of the Hyperloop transportation network has given us the early signs of how we will traverse vast distances more quickly and electrified air travel has cut carbon emissions by over 80 per cent for this form of travel.

Bioengineering has enabled plants to grow more quickly, more sturdily and with minimal irrigation and soil utilization.

Advances in human genetics and biotech have given us longer and more healthy lives already. We're seeing a five-year uptick in life expectancy in the Western World (arresting some of the 2020 declines through obesity and mental ill-health) with 15-year upticks in Africa, South America and parts of Asia.

Early experiments with Universal Basic Income have stuttered but the new ways people are incentivized to work for a form of state-aided support have shown that the 'workless class' was a system product not a natural human state. Local community work, helping the older members of society and those with specific needs, and working in a more conscious food industry have created roles for people to find esteem and learning on the job.

Criminal rehabilitation and integration into society with more advanced psychology and use of human and robotic assistance has lifted many from a destructive criminal past into a more connected community-based future.

Nation states have decentralized much of their governance and localized, regional representation has breathed new life into politics after the disastrous period in the late 2010s proved a new model of governing was needed. Youth councils, People's Panels and Citizen Assemblies are mixed with mature community members in a system reminiscent of tribal days of yore.

Three key elements to 2050 citizenship

Overall, life appears to be more balanced than in a long time, partly because human beings and machines have created three key factors:

ABUNDANCE, AUTONOMY AND ALTRUISM
We learned in the mid-2000s that **autonomy** was becoming critical to how people worked. We saw that allowing people to direct themselves rather than feel constantly supervised was the key to unlocking what was then called 'Human Capital'. Early experiments found the transition from *managed* to *liberated* hard, but some of the more successful enterprises of the latter 2020s showed this to truly be the

way forward for workplace culture and operating modes. With this new sense of influence over self and things around us, we acted in a way that was a surprise to many – we became more accountable, responsible and took ownership of things that mattered. No more layers of management were needed so people were reskilled into coaches, advisors and facilitators.

We then developed such powerful making capability through miniaturized and intelligent machinery (often using deep or machine learning and therefore becoming more artificially intelligent) that we flattened production costs, speed and quality of production and were able to tackle larger issues like energy creation and planet repair more rapidly. With this came the sense of **abundance**; more was available to more for less, so we became less greedy by this nature of *availability*. Abundance created, ironically, less envy and therefore less of a need to prove your merit in society by what you owned. It became more about *what you did* that mattered. Of course, luxury goods are still available but their place in society was questioned so that even the most ardent capitalist companies became conscious and did more with their wealth, for the planet and society, and became more '*Patagonia-like*'.

Through this, we became more **altruistic**. Companies who couldn't show a true and genuine purpose in making the world a better place to be part of, withered. Many collapsed and others morphed into a more conscious version of their former selves. Rutger Bregman's famous 2019 World Economic Forum outburst[3] (about higher taxation for the super-wealthy) led to more consideration of taxing the mega-rich and therefore the benefits of such wealth were likely to be grabbed by governments. Voluntary schemes became the norm, where companies would avoid straightforward taxation by being included in large philanthropic schemes to boost the developing world (as we referred to it in 2020) and local communities, health and social care, and education and privilege. Companies went from sponsoring a road-traffic hub near their factory, to entirely funding local and international schemes that supported their workers and their families, their communities and those of their supply chain, using Blockchain technology.

Funding such ventures cut out governmental tax schemes and instead created more community and active participation, as Corporate Social Responsibility became an industry within industries and a parallel human investment company was run alongside big banks, big pharma, big industry and big tech.

This '3A' effect led to a '3E' model for society built around it:

- **Economics** (of a much more distributed and regenerative sort) inspired by British economist Kate Raworth's 'Doughnut Economics' theory of regenerative use of the planet's resources – not just recycling but regenerating where extraction was the product of mining, farming and production.[4]
- **Education** and a more humanist, discovery-based model that advantaged everyone and not just those with wealth privilege.
- **Enterprise** – organizations and individuals collaborating to achieve more than profitability and deliver what was previously called the *triple bottom line*.[5]

Economists and historians alike would have been aghast at how quickly things shifted had they not lived through it. Such was the power of the new ways of using machines, human creativity and capacity and a recognition of a common adversary (climate/ecological damage) that we saw 2050 as a new era – **the age of enlightenment**. A rediscovery of things that were previously the domain of eastern mystical arts.

Society still had problems – some warlords, religious zealots and despotic leaders trying to force their way to power. Yet there was a power and solidarity in people of 2050 that came from the generation who lived through more suffering than their parents (for one of the first times in history not connected to war, disease or natural disasters). This fundamentally shaped a new form of consciousness that started, in all places, in the workplaces of the 2020s.

Digital capability and connectivity – much as Tim Berners-Lee aspired to with his early vision for the World Wide Web[6] of decentralization, non-discrimination, bottom-up design, universality and consensus – set the infrastructure for abundant clean energy, which in turn gave us more distributed and mechanized making capability through our work, which led to more distribution of influence and less desire to simply acquire wealth with the realization that we're all in it together to put right what the previous 100 generations had exploited and over-used from our planet.

Utopian or protopian?

Wired magazine editor Kevin Kelly introduced the term *protopian* in 2011[7] to explain that the future is likely neither *utopian* nor *dystopian* as many predictors of the future believed it to be. Protopia is:

> a state that is better than today than yesterday, although it might be only a little better. Protopia is much much harder to visualize. Because a protopia contains as many new problems as new benefits, this complex interaction of working and broken is very hard to predict.

A dream state?

Before this narrative is dismissed as overly optimistic and ideological, even the most ardent scientific minds would agree that this is all **possible and plausible**. The only thing to stop this would be ourselves and the advancement of natural disasters.

Work, crucial to so many of us for economic stability, is the key to this as we need to be put to work to enable it to happen. So far from subscribing to the view that more machines will lead to displaced people with riotous tendencies, machines will lead to capacity and capability like never before. It is this ideology and theory that I believe will see a new dawn in 2050.

Work – at the time of writing this book, a pretty demonized force (and perhaps rightly so with the Gallup-type reports of disengagement we talked about in the introduction) – **will emerge as our saving grace**.

Our work will mean something bigger than ourselves and this will see us move from functioning parts of a machine to a living part of an ecosystem that needs more sustainable ways to flourish, as do we, as a people. We need something that isn't stressing us to the point of premature death but instead is a way to – as 20th-century philosopher Howard Thurman describes – makes us come alive,[8] whether you think this is self-indulgent or actually in pursuit of what the world really needs.

I've long subscribed to the theory that we are all self-motivated. When we say 'make the world a better place', what we probably mean is 'I would like to work on things that make me feel good because I can make others feel good in that process of making the world a better place'.

There is nothing *wrong* in starting with your needs and this just happening to ripple out positively to others. We fool ourselves that we are true altruists or philanthropists, when even that sentiment to be charitable is driven by our desire and design to be so. It is with this in mind that we often say *'fit your own oxygen mask first before attending to others'*, which I think differentiates 2050 from 2020 or even 1990.

We will come to appreciate that what I work on, what I do for a living, is what I need as a human being, and it just *happens* to be what the planet and those who live with me on it also need.

That is truly an optimistic viewpoint and yet is perhaps the truth behind all motivation to achieve this 2050 vision. Maybe a huge dollop of reality is what will see us through the current turbulent times – **we need people to want to be this way**. And I believe helping people find themselves through the work they do is the secret to this new-found enlightenment, just as artists and scholars found their way in the Renaissance. Three new 'R' words will lead us to a new dawn:

- Realignment.
- Recalibration.
- Reinvention.

These 3 Rs are what life, the universe and everything are really all about – helping us be at our best, and the world gets to be a lot better in the processs.

As such, we need an energized workplace to achieve this realigned, recalibrated and reinvented work proposition.

We need to design work that stimulates and creates human energy rather than merely depleting it. We need to position ourselves as designers, architects and proponents of a more sophisticated way to bring people, their talents and their desires to the position of most need in organizations, be they in service, production or administration of the factors affecting people's lives.

We need to align behind the 5th-century BC term from ancient Greece – *Eudaimonia*,[9] or human flourishing.

Endnotes

1 OECD (2018) Job creating and local development 2018. Available from: www.oecd.org/cfe/job-creation-and-local-economic-development-26174979.htm (archived at https://perma.cc/UJ9Q-Q6AG)

2 Spiller, P (2017) Could subjects soon be a thing of the past in Finland? *BBC News*. Available from: www.bbc.co.uk/news/world-europe-39889523 (archived at https://perma.cc/HY4M-QAP6)

3 BBC News (2019) Rutger Bregman: The Dutch historian who went viral. Available from: www.bbc.co.uk/news/av/world-47077624/rutger-bregman-the-dutch-historian-who-went-viral (archived at https://perma.cc/BA43-EA5K)

4 Raworth, K (nd) What on earth is the Doughnut? [blog] Available at: www.kateraworth.com/doughnut/ (archived at https://perma.cc/E62S-T4D7)

5 The Economist (2009) Triple bottom line. Available from: www.economist.com/news/2009/11/17/triple-bottom-line (archived at https://perma.cc/25WM-FGLZ)

6 World Wide Web Foundation (nd) History of the web: Sir Tim Berners-Lee Available from: https://webfoundation.org/about/vision/history-of-the-web/ (archived at https://perma.cc/3KYF-B2KR)

7 https://kk.org/thetechnium/protopia/ (archived at https://perma.cc/RP6Y-CLJA)

8 www.goodreads.com/quotes/6273-don-t-ask-what-the-world-needs-ask-what-makes-you (archived at https://perma.cc/J69L-XBQ2)

9 www.britannica.com/topic/eudaimonia (archived at https://perma.cc/Y4BK-8ND9)

02

20th-century design flaws

A look back at the history of the design of work

> In this chapter, we will look back at the foundations of the exciting and challenging changes ahead. It is important to understand what has happened before we plan a better our version of a workplace and the plan to get there.
>
> Turning our thoughts into actions inspired journalist, author and poet Khalil Gibran to say, 'Work is love made visible'.
>
> Many of us are burdened by work and it is not an act of love made visible. Historically, in wartime and during crises, we did not think about a 'love of work'; we worked to protect who and what we love (family, community, freedom, justice).
>
> We will look back as far as the post-World War II state of the world to give us almost 100 years of (largely) peacetime existence where the forces of human endeavour and ingenuity have us living in a connected planet about to exploit the biggest shift in industry since the development of the loom, steam engine, electricity and, more recently, the microchip.
>
> And we look to the new forms of work that require more adapted ways of being and work than the overly programmable mechanics of 19th- and 20th-century work.

A psychological theory of human evolution

Many people have given us a range of theories on what we mean by 'human evolution', with one psychologist in particular creating significant interest in not only the past traits of evolution but also a realistic approach to how we might be in our next stages.

Professor Clare Graves captured this in his work in the 1950s, which started from his teaching of psychology in New York.

It was during constant questioning from his undergraduate students that he realized there was a missing element in the frames that described evolution in human psychology. He was unable to answer the simple question: **which of the psychological theorists was the *right* one or the *correct* one?** So many theorists and their work appeared to be in contradiction or competition with others, making it difficult to decide which theories to apply and believe in.

Prompted by this lack of clarity, Graves set out to develop something that would be as truthful, fair, right, just and accurate about human psychological development as it could be at that time: an epistemological model of human psychology. No mean feat, especially with the world emerging from war with new-found hope and energies.

Graves persisted and seemed to relish the challenge as his life's work. The result was the 'Emergent Cyclic Levels of Existence Theory',[1] a fascinating concept that shows how humans have evolved through external influencing factors and their own internal agency and counsel.

Essentially, we have a cyclical series of bio-psycho-social coping mechanisms that depend on the external environments we find ourselves in (physical circumstances and mental states). We respond to these based on our intellectual, psychological and emotional developed states, which includes a *regressive* adaptation and not just a constantly *progressive* developed state. That is, we can go backwards – psychologically – if the environment causes us to do that. Going against what we may have learned, what we once believed was right, fair and just.

In bringing this to life, if Graves hypothesized a situation – such as having to survive in a drug cartel environment – he would adapt and somewhat regress his methods of how he needed to be to cope in that violent, tribal culture. Of course, he might be more intellectually, psychologically and emotionally developed than those gang members around him – and therefore *know* there are ways to exist that have developed beyond warlords, violence, oppression, fear and aggression – but that doesn't mean he couldn't adapt and cope to this way of being in order to survive, via a regressive state of being.

Graves' theory also answered (somewhat) the concept of Nirvana or the peak of human existence, so often desired but thought to perhaps be a never-realized ambition. Graves' work set out to describe that yes, this could be achieved but it was unlikely to be a permanent state.

Graves' entire work was built around this cyclical nature of the human state and that we find ourselves in constant motion between levels of psychological development. Therefore we should accept that at times we will have to act and be in a way we thought we had developed beyond, in ways we thought were regressive, backwards, primitive even. Yet the external environment we find ourselves in determines the need to be that way in order to cope with the external forces.

It is a fascinating theory that has given life to a number of subsequent psychological frameworks and adaptations; Professor Don Beck, Christopher Cowan and Ken Wilber worked Graves' theories into the concept of *Spiral Dynamics*.[2]

Now is not the time to unpack this entire work, but spiral, cyclical – both meaning to show how we as humans advance – sure. *Yet we can and do regress*.

We only have to look at the 2019 state of socio-political mindsets – the rise of the Far Right, climate change deniers, flat-earthers, fascists, sexists, racists, anti-Semites, homophobes – to show how we can wilfully regress.

Progressive ways of being are challenging for some people's sanctuary and belonging. No matter how facts, science and literature can reveal a 'right' state of thinking about a topic, people can – and now so publicly do – deny such states/matters.

People are therefore *choosing* how to think, feel and be about a topic even when confronted with forceful alternatives to their 'truths'.

How we feel about the systems of work

Faced with this fascinating view of the human state it is important to understand the environments that create progression and regression of the psychological state that guides so much of how we behave in the world of work.

If you are schooled in a strict way, if you work in a highly regulated environment, why would you believe in a state that gives people unbridled choice? You did well through being regulated. Yet you've never developed or experienced a world where the ultimate choice was yours and any actions you took were determined by an advanced state of understanding, not by being controlled by someone else.

Pavlovian conditioning[3] exists and proves how we respond to regular stimulus. School bells and factory buzzers indicating breaks could be either the oppression tools of forced regimes or the guiding interventions to focus easily distracted heads and hands.

The quiet crises I referred to in Chapter 1 (Peak Work) may not even be recognizable to some, and certainly those old enough might point to the lack of unionized disputes as proof that things aren't as bad as they were. They might conveniently overlook that union power has been disassembled, stifled and regulated over the last 30 years or so.

Indeed, some people may pick up this book, look at the cover and the words 'Designing organizations where people flourish' and think it some pipedream, restricted to bro culture in Silicon Valley/ Shoreditch, a community farm in Kanazawa, a family business in Mombasa, an art gallery in Marlow, a tea shop in Agra.

Big pharma, large retail, huge governmental organizations, even smaller family businesses may not create the flourishing experiences people could get from their work.

Why would people even think workplaces where people flourish could be a thing?

When generation on generation have found themselves in unspectacular working conditions, what right does anyone have to experience this even if it did exist?

The *conditioned mindset* might be that work is a toil to achieve credits to spend on enjoying some safety, joy and all those things that constitute life. We have vacations, weekends and public holidays to 'live'; work is what interrupts that. Just as learning at school perhaps interrupts play.

Many people (around 66 per cent[4]) believe their work to be a tolerable economic necessity with conditional loyalty that any additional 'discretionary effort' is effectively giving away more to others for free. Sixteen per cent of their colleagues are actively disengaged, meaning they are negative about virtually all parts of their work apart from some relationships with colleagues and the fact that they get some pay (though in their mind, probably not enough for their efforts).

When people appear to be put into intolerable situations of oppressive supervision and distrust, where management are inconsiderate to everything except targets, performance indicators and delivery, it is truly understandable how (at best) one in three of us report this system of factorized work to be unsatisfactory.

As acclaimed author Nilofer Merchant said on stage at the HR Directors Summit of 2018: 'We've become atomized, not actualized'.[5]

Knowing the history of work – a personal story

The history of work, in academic terms, has only recently become of interest and taught in business schools and universities. The emergence of a fascination (some may even say fetishization) of work is an even newer phenomenon.

History was taught (even in my early years in the 1970s) around major socio-political events. I studied Ancient Egypt, the Roman Empire, the colonization of North America (which to be fair did provide a healthy amount of Native American culture and sparked my interest in that topic), British Monarchs, the rise of Hitler and World War II. It fascinated me and continues to do so to this day.

What I *wasn't* taught was Industrial Affairs (bearing in mind I grew up with strikes, power cuts, miners' disputes, Thatcherism/Reaganomics – that was a missed opportunity), the (former) British Empire, past slave trades and mercantilism, then Windrush immigration into the UK, communism and the Warsaw Pact, Suez, oil and the Arab–Israeli war, class and social structures in 1970s Britain, and of course *the history of work*.

I found about Taylorism,[6] the Hawthorne Experiments,[7] Maslow's Hierarchy of Needs[8] and more whilst in the workplace – often after being there for 10 years or more.

These longstanding, fundamental shaping elements to work would have been really helpful to me before embarking into the world of work and during it. I had no idea there were management sciences until a lot later in my career. I took on my first management role aged 21 and full of naivety. I made it work, but I would have benefited from much of this theory. That I didn't go to university may have contributed to this but I wasn't alone in that unknowing state.

All of this was a sudden realization that I had become really interested in work in a different way: beyond what I was doing and into *how* I was doing it.

I started to look seriously at business books, heard about this thing called the *Harvard Business Review*, and found courses, conferences and features on things like Lean Process Improvement, Business Process Re-Engineering, Business Strategy and more.

I bought myself early productivity tools like a faux leather-bound work planner, scheduler and organizer that made filofaxes look like a rather low-functioning diary. *Wall Street* – a film about greed starring Michael Douglas as Gordon Gekko, with braces, slicked-back hair and striped shirts – provided me and many of my colleagues with wardrobe iconography and a desire for first-generation mobile phones.

Of course, the technology we were putting together at the time (1994, seven years after *Wall Street* came out) was primitive compared to the tech of now, and yet it was already emerging that these methodology-framed, intellectually stimulating, psychologically aware approaches I was experiencing would reshape the rest of my approach to work.

Organization development – a discipline most powerful

Organization development has no better description, which also sums up my belief system, than the opening line from the UK NHS Employers' approach: *Organization development (OD) enables people to transform systems.*[9]

These extracts from the CIPD's factsheet[10] are helpful in explaining more to those who are not that familiar with OD:

> Organization development focuses on **maximizing the value gained from the organization's resources** – for example, in an automated manufacturing plant, the development might focus on mechanical efficiencies, whereas if the organization produces people services, it might focus on people capabilities.
>
> Organizational development focuses on **an organization's strategy, goals and core purpose** – all development is carried out to achieve these things to a greater extent. Development that's undertaken without such a focus can become incongruent with the rest of the organization and can cause issues in other areas.
>
> Where an organization's main competitive advantage is delivered through their people (as opposed to technology or machinery), organization development will involve **applying behavioural science knowledge and practice,** such as leadership, group dynamics and work design. This ensures that people practices are developed in a way that uses research-based insights and scientific understanding of how and why people behave the way they do.
>
> Organization development is related to change management in the sense that many developments would be implemented using change management practices but also, because it is being done continuously, organization development is a kind of **planned, ongoing, systematic change that aims to institutionalize continual improvement within organizations**.

It was only on entering the professional field of Human Resources in 2003 that I really became attuned to the *how* of work.

My move was to Learning and Development – the field that shaped my early thinking on managing other people in the mid-1990s. I went from recipient of the product of their endeavours to the creator and deliverer of that insight. Having now had 15 years of managing others, of applying methodologies, of understanding more about the systems at play in work, did I find my 'space'?

Indeed, in 2018, I was awarded recognition for article of the year about OD.[11]

This synopsis of my past is intended to demonstrate that we did not – and may still not – teach people enough of the 'how' of work, and OD is a hugely insightful part of that teaching.

From flawed design to designing from the 'floor up'

Whilst researching, designing and delivering learning interventions became a rewarding part of my work in my early days of HR, I was more interested in the prevailing systems that gave rise to the need to learn, that made applying that theory, of learning to change, easier or more difficult, and how the way people behaved towards each other was influenced by many elements of the design of the system they were operating in.

Which is why I declared in Chapter 1 that the design of work is flawed and has been for some time. I realized this most profoundly in 2006 when I discovered the book *Maverick* by Brazilian engineering CEO Ricardo Semler.[12]

It was in this book that I found a rule breaker who had made a success out of an entirely unorthodox way to run an organization. In short, Semler created an environment where teams set their own production quotas and shared profits throughout the enterprise, not just to those in the more senior positions.

There were so many other designed elements introduced (democratic voting on key decisions and self-setting of salaries being two examples) that this firm delivered more than its fair share of departures from working norms. Many hailed this as a sign of things to come; others as a fantasy full of gimmicks that would not be taken seriously.

Bearing in mind I arrived at this book 13 years after it was released, not much had changed (to my knowledge) since its publication. However, it had inspired many entrepreneurs and is held in high regard by many of the more 'enlightened thinkers' that make up business school academics and authors.

From this moment on, I could see the 'psychological drag' presented by much of the traditional organization design and the same when observing others. It was the start of a research trail that continues to this day, with a growing group of alternative models for how to structure an organization.

I just hadn't realized it was organization design at fault until I read Semler's book. In thinking about how to change things, I had my sense of alternatives that seemed to be unable to take hold beyond my own thoughts until this book, which was way more ambitious than any of my ideas or hopes. I felt both inadequate and enabled.

My belief in a flawed organization design was further embedded in two ways; one an experience and the other, a methodology.

Experiences were in something which became a regular 'ask' of HR – **restructures**.

It became an almost monthly occurrence that some business leader wanted to restructure their teams, divisions, directorates. So why fix a structure if you're then going to restructure some time again soon? Keeping it fluid seemed to be a better model. No one seemed to know how or want to do that. So merry-go-rounding on unfreeze, change, refreeze and repeat seemed to do three things to people:

1 distraction;

2 uncertainty; and

3 fear.

Some of the requests for restructuring came from a slightly more underhand starting point: to remove someone from a senior position rather than manage their poor performance or behaviours.

So an entire division was put into a state of alert that they may be restructured to who knows what, because one manager couldn't properly manage another? Now that's a flawed process and design in combination.

Yes, the restructures continued and the state of convulsive change with who knows what as a consequence ensued.

The other was a methodology I've now become accustomed to: **Agile**. I bought a book in 2008 whilst doing some research into Agile: *Scrum: A breathtakingly brief and agile introduction*.[13] I was hooked and wanted to use this approach wherever I could.

I got some traction and use and some ideas of how to work in the (now) expanded team I had at the time; dispersed, with a range of roles, a range of projects underway, different specialisms, experience levels, likes, ways of operating. I had a team of 12; we needed to be responsive but planned, creative but channeled. Introducing Agile was tough then and it would be tough now. Nevertheless I learned so much from my attempts at creating autonomous yet aligned ways of working.

It really came to the fore several years later when working with a learning design team who were keen to try this out. We hit 'paydirt' as we reduced design and development times in digital learning content creation from six months to five weeks. It was like magic.

Yet, it was all in the design

And not just the design of the tools and approaches we worked to, but in the design of **how we were with each other**. How we made decisions, got creative, took on ownership and responsibility for each other's well-being and application of effort. It was like our micro version of Semco (the company Semler features in his book, *Maverick*).

From this moment on I knew Agile – as an operating system, methodology, mindset and all the associated elements of it – would become my 21st-century design approach; to design for the fluidity I longed to offer those constant restructures I had to help engineer in the 2006–2012 period.

Researching the Agile Manifesto,[14] reading the Cluetrain Manifesto[15] (an early view on connecting technologies like the World Wide Web and content and communities in the early days of the internet) and other early publications on the socialization of work (manifested by the increased use of social media by us all) only enforced my view that we were shifting towards that Semco model of being – autonomous, liberated, empowered. And ultimately, self-managed.

By now I was reading about the Morning Star self-managed model,[16] where colleagues contracted with other colleagues, negating the need for management to intervene and decide. Discovering WL Gore[17] (with their own version of self-management and delegated decision making) felt like I was discovering things I always believed in and didn't believe possible – designed organizational models of operating that liberated people and culled bureaucracy and the machinery of 60 years of management science that no longer helped people and organizations flourish.

I could see a revolution dawning, a call to arms of those who believed in the alternatives, of which, in the early part of the 2010s, there was a growing band.

And then in the summer of 2012, I attended an event that shifted my view of the world of work forever. It was a simple gathering of (mainly) HR folks in a disused bed factory in South London under the banner of Connecting HR.[18] Organized by Jon Ingham and Gareth Jones, this collection of people with job titles and their own enterprises took my breath away. In the format of an Unconference[19] (where no agenda is set except by attendees during the day to a series of facilitated sessions) I had more epiphany moments in one day than in several years of hoping for them.

There were sessions on all sorts of topical business elements – trust, leadership, empowerment, inclusion. The assembled participants listened to the Barrett Values Centre[20] about the reconstruction of Iceland's entire societal and business proposition, to WorldBlu[21] and their freedom-centred democracy at work. I had found my tribe to go along with my mindset.

I saw so many options to do alternative things, I knew corporate life was no longer for me. I could see that I had a path to a different way of being and that was the beginning of the end of my role in a job. OK, too much pressure, work and a combination of poor decisions on my part led to my ultimate departure from a job I had previously loved, led me to the world of independent practice and immediately into hackathons, consulting advice and designing and delivering for a more liberating sense of how people could be assembled to work together.

Since joining the freelance world, I've been even more acutely tuned to the shifts in the way work is designed and organized. More examples appear to have surfaced that have challenged the orthodoxy of work design and how organizations are structured, and this book will contain many of those when we get into practical applications of organization design and work (and to a degree role) design. And all of the examples of new thinking in work design equate to a hugely energetic approach people have in their work. A committed, dedicated and fulfilling working lot in their life.

From mechanics to heuristics

The easiest way to define the way we need to shift the design of organizations, work and all the associated behavioural elements, is to look at Mechanics contrasted by **Heuristics**.

A heuristic is defined by 101computing.net as 'any approach to problem solving, learning, or discovery that employs a practical method, not guaranteed to be optimal or perfect, but sufficient for the immediate goals'.[22]

To briefly summarize again the mechanics of work: Taylorism has made sure we look at human effort, in a work sense, as part of a machine. Smaller component parts of the larger whole. Repetition to boost competence and accuracy. It has been that way since the dawn of industry but particularly the production line concepts of the early part of the 20th century.

If we look at pre-economic crash statistics from the US Bureau of Labor Statistics, 1950 saw 40 per cent of people in knowledge work and 60 per cent in either trade, transport or manufacturing. Fast forward to 2007 and that is reversed.[23]

A 2013 Oxford University study reported that 47 per cent of work currently done by humans is automatable. Other studies have since predicted a range between 9 and 35 per cent.[24] So at even the most conservative or radical end we may see more mechanical work headed to automation, so the 'knowledge' worker percentage could grow or reduce.

Most predictions, like those from World Economic Forum,[25] describe the roles that are unlikely to be automated as having creativity, critical analysis and problem solving, compassion, empathy and communication skills as primary features.

Heuristics, as defined earlier, seems the perfect opposite to mechanistic approaches. Mechanics is about predictability, managed efficiency, optimized and integrated connections and reactions. Heuristics is about intent, direction and an uncertain but discovery-based approach to finding a solution or completing an action.

With so much of our world guided by the laws of physics, it is easy to see how mechanics has become the order of the efficient world we know:

- We have conquered chemical – even atomic – reactions to provide power, making capability and more. It has even been said that we have enhanced ourselves through mechanics.
- We have developed the technology that is the oven to provide a supplemental aid to food consumption. We have effectively engineered an additional stomach through a technology we call cooking.

So, as we think we can make all around bend to our will, desire and need, we often realize that we are still not masters of our universe as the power of nature, the unpredictability of mutations and the 'unknown unknowns' mean we should be far from complacent.

Which is where heuristics techniques can help.

There are three main types of heuristics: availability, representativeness, and anchoring & adjustment:

Availability is the most obvious one and is where we recall what we know or have experienced. It is about mental shortcuts, existing biases and wired preferences, and is something to both utilize and watch out for.

Representativeness is where we catalogue, store and categorize things, our thoughts and experiences and of course other people. Again we can find ourselves somewhat assumptive when we make representative assessments but also we can use them to nicely create some sense of order out of disorder.

Anchoring & adjustment is about numerical aids to certainty and assessment of likelihood. So for example, if we have a new member of the team and we recognize that in the first three days they are likely to make their mind up about whether they have connected with the team (based on the prior experiences of the other four team members), we'd make sure we did all we could to make those three days the optimal bonding experience. We anchor that experience through the application of those optimal numbers (in this case three days).

We can and will also adjust this, based on the fact that we recognize the new team member is coming to this role after three years of caring for an elderly relative and may need more than three days to overcome any uncertainties they may have. Therefore from our anchored three we adjust to six and make sure the most enlightening experience they could have goes beyond the weekend and into week two (checking how they balance their work and life commitments in this first week as an indicator of how things would be continuing in this manner).

Heuristics, in the main, is that adapting way of handling things. Not the mechanistic, highly predictable way, yet still a process.

This is very much at the heart of digital production methods such as iterative, agile development.

A prototype is put together with the knowledge it has flaws but aiming to gauge reaction, assess usability and bring forward that all-important feedback and suggestions to improve the product. What comes back may very well be unexpected and if we adopted a mechanistic approach, this could make such feedback difficult to take on and deliver.

Heuristics appears to be very much the way we are having to set ourselves up in this world of unpredictable 'Black Swan' events[26] (phenomena named after the first recorded sightings of black swans in Australasia, where previously only white swans were thought to exist) and random occurrences tagged with the (now) cliché Volatile, Uncertain, Complex and Ambiguous (VUCA) world.[27]

A mechanistic approach, then, is aimed at capturing the optimal energy of people as part of the machine-like thinking that has process as the overlord. The management approach to this is to create an archetype (role) to focus on the processes and ensure there is compliance and consistency of application.

A heuristic approach creates a different kind of energy, one that will need to adapt, emerge and be more individually determined;

therefore management is about allowing discretion, analysis, decision making, experimentation and attention to adapted alignment to the overall desired outcome and expected results.

This is a huge shift in energy – from compliance and predictability to emergence and adaptation.

Instead of people being focused on repetition and being managed, they will be expected to take more ownership but have less supervision and more support and enablement. Many social scientists will say that in order to be efficient, people need repetition to provide that consistent and predictable application, yet they suffer through boredom and the inflexibility of approach and will not cope well with deviances and exceptions.

Whilst the variety and unpredictability that comes with a heuristic approach may be more interesting, stimulating and challenging for people, it presents a very different expectation on economies of scale – ie that nothing is truly standardized, therefore it cannot be optimal in efficiency of process.

Yet, if there are repeat tasks, people will still become competent and confident in them and it could be a ready switch between mechanistic and heuristic which still provides variety and stimulation alongside efficiency and certainty of outcome, thereby energizing people through natural human traits like curiosity, determination and creativity.

Indeed, many call-handling scripts have been adapted to become not the entire *gospel* of how to communicate with customers, but more a set of core principles to enact with tailored approaches to each individual caller. As a customer, I definitely prefer a more individual, attentive and listening call handler rather than a canned, scripted agent, even if my query is an exact match for a mechanized response and resolution.

So heuristics, whilst seemingly a departure from efficiency drives from the 1980s systems methodologies (like Business Process Reengineering, Total Quality Management (TQM), Kaizen, and Lean), is actually showing how to create adaptive, customer-centric and human-centred design principles as winning strategies to delight customers, enhance reputation, demonstrate an interest in employee experience and provide a more human feel to interactions.

The randomness of human beings is perhaps what we have finally stopped trying to conquer and now we aspire to work with those variable energies and nuances. In my book *Transformational HR*, I referred to HR as 'white-water canoeists' of this energy rather than their previous attempts to channel compliance by being dam builders. Going with a flow, not trying to blockade it.

The emerging field of *Robotic Process Automation* promises to enhance production of algorithmic elements of work and, as many argue, could create significantly more capacity for us to do more heuristic work as required by an ever more complex, intertwined and demanding world.

We most certainly know a lot more about our motivations, our energy levels and how we can be optimized doing the work we are tasked to do; the impacts of over-work (or Peak Work as I've called it), of higher levels of recorded workplace stress, and those 66–87 per cent levels of disengagement that result in a rather sad state of affairs.

WHAT WE LEARNED FROM THIS CHAPTER

1 We have many inherited design flaws from the 20th-century version of work, which still haven't been adapted despite being in the third decade of the 21st century. It is the assertion of this book that we may be preventing progress with deliberate or accidental neglect to the design of work. We are urging readers to look critically at the design of their organizations and how things might be adapted to the 2020 world and beyond.

2 Much of the narrative and some research over the last few years has pointed us to the increasing rate of automation of mechanistic work, and the need to look at how we can better support and adapt our people for the remaining heuristic work. We are urging readers to think analytically about the skills development they and their colleagues are undertaking in order to be better prepared for that more heuristic future of work.

3 Including others in design conversations, workshops and implementation appears to be our most under-utilized option in this area. Whilst it may seem like a more chaotic way to manage the design of an organization, with people involved there is (a) more ownership; (b) a wider pool of insight from people actively involved in a range of areas across the

organization; (c) innovation and energy towards organization redesign over inertia, suspicion, fear and anger over restructures. We are urging an inclusive, agile and highly participative programme of organization design as a norm and a move away from constructed restructures which cause anxiety, uncertainty and psychological trauma to many.

Endnotes

1. www.clarewgraves.com/home.html (archived at https://perma.cc/BJ7M-QA2K)
2. Beck, D and Cowan, C (1996) *Spiral Dynamics*, Blackwell Publications
3. McLeod, S (2018) Pavlov's Dogs, *Simply Psychology*. Available from: www.simplypsychology.org/pavlov.html (archived at https://perma.cc/8944-6LT4)
4. Harter, J (2018) Employee engagement on the rise in the US, *Gallup*. Available from: https://news.gallup.com/poll/241649/employee-engagement-rise.aspx (archived at https://perma.cc/K4AV-USGL)
5. http://nilofermerchant.com/ (archived at https://perma.cc/Y3F5-FELQ)
6. www.businessdictionary.com/definition/Taylorism.html (archived at https://perma.cc/F96L-W67K)
7. *The Economist* (2008) The Hawthorn Effect. Available from: www.economist.com/news/2008/11/03/the-hawthorne-effect (archived at https://perma.cc/6VSJ-29Q8)
8. McCleod, S (2018) Maslow's Hierarchy of Needs, *Simply Psychology*. Available from: www.simplypsychology.org/maslow.html (archived at https://perma.cc/X8SM-Y3UL)
9. NHS Employers (nd) What is organizational development. Available from: www.nhsemployers.org/campaigns/organisational-development/what-is-organisational-development (archived at https://perma.cc/DD2D-REHW)
10. CIPD (2019) Organisation Development. Available from: www.cipd.co.uk/knowledge/strategy/organisational-development/factsheet (archived at https://perma.cc/ME7Q-7ZSZ)
11. Timms, P (nd) Organisational development in strategic HR: is now the time we all become OD practitioners?, *The HR Director*. Available from: www.thehrdirector.com/organisational-development-strategic-hr/ (archived at https://perma.cc/CYK7-JGP7)
12. Semler, R (1993) *Maverick: The success story behind the world's most unusual workplace*, Time Warner
13. Sims, C and Johnson, H (2012) *Scrum: A breathtakingly brief and agile introduction*, Dymaxicon

14 https://agilemanifesto.org/ (archived at https://perma.cc/K84K-FTF6)
15 www.cluetrain.com/ (archived at https://perma.cc/39EX-CB9R)
16 Hamel, G (2011) First let's fire all the managers, *Harvard Business Review*. Available from: https://hbr.org/2011/12/first-lets-fire-all-the-managers (archived at https://perma.cc/CJ9T-BGHY)
17 Hamel, G (2010) Innovation Democracy: W.L. Gore's original management model, *Management Innovation Exchange*. Available from: www.managementexchange.com/story/innovation-democracy-wl-gores-original-management-model (archived at https://perma.cc/Z4X4-53DU)
18 https://twitter.com/connectinghr?lang=en (archived at https://perma.cc/27Z4-CB93)
19 Zander, R (2017) How to run an un-conference, *Medium*. Available from: https://medium.com/responsive-org/how-to-run-an-un-conference-92e7cf089831 (archived at https://perma.cc/7PDN-GE4B)
20 www.valuescentre.com/ (archived at https://perma.cc/7S32-9CBW)
21 www.worldblu.com/ (archived at https://perma.cc/Q38X-JRQ5)
22 101 Computing.net (2018) Heuristic approaches to problem solving. Available from: www.101computing.net/heuristic-approaches-to-problem-solving/ (archived at https://perma.cc/59TF-GQ64)
23 Dawson, J (2016) What is the percentage of desk jobs to manual labor jobs in the USA? *Quora*. Available from: www.quora.com/What-is-the-percentage-of-desk-jobs-to-manual-labor-jobs-in-the-USA (archived at https://perma.cc/F333-UB3X)
24 Osborne, M and Frey, C (2018) Automation and the future of work: understanding the numbers, *University of Oxford*. Available from: www.oxfordmartin.ox.ac.uk/blog/automation-and-the-future-of-work-understanding-the-numbers/ (archived at https://perma.cc/L35M-JF6C)
25 World Economic Forum (2018) Future of Work report. Available from: www3.weforum.org/docs/WEF_Future_of_Jobs_2018.pdf (archived at https://perma.cc/T2TF-TJVE)
26 http://blackswanevents.org/?page_id =26 (archived at https://perma.cc/YB69-T542)
27 Bennett, M and Lemoine, G (2014) What VUCA really means for you, *Harvard Business Review*. Available from: https://hbr.org/2014/01/what-vuca-really-means-for-you (archived at https://perma.cc/5KY3-EUEN)

03

80/20 variances

How we're reshaping the design of how we work and live

In this chapter, we look at the almost mystical quality of Pareto's 80/20 rule as it relates to the design of work, workplaces and how we live our working lives.

We look at Pareto's original theory, and at how statistics around the state of the workplace are shaping our thinking but also manifesting in our frustrations around our perceived inability to address the decline in fulfilment and satisfaction from our work.

We look into the stark realization that 80 per cent of us are enduring a troublesome approach to our working lives with new-found fragility in the 'deal' that's struck between the employer and those in its employ. Whilst we have 20 per cent of the working world in a state of engagement, have they found a recipe for some form of human flourishing (eudaimonia) and a near nirvana, or as Maslow stated, a 'self-actualized' state of being?

Whether the answer lies in a mathematical equation and probability, or a combination of this and human-centred psychology and work design, this chapter aims to give us some sense of the way to present our arguments, theories and applied thinking into doing. Whilst this chapter will not necessarily provide the tools which will be found in later chapters, it will aim to stimulate the logical processing aspects of our brain and combine this with the theory of change and design.

Numbers are framing the world: percentages of rain forest loss; the rise in temperatures that frames the climate emergency; the S&P/Dow/FTSE/Nikkei/Hang Seng; GDP; interest rates; reserves; the Human Poverty Index; or the United Nations 17 Sustainable Development Goals (SDGs).

> We are surrounded by, guided by and obsessed by numbers, so does 80/20 carry any true weight or influence? Is there an energy source that sits somewhere in this ratio?
>
> How can we leverage this numerical phenomenon to help us design for better?
>
> And how can we use numbers more wisely in the way we rescue the human race from a self-inflicted dissatisfaction, discord and even early demise because of poorly designed and deployed systems for work?

We all know Pareto's rule[1] – or do we?

Picture the scene: 19th-century Italy, and Vilfredo Pareto is harvesting peas when he notices some pods are way more stacked with peas than others. And upon counting them, he realizes that 80 per cent of his pea crop comes from 20 per cent of his pods.

Interesting in and of itself. But Vilfredo was no vegetable farmer – he was a late-1800s economist. He took this finding into the world of economics and found that 80 per cent of Italy's wealth was held by only 20 per cent of its citizens.

Since this discovery, various statistical analysis programmes have revealed similar ratios: 80 per cent of crime is perpetrated by 20 per cent of known criminals[2] (the so-called repeat offenders). If you are a charity, it's likely that 80 per cent of your donations come from 20 per cent of your donors.

It's often called a law or a rule but in reality it's more a **defined phenomenon**. There is no statistical certainty behind 80/20 and we often label things that are similar (90/10; 70/30) as if it were part of this same phenomenon. So the numbers may vary but the point being made is the same: focus on the smaller number because it is largely responsible for the creation of the larger number.

Peas and Italian lira gave rise to this belief and applied theory in some – clearly not all – cases.

And so to work, and the aforementioned Gallup annual survey on employee engagement that so many of us rely on for our statistical referencing on the state of the workplace and its impact on people.

Seventeen per cent of us report being fully engaged in our work.[3] You could say that's as near to 20 per cent as we can get to apply this rule to the workplace, meaning more than 80 per cent of us are only partially or not at all engaged in our work.

If we then look at workplace productivity, it appears to be stubbornly flat and in many cases declining[4] despite the advent of advancing technology. This could help us understand that the contribution of the *vital few* (to use a Pareto term) is not compensated for by the *trivial many*. It seems harsh to label 80 per cent of the workforce trivial and indeed it is.

That 80 per cent is wasted human capital (a phrase I don't like but hopefully it makes the point). It's not that 80 per cent of your workforce are careless, carefree or useless let alone trivial. It means that in a huge majority of cases, the work that has been designed for them to do is unengaging, leading to a very basic level of compliance and an underwhelming level of performance.

A vicious circle of uninspiring work that needs doing and an uninspired worker doing that work.

We have to face the fact that we cannot simply design all work to be engaging and inspiring. Or do we? Are we stuck with an 80/20 ratio of less engaged/engaged because we can only truly design inspiring work situations for 20 per cent of our people?

So is it boring work or bad work design?

Even if the work we have to do appears to be a loathsome and boring endeavour, does it really have to be endured by people or can we not look at a range of variations and stimulus to help make **all** working lives more interesting?

According to a careeraddict.com article[5] the most boring jobs in the world are:

1 Security guard
2 Bank branch manager
3 Data entry
4 Accountant

5 Nanny

6 Dishwasher

7 Truck driver

8 Cleaning and housekeeping

9 Waste and garbage collection

10 Teacher

The basis of this research is not given and eight comments to this article challenge the assertion that these jobs are boring.

I'd surmise that being a nanny or a teacher is boring if you don't like children but then why take the role if you don't?

Boring work, a dull job, tedious routine tasks – it's all relative to the individual; there are people I know who've been happy to be a data entry clerk, a security guard or a truck driver.

People often find themselves in a situation where they believe there are better things they could be doing and find they don't have the means or the wherewithal to facilitate that change.

Therefore, whilst some work seems boring and the make-up of a job is dull and uninspiring, there are still things we can do to create stretch, variety, stimulation **where it is needed**.

But how do we find out what is needed?

I believe that many people (probably 80 per cent) are like me, and entered the workplace with little certainty about what they wanted to do in their working life. Some enlightened souls (probably 20 per cent!) are clear from their university or school studies, their sporting or hobby pursuits, or their parents or family business ventures. These factors are still not definite but the sons and daughters of lawyers often become lawyers themselves and so it goes.

When I entered the workplace I had a general interest in the law, journalism, and teaching. I now find myself working with legal constructs (companies), writing books and features (about people at work), and helping people learn new things that make their life more fulfilling (consulting, advising, training and coaching). So you could say I ended up where my interests took me.

But I'm no lawyer, journalist or teacher. I'm a variation and combination of all those things.

Many people don't truly know what their full potential is and that's part of the wonder of being a discovery-based human being.

Who am I and what am I here for?

This is the question that has perplexed and baffled philosophers, dictators and religious leaders for centuries.

Of all the phrases I believe sums this up (and there are many) it is this from legendary American football coach Vince Lombardi: *The measure of who we are, is what we do with what we have.*[6]

Which may lead people to discuss this with the concept of **existentialism**.

Existentialism is defined as a philosophical attitude associated especially with Heidegger, Jaspers, Marcel and Sartre, and opposed to rationalism and empiricism, which stresses *the individual's unique position as a self-determining agent responsible for the authenticity of his or her choices.*[7]

The unique position we find ourselves in is in *being* ourselves. Not the daughter, the husband, the employee, the Officer, the Doctor, the Mayor, or similar appellations. Existentialism is about finding our true selves through the choices we have and make.

We develop a sense of personality and we forge ourselves into the human beings we are – completely unlike any other human being there ever was or will be.

With that in mind, we still have to *find* ourselves in a life and work sense. We have to discover who we are through a range of interactions and events, tests and challenges.

Eventually we find out what socio-political persuasion we might take up, the type of lifestyle we want to lead and, of course, the work we want to do.

It may well be that 20 per cent of our life is spent working out how to make the most of the 80 per cent we have left.

By the time we're 20 years old, though, we still don't TRULY know ourselves. So maybe 80 per cent of our life is spent working out what is our best self, and 20 per cent of our time is spent maximizing that to achieve what we want from life.

Anyway, 80/20 might apply to life, but in order to illustrate my point on discovering who we are and what we're really meant to do in life that enables us to truly flourish I will use the power of a story to get us there.

Work helps us find out *who we are and what we're here for.*

The story is of a phenomenal singer from a phenomenal era: Marvin Gaye and the Motown musical empire of the 1960s and '70s.

Born Marvin Pentz Gay Junior, April 2nd 1939 in Washington DC, Gay (who added the 'e' to his last name later on – like Sam Cooke did) began his singing career, like many of the time, in church (Marvin's father was an ordained minister).

Gaye had a troubled childhood, with his father at times being brutal towards his family with beatings and violent outbursts. Having performed in some of the vocal doo-wop groups of the time, Gaye's more secular musical choices led him to explore that avenue as a career. However, it was around his 17th birthday that Gaye left the family home and dropped out of high school to join the Air Force.

Somewhat jaded by the menial tasks he was given as a basic Airman, he was discharged on mental health grounds and he returned to his singing passion. He would then meet up with a burgeoning music aficionado, Harvey Fuqua, who enlisted Gaye into his doo-wop group The (New) Moonglows. Fuqua was one of the pioneers of the African American music scene in the late 1950s that came to Berry Gordy Jr's growing Tamla and Motown venture in Detroit.

Fuqua brought Gaye and others to the Motown stable where Berry Gordy Jr could see star potential in this charismatic young man. Until Gordy worked out Marvin's true place in his plans, Gaye was a drummer, songwriter, backing singer and was kept busy albeit somewhat in the wings.

Then, in 1961, Gaye was given his first recordings and, whilst they didn't exactly ride high in the charts, they proved his potential.

There was, however, one problem.

Gaye wanted to be 'the black Frank Sinatra', singing jazz standards and mellow swing in a way that appealed to older music listeners.

He had no desire to become a Rhythm & Blues (R&B) icon. And Berry Gordy Jr wanted to build his empire on the Sounds of Young America. The affluent, hip and demanding young white American teenagers.

So, Gordy did something that could be construed as a good piece of mentoring, performance enhancing and talent spotting. It could also be construed as manipulating and using someone as an asset in the pursuit of corporate gain.

What Gordy did was stretch his performer. He asked his songwriters and producers to ensure they scored all of Gaye's songs **one octave higher**. Brian and Eddie Holland, Lamont Dozier, Smokey Robinson, Norman Whitfield – all producers and writers who knew how to get more from Gaye's vocals. **One octave higher**.

Gaye was helped by having a five-octave range anyway, so to him this was nothing too challenging – just not what he thought he'd be recording. No swing standards, or supper-club jazz. Hip, young, vibrant and church-like R&B. 'Can I Get A Witness', 'Ain't That Peculiar', 'I'll Be Doggone' and many more.

Did Gaye like his new-found fame? He certainly seemed comfortable as headliner for the *Motortown Revue* concert tours and was soon to become the partner for duets that really appealed to the music-buying public of the United States and beyond. Mary Wells, Kim Weston and perhaps most famously Tammi Terrell, joined forces with Marvin to record some of Motown's bestselling duets.

This glorious state of affairs lasted through epoch-defining moments like 'I Heard It Through the Grapevine', 'Ain't No Mountain High Enough' and 'You're All I Need to Get By'. The latter two were performed with his singing partner Tammi Terrell, who tragically collapsed on stage in Marvin's arms and never recovered from a brain tumour, dying tragically young (aged 24) in 1970. Marvin was clearly devastated, and withdrew somewhat from the public eye.

Around this time, American lives were hit by race riots; Malcolm X and Dr Martin Luther King Jr were leading a fightback on civil injustice and the continued struggle for social equality, especially in many southern US States.

Marvin saw brutality on the streets and on TV screens and it troubled him.

He started to write about the experiences as songs, and in conversation with (one of the Motown group The Four Tops) Obie Benson, he realized they had a perfect combination: an elegant piece of music and the poetic, socio-political consciousness of a song.

Gaye took it to Berry Gordy Jr, the founder, owner and leader of Motown. You remember, the leader who took Gaye beyond what he thought he could do as a recording artist.

It is reported that Gordy rejected the recording, stating that Motown was about fun and enjoyment, not socio-political statements and movements. So Gaye withdrew his energy and his labour; he went on strike and refused to record anything else. Faced with one of the most appealing artists on his roster no longer recording, Gordy eventually reneged.

The song was 'What's Going On', one of the landmark songs of the 1970s and still poignant and relevant to this day (maybe even more so with current political polarization).

Stevie Wonder followed suit with 'Living for the City', Chicago's Curtis Mayfield with 'If There's a Hell Below (We're All Going To Go)' and over in Philadelphia The O'Jays with 'For the Love of Money' – all called out the injustices, division and decay in society.

Gaye's epic paved the way for more protest through song, more awareness of injustice through hit records and more stances by artists using their fame to raise others' consciousness.

Yet he had to withdraw this labour, his energy and his creativity from an enterprise that had made him capable of taking on this fight through the power and artistry of song. The label gave him fame and stages, and eventually had to give in to him so he could have his platform.

What this story tells us is not of one artist's fight over an oppressive employer. Arguably, Gordy was a hard task master but ultimately gave many people a shot at fame and fortune they couldn't have earned in other ways.

No, this story talks of knowing and design. Knowing your true worth, value and reason for being doesn't come easily and you may need some help along the way from your friends, family, and employer. *Design* is the secret to all things improvement yet again comes better with experience and creativity combined.

Gaye was a brilliant performer yet he could have disappeared into obscurity had he stuck to 'crooning'. So his work was designed by his employer (one octave higher), knowing that his capability lay beyond what he believed was best for him or indeed what he was capable of.

However, had this continued to be the state of affairs (employer dominance over an employee), the world would have been denied an epic moment in song and music. Had Gaye not developed the confidence and competence to take on his employer over what he deemed artistic suppression, we would never have experienced a song that was as profound as 'Strange Fruit', 'A Change Is Gonna Come' or 'Imagine'.

So the result was an ultimate in *design* by the employee, now in a state of *knowing*; knowing his true value and worth, and what he was able to do through his talent, determination and creativity.

80/20 and the *What's Going On* factor

The 80/20 in this story is that (probably) 80 per cent of Gaye's fame was down to his employer in the first instance – designing things to make more of Gaye's talent than he would have ever done alone.

And then in an about turn, arguably the more lasting memories of Gaye's musical genius legacy, came from the 20 per cent of his career where he took control. Twenty per cent of Marvin's career that – without the 80 per cent initial input from his employer – may never have happened.

And as such, that is the case for many of us.

Eighty per cent of us, shaped by our experiences and what the workplace 'gives' us. I use quotes there as the employer doesn't gift these to us without some return on that investment. In the name of getting more from us, the employer helps by giving us things to get more from us. It utilizes our energy, our endeavours and our applied efforts to do more of why it exists: to either make more money (for-profit enterprises) or operate within tighter margins (non-profits, governmental or charitable).

So this 'gift' is not some societal giving or humanist gesture; it's economics. Numbers. Productivity boosts through enabling and skilling people through development initiatives, stretch assignments and skills programmes.

We could say that 80 per cent of what an employer does for you as a worker/employee is to create gain for them and the other 20 per cent is what we can gain out of this 'deal' or exchange. Whatever the motive or the outcome is, like Marvin Gaye's story, it is one of experience, viability to achieve what your employer needs of you and then ultimately, through that, of self-discovery and self-actualization, as Abraham Maslow described it. A peak. A pinnacle. An apex.

So maybe we'll take that 20 per cent and be happy to put the 80 per cent to work for our employer as part of that deal – discovery whilst getting some form of recompense financially.

When we eventually find ourselves like this, we'll want to give the best of our most creative and applied self, and then it's down to the employer and (the now) *knowing* employee to work out whether that's an adapted deal (like Gaye's) or whether that means the employee has to find their new place of worth in another venture.

It would explain why many people move to freelancing in the latter stages of their career. They realize who they are, what they want from their work and life, and find that the employer is not the place with which to find/do those things.

So we may spend 80 per cent of our time with an employer, and look back and think what little we have got from all that effort and time. But in reality, we may have *found ourselves* entirely – what we believe in and value most. What we are best at and what we love doing. Who we truly are and what we're inspired to be in life and in our work. That may only have come from 20 per cent of that time whilst toiling under contract. But what a 20 per cent if it was! The 'What's Going On' times of our career.

It's also – of course – the 80 per cent of disengaged people that could be used to unlock the productivity equation and the puzzle of flatlining and declining rates of productivity. Eighty per cent of us coasting through our working lives or suffering through some form of endured servitude.

If we can flip this into 80 per cent of people celebrating fulfilment and flourishing from our work, with only 20 per cent of us still in some state of uncertainty, it's certainly a big shift from over a decade of 80/20 in favour of being disengaged.

More than numbers

The majority of the rest of this book is about how we might do that, how others have unlocked much of the engagement and energy quotient in their people who are experiencing work in a way many now think is not possible. We have significant recalibration to undertake before we can go beyond merely dreaming of this possibility.

For a start, the numbers are against us. Up to 80 per cent disengaged has been the case for a long time now despite increased life expectancy, standards of living, and understanding of what we're all about as people and as employees.

Then we have the numbers for profit or economic performance, which have been incredibly short-term and binary (profit/efficiency or else demise) and have driven recent decisions to cull staff numbers, to sell off unproductive parts of businesses to outsourcing or offshoring. We have been dominated in our thinking by those numbers.

And there is no such number for the energy people give to their work and the value this creates, nor have we truly measured the numbers that become the value lost when we abuse that energy in people.

We also have the numbers of productivity to contend with; GDP and the Davos-going leaders' obsession with it as the ultimate in measurement.

There is hope though.

New Zealand is a nation very much revered as the 2020 and beyond version of a nation state with a compassionate and capable leader, an open, tolerant and just society, and an ambition to be a country fiercely protective of its people, natural assets and its place in a more just world. Not just because of, but largely led by, Jacinda Ardern as Prime Minister.

The New Zealand government recently declared it would be focusing on well-being as a measure of success as a nation and not just GDP.[8]

It demonstrates something like 80/20 in this thinking; there's probably an 80 per cent obsession on the economic factors that impact on GDP, when in reality there's a 20 per cent slice of this that's being overlooked. Like how well people are, how mentally stable and flourishing they feel, how connected they are to their employer beyond mere financial/labour exchange, and how innovation and active participation in growth are the 20 per cent that could make the difference between a good organization and a thriving one.

It's all speculative of course, yet instinctively many feel that if a company has an explicit duty of care, and consideration for the wellness of their employees, the repayment of that support is something beyond the transactional stuff that's exchanged begrudgingly by both 'sides'. Indeed, a study of the economic performance of WorldBlu listed companies in 2013[9] reported a huge difference in economic performance and resilience compared to their conventional counterparts – 103 per cent growth compared to 15 per cent.

Could WorldBlu's freedom-centred working and the nation of New Zealand be onto something with this move to inclusion, freedom and well-being over an obsession with the mechanics of work and GDP?

Time will tell, and maybe 20 per cent of us think this is awesome and 80 per cent believe it's madness and counterproductive.

Let's take a look at another nation: Iceland.

In the early 2000s, Icelandic banks appeared to suddenly become an investment hub like some *El Dorado* of wealth management. And then, boom. It all fell apart. Iceland effectively became bankrupt.

What happened next was something not seen in other nations where their economic engines ground to a halt and pistons froze in their chambers. The government bailouts and the public ownership of banks became the engine-rebuild package for commercial entities who overstretched themselves and required significant support to return to functioning, profit-making ways.

The nation of Iceland, though, looked at itself in the mirror and said, 'How can we do this?' They enlisted the help of a UK/US consultancy, the **Barrett Values Centre**,[10] who came to the nation's rescue by looking at the values set of a nation with a smaller headcount than some global companies.

They wanted to understand how much of the nation's road to recovery was in Icelanders' understanding of how Icelandic values could influence behaviours and change the culture; from one of financial ruin and embarrassment to a once-again thriving economy and a more conscious way of handling money, trade and commerce.

The initial cultural assessment revealed the nature of the shock and disturbing anxiety the people of Iceland now felt after their banking industry collapsed and was a co-facilitator of the 2008 global financial crisis.

An espoused set of values were sourced (personal and national levels) and these were used to plot the trajectory between actual and desired values in order to start the country's journey to recovery. A bold move by a nation to treat itself in this way (like a corporation) that led to the identification of *Seven Levels of National Consciousness* with clear shifts needed and plotted using the indices provided by the *Barrett Model*.

Using this source data as proof of the gap to close and how to measure progress and plot a course, there followed around a decade of actions, including criminal prosecutions of their Prime Minister (overseeing the nation's finances) and the banking leaders who facilitated the collapses.

The recovery started after the new government let its three major banks collapse and did not bail them out like the US and UK governments did. Using IMF funds and capitalizing on its low-value currency to build a stronger export and tourist economy were major aspects of its recovery and yet it was also clear that people needed a restoration of their belief in the politicians and economic leaders who played a similarly huge role in rebuilding faith and galvanizing the spirit of Iceland's 350,000 people.

Using the 80/20 rule would be difficult to apply to Iceland's collapse and eventual recovery. And yet, at least 80 per cent of its population had no direct part to play in its collapse, but still paid the price of having to work through to recovery and adjust moral and social values to oversee a new way to live the Icelandic way through centring on a more solidly defined and acted out set of values.

And it is the effect of values that interests me most in connecting to the premise for this book and its focus on energy. Values are, of course, our guiding forces. They mean something to us. They have resonance and a strong, almost magnetic force.

Values are an energy source and indeed a manifestation of our energies

We find energy when we have our values known and defined by us, and they compel us to act in a certain way. That magnetic force, that immovable cornerstone of what we hold most dear and adhere to.

When we look at actions that are arguably misdemeanours (forcing people to work longer hours than they should optimally be working), that are ordained processes (a focus on selling even when customers don't want to buy the product), that cause us to do immoral, illegal and unfair things to others, we can blame the process all we like and yet, if we take our values as an overriding factor, we may not see so many corporate crimes and inappropriate actions.

Of course, values are subjective and they are ours. They may appear to be in conflict with what others believe to be fair and humane:

- What values are at play when people choose to hunt and kill a beautiful animal for a trophy?
- What values are being displayed when people show bigotry and hatred towards others based on the colour of their skin?
- What values are being channelled in the deliberate misuse of people's money simply to try and make more money for clients?

We may think there are some people who have no values, except they do – just a very distorted version compared to our own, perhaps.

What Iceland did was channel the positive and restorative nature of values to energize their people to create the conditions for recovery – sustainable recovery – of a nation's wealth and reputation.

With the current investment in cryptocurrency and tourism, new forms of growth saw a pretty staggering 7.6 per cent GDP growth in 2016 – just eight years after the turmoil and six after the volcanic eruption took most Atlantic flights out of action. An incredible story with more to come, through the energy of people and their belief in the values that bind them and the collective energy to overcome a seismic shock to this small and proud nation.

From numbers into songs and into values has been quite some journey for this chapter. It has, though, attempted to show a range of tangible and intangible factors that shape the energy we have, use and regenerate in a range of circumstances. When we feel we have control and are values-led – like Marvin Gaye or the people of Iceland – we can perform extraordinary feats of creativity, resilience and artistry to create lasting impacts for others.

> WHAT WE LEARNED FROM THIS CHAPTER
>
> 1 Pareto's rule shows some interesting numerical values for the phenomena we're experiencing with employee engagement. We can accept that we're unlikely to ever see 100 per cent of us report being engaged in our work, yet less than 20 per cent of us for over a decade is a sorry state of affairs, We all have an obligation to look at reversing the current 80/20 in favour of disengaged/engaged to 80/20 engaged/disengaged. One employee, one team, one company at a time.
>
> 2 We can see that how much of who we really are as people can be helped by the discovery elements of our working lives. The story of Marvin Gaye as a recording artist shows how we can be stretched and channelled by our employer and then how we can establish our confident, competent and creative self to truly do what we believe in and love. We should expect our employers to help us discover our talents (our 'one octave higher') in order to then establish our true purpose and reason for being in our work (our 'What's Going On' moment).
>
> 3 Through all the 80/20 applications, the discovery of our true talented selves and our journey through to doing the best work of our lives, we need to understand the power of our values and the energy source that they are and drive us toward. We would be well served by our mindful understanding and utilization of our values as we discover how powerful they are for us and in helping direct the efforts of others to achieve lasting, positive outcomes for ourselves, those nearest to us and the world more generally.

Endnotes

1. Policonomics (nd) Vilfredo Pareto. Available from: https://policonomics.com/vilfredo-pareto/ (archived at https://perma.cc/9K5W-EAZN)
2. Parker, F (2016) Just 1 in 5 of population commits 80% of crimes, *Stamford Mercury*. Available from: www.stamfordmercury.co.uk/news/just-1-in-5-of-population-commit-80-of-crimes-1-7731202/ (archived at https://perma.cc/HQS3-DD83)
3. Gallup (2017) State of the Global Workplace. Available from: www.gallup.com/workplace/238079/state-global-workplace-2017.aspx?utm_source=link_wwwv9&utm_campaign=item_231668&utm_medium=copy (archived at https://perma.cc/4DMG-9H57)
4. OECD (nd) Productivity statistics. Available from: www.oecd.org/sdd/productivity-stats/ (archived at https://perma.cc/Z3PL-WUFC)
5. Harrison, K (2016) Top 10 most boring jobs in the world, *Career Addict*. Available from: www.careeraddict.com/top-10-most-boring-jobs-2015 (archived at https://perma.cc/BZ5V-27F5)
6. www.goodreads.com/quotes/968021-the-measure-of-who-we-are-is-what-we-do (archived at https://perma.cc/73PP-896U)
7. www.dictionary.com/browse/existentialism (archived at https://perma.cc/R65L-DME4)
8. Charlton, E (2019) New Zealand is publishing its first 'well-being' budget, *World Economic Forum*. Available from: www.weforum.org/agenda/2019/05/new-zealand-is-publishing-its-first-well-being-budget/ (archived at https://perma.cc/24KK-UDNE)
9. WorldBlu (nd) Introducing WorldBlu certified freedom-centred workplaces. Available from: www.worldblu.com/certified (archived at https://perma.cc/2UPW-GWRN)
10. Barrett Values Centre (nd) The Barrett Model. Available from: www.valuescentre.com/barrett-model/ (archived at https://perma.cc/P5VB-DH7L)

04

1/20 or a 20 per cent probability

What are the chances that your work energizes you?

In this chapter, we look at the sad state of affairs in our work, workplaces and organizations providing us with something that should give us a flourishing life.

As described in our previous chapters, with only around one in five of us experiencing an engaging experience of work, isn't it about time we addressed these chronic shortcomings?

Illnesses brought on by stressful ways of working; broken families due to absent parents always working; devices meaning we're 'always on'. Whilst it might not look like anything other than a first world problem, we have an epidemic of the proportions of plagues and influenzas on our hands and we've designed it like this.

Indeed, there are even worse signs to come where there are some predictions of a workless future, of people no longer needing to make anything and of artificial intelligence and robots of the physical and logical sort taking our jobs. To many this means no economic viability, and therefore no quality of life. No money to pay for things and experiences which the robots provide. This is the dystopian view of the future. Others predict a slip into purposeless, hedonistic ways of living which will see some bleak Blade Runner-esque or Matrix-like dismal or even fake reality.

Whether the science fiction book and movie industries have any truth in them, we shall have to see. What is clear is that there are already signs and incidents where some form of addictive, intrusive, malevolent technological interference with our lives is happening. Be it data and voting manipulation, be it gambling and pornography addiction, or be it the constant screening

> we seem to live our lives through, none of these appear to paint a rosy picture of the future yet to unfurl.
>
> So in this chapter we take a look into research, opinions and stories of how the world of work is making us ill, live shorter and more unhappy lives, and the crimes against humanity in how people are treated as commodities instead of human colleagues and part of a united team doing great things together in the name of work.

Introduction – a stress pandemic

The CIPD is one of the biggest membership organizations for the HR, OD, learning and people professions in the world, with over 150,000 members globally. It has a strong future-focused agenda under its mission of **better work and working lives**.[1]

It regularly researches hot areas and topics impacting on the world of work and people's experiences of it, so that its professional HR members are informed and inspired to act in the most appropriate way on things like evidence rather than tired best practice or anecdotes.

One piece of research culminated in a report published in 2019[2] which demonstrated just how toxic workplaces have become. This extract is particularly telling:

> Within UK organizations, the last year has seen an increased focus on employee mental health combined with employee wellbeing featuring on more senior leaders' agendas (CIPD, Health & Wellbeing at Work, 2019).

These positive steps are, however, set against a backdrop of increasing levels of Presenteeism, Leaveism, and resultantly, increased stress. Employee burnout is becoming more common. Employers within the UK may indeed be taking mental health more seriously but with a workforce facing blurred lines between work and home (CIPD, Health & Wellbeing at Work, 2019), what will this situation look like in 2050? Furthermore, with AI advancing and replacing humans in some industries, how will humans be affected; both in terms of wellbeing and physiological and psychological energy expended at work?

The CIPD report mentioned above also reported that over a third (37 per cent) of employers have seen an increase in stress-related absence, with heavy workloads and poor management styles to blame.[3]

In support of this assertion, in May 2019 the World Health Organization published a declaration that **burnout was now an officially recognized ill-health phenomenon.**[4] Classified as a disease. Stress-filled working is now an illness like bacterial and viral infections. An officially recognized disease where the infliction of circumstances in modern workplaces is the cause, is a travesty of modern workplace design.

Who is to blame?

Is it:

- HR, with its pro-employer policies treating all employees as work-shy payroll plunderers?
- Management, with its heavy-handed and oppressive supervisory tactics?
- Senior leaders, with their eye only on operating overheads and costs/profit?
- Society, with its fetishization of consumer products and lifestyles and its fixation on success being how hard you work and how high up the ladder you're climbing?

I think the answer is you.

Well, you, me and all of us.

We're all somehow to blame for this situation – through not being aware, being involved in such bad practices ourselves, for not calling out others who do such oppressive or self-harming things, and for not having our minds cleansed by alternatives.

We've knowledge that says things like overly long hours aren't good for the work we do, the people we're doing it with or the people who are waiting at home for us. Yet we persist.

So again, a pandemic. A self-designed one at that.

An extract from the WHO report mentioned earlier says this:

> Burn-out is a syndrome conceptualized as resulting from chronic workplace stress that has not been successfully managed. It is characterized by three dimensions:
>
> - feelings of energy depletion or exhaustion;
> - increased mental distance from one's job, or feelings of negativism or cynicism related to one's job; and
> - reduced professional efficacy.
>
> Burn-out refers specifically to phenomena in the occupational context and should not be applied to describe experiences in other areas of life.

So the initial dimension is **energy depletion or exhaustion** – the entire premise of this book is in those words. We're exhausted not just by physical exertion, but by mental overload and stressful ways of being.

Let's take a look at this and, for a short time, explore how human energy is created, used, wasted and then regenerated.

Use of energy/depletion of energy at work

As a guide, an *average* man needs around 2,500kcal (10,500kJ) a day to maintain a healthy body weight. For an *average* woman, that figure is around 2,000kcal (8,400kJ) a day.[5]

The number of kJ varies depending on age, sex, activity level, body size and geographical location.[6] The brain represents 2 per cent of a person's body mass, yet uses 20 per cent of oxygen and calories.[7]

Knowing that much of the work we do is now logical and not so much physical, how do we utilize and sustain our energy when our thinking 'muscle' is using 20 per cent of our energy source in 'normal' day-to-day circumstances? At times of pressure, intensity and long hours, we're using our mind in a way that depletes our energy without us truly realizing this until we are near to collapse. And how can we recharge our energy source to give that hard-working muscle more to keep us going?

In proving the impact of over-working, Stanford Professor Jeffrey Pfeffer (2010[8]) called for a *better understanding of the human dimension of sustainability*; and Fritz, Lam and Spreitzer[9] attempted to answer this by looking into sustaining human energy at work.

The authors looked at employee strategies to sustain energy. They concluded that strategies relating to **learning** and **positive workplace relationships** were most strongly correlated to employees' energy (rather than switching to simpler tasks, for example browsing the internet, as some form of a break).

Fritz, Lam and Spreitzer also discussed factors that lead to a depletion of human energy at work. They cite the human energy crisis[10] as the term used to describe employees who are depleted of energy. Fritz *et al* mention:

- increased workloads during recessionary times;
- service sector jobs requiring more emotional labour; and
- attachment to mobile phones/laptops and connecting to work outside of 'working hours'.

Either individually or collectively, these are causes of depleted energy in people at work.

Firms who are struggling financially cannot offer employees perks that would allow them to replenish energy, such as additional vacation time, bonuses, study programmes and even leave for family or caring needs. This severely impacts on morale and can create resentment and negative energy use.

In 'Task planning and energy expended: exploration of how goals influence performance', Earley, Wojnaroski and Prest[11] found that:

> their studies demonstrated that goal setting and task training influenced the dependent variables. In addition to influencing an individual's energy expended (effort and persistence), a specific goal led an individual to plan and organize more than did an individual given a general goal (ie 'do your best'). The results of both studies suggest that goal setting and task-relevant information influence performance, in part, through their influence on energy expended and planning.

These studies and declarations show there is something wrong in the way we view human energy at work – as a commodity that is full on arrival to, and a whole lot less on departure from, the workplace.

We know human beings are complex and that through illness, home life, financial problems, being a victim of criminal or anti-social behaviour, bereavement or a range of other life events and challenges, 100 per cent may be a lot less on arrival and therefore considerably less during, and at the end of, the working day.

We already know from Taylorism[12] that we are largely bound by a set of scientific management models and work efficiency as our default position for work design. Taylorism treats human beings quite literally as robots. Programmable, and once programmed, functioning at an optimal level (subject the right punitive or reward measures either side of bad or good performance). The disassembly of production into finite, smaller tasks, leaves a study of efficiency more sharply focused on the famous shorthand phrase 'widgets per hour'.

What it fails to take into account is that a human being, who happens to be a member of your workforce, may arrive into work tired from some outside-work troubles. So they will not only be temporarily distracted by this, they will also be subject to other variable factors such as boredom and distraction whilst on repetitive tasks, and/or stress and anxiety over oppressive supervision of the work they do. Both of these factors will impair us as a human being, yet would not impact at all on a programmable robot.

Taylorism was perhaps the best approach we had at the time of mass production techniques replacing artisan production, and being more efficient and thereby proliferating profits through less costly production, but at a huge cost to us as the very people the products were intended for.

And whilst we all know or believe that this approach has its flaws in the modern working world, Taylorist practices endure and thrive and are still the (main) force in efficiencies in the workplace, irrespective of the psychological trauma to the human beings in our employ, or the gross inaccuracy of this so-called science. Taylorism is simply too simplistic to be our 'go-to' methodology for the measurement of human effort in the 21st-century workplace. It is also infamous for energy use only – with little or no recognition (beyond scheduled breaks reluctantly offered to people) of the regenerative power of a shorter series of breaks beyond food and drink with talking, a pure state of rest and of course walking/exercise.

We have admittedly introduced more variety through regularized breaks, better lighting, rest rooms, foodstuffs, hydration and now fresh fruit, foosball tables, meditation spaces and even sleep pods, which are the norm in many newer companies and start-ups. These help employees regenerate their energy. Legislation has even been introduced for machine operators, pilots, haulage drivers and surgeons to make sure these people are not too tired to do a good job.

Yet things like a lack of sleep in people pushed hard in their life and work are largely ignored when it comes to making sure the factors of human performance are a closely respected and channelled part of organizational life. Indeed, researchers at Harvard Medical School[13] found that sleep deprivation is annually responsible for 274,000 workplace accidents and errors, costing employers $31bn a year.

One costly example of this occurred in June of 2017, when one of the world's largest airlines, British Airways, was hit by a computer outage that forced the cancellation of over 800 flights with £80 million lost – not to mention thousands of passengers' travel plans in ruin.[14]

It was not a mechanical failure or glitchy software, but a maintenance contractor accidentally unplugging an uninterruptible power supply. One report said that the contractor was panicked into this action.[15] Stress or incompetence? It sounds to me a lot like stress that could have links to sleep deprivation, anxiety or oppressive management.

It is well documented in medical research that fatigue in the workplace is a hazard, leading to reduced attention spans and lessened concentration, as well as impaired decision making.

Typing into a search engine 'Tiredness as a killer in the workplace' retrieves 334,000 results ranging from the oil and gas industry, to transportation, to energy. Indeed, in 1979, the United States' biggest nuclear disaster on Three Mile Island was apparently caused by tired workers.[16]

There are likely many more unreported failures than reported, down to people being overworked, stressed, anxious or pressured into something which costs others dearly. Many people have probably lost their jobs because of such failures, potentially induced by a high-stress environment forcing people into panicked decisions or actions which are deemed corrupt (but could be errors or overlooking things because of stress or tiredness). Of course, not all corruption is caused by such workplace stress – some can be down to mischief, criminality and even industrial sabotage.

There is little doubt that being under tired and/or under stress causes people to act in some unorthodox ways. *Harvard Business Review* featured the impact of decisions under stress in their 2017 feature 'Stress leads to bad decisions: here's how to avoid them' by Ron Carucci.[17] In this feature, Carucci shares previous research which looked at huge corporate failures and the brain science that helps us understand how we make decisions.

In simplistic terms, we use *pattern recognition* and *emotional tagging* in order to make decisions.

Pattern recognition is the reliance on past experiences and judgement calls.

Emotional tagging is where we attach a replayed emotional response to those thoughts and experiences.

Both can be effective in helping to chart a course of action; together and individually, they can also be hellishly misleading, convincing us to act in a way that turns out to be disastrous.

Add in heightened anxieties, stress and pressure, with adrenalin, cortisol and other chemicals rushing through our systems, and we are in a lower cognitive state of functioning. Blood – vital to powering the brain to do its best work – is pushed towards the limbs in case there's a *fight or flight* needed. We are less intelligent when we're experiencing fear induced by stress. Creative designer Henri Hyppönen's research shows that when we're in a fearful or anxiety state, we lose about eight points from our IQ. We become more stupid.[18]

We also need people around us more. The other chemical that is released during a stress response is oxytocin. This is often called the hugging hormone, as it is released when we embrace or are in close social contact with others. It urges us to seek others' company. Whilst understandable, this can also be confusing to us. A programmed sign of need when we should be at our optimal best to make a decision? And we can reject the one thing that may help us – other people.

So there is an individual, programmed response to stress; instead of a 'danger' response and the panic and heightened anxiety state, we can reprogramme ourselves to focus on a positive stimulus and response to stress to bond with others. Yet we often ignore it.

Hyppönen's research describes how, in an anxious state, whilst we have a bonding chemical (oxytocin) in our system, we seem to reject the social urge and withdraw even more from others.

Imagine the stress of a deal around a merger; hiring a critical new team member and knowing they're in demand from your competitor; a new product launch; a catastrophe in a health and social care environment and deciding how to respond and take action.

At the precise moment you need every ounce of capability and energy, you're losing it because you're in fear and being overtaken by your bad stress reactions when you could channel that energy for your benefit. Gripped by tension, you will make a decision that gets some strange responses from the team, so you are now even more frightened or angry with their response. You don't have the time or the energy to discuss this with your colleagues and the last thing you need is another meeting to discuss it all.

You may have had some doubts but now you dogmatically stick to your course of action. Because you're the highest-paid person in the room, your opinion is the one that counts. So you go ahead with the merger, make an outlandish salary offer, sign off on the risky new product or immediately fire a senior manager.

And it all backfires. And things go even more wrong than before. And people – you included – will say, 'How was such a poor decision made?'

Stress, fear, anxiety, burnout, not enough energy or the wrong kind of energy at play.

Psychological and physiological energy

At work, our brain uses more energy than it would relaxing at home on the sofa. Mental activities require more brain power than our leisure time. 'As an energy consumer, the brain is the most expensive organ we carry around with us', said Dr. Marcus Raichle, a distinguished professor of medicine at Washington University School of Medicine in St. Louis.

As we said earlier, whilst the brain represents just 2 per cent of a person's total body weight, it accounts for 20 per cent of the body's energy use, Raichle's research has found. That means during a typical day, a person uses about 320 calories just to think.

Ampel, Muraven and McNay[19] argue that a hard 'thinking' day without the right breaks and foodstuffs, can result in diminished brain glucose supply, and this creates a physical limit on neural activity. This supports the proposition that decreased cognitive ability can occur if a person is bereft of energy. When we're physically and mentally tired is when we're most likely to drop the mug of tea, forget to lock the window or forget to set our alarm for that earlier rise we needed. Exhaustion impacts negatively on our conscious choices, actions and behaviours.

How to replenish and utilize psychological energy

How do we replenish and utilize psychological energy without over-reliance on stimulants like caffeine?

Using another internet search, this time 'maximizing energy levels', you are faced with a barrage of information suggesting you try to control stress, undertaking such measures as eating well, exercising more, avoiding smoking and alcohol and ultimately 'lightening your load'.

What happens if you cannot avoid having too much to do and are overworked, resulting in fatigue? How can we replenish our finite daily psychological energy?

A study on when and how nurses best recover from work stress stated that a respite experience replenishes psychological and physical resources that work may have depleted.[20] Albeit focused on the nursing profession, this study concluded that leisure experiences do positively impact recovery from exhaustion caused by work fatigue.

Through an empirical study, ten Brummelhuis and Bakker[21] argue that off-job activities enhance next-morning vigour and energy (supporting the 'Effort-Recovery model'):

Our results support the assumption that recovery occurs when employees engage in off-job activities that allow for relaxation and psychological detachment. The findings also underscore the significance of recovery after work: adequate recovery not only enhances vigour in the morning, but also helps employees to stay engaged during the next workday.

Psychological detachment from work is important to ensure employees restore and replenish their individual resources. Fritz *et al*[22] argue that work breaks need to be embraced to prevent this detachment. The article looks at 'breaks' as in holidays, weekends, evenings and breaks at work.

Fritz *et al* argue that those who are highly involved in their jobs tend to find it harder to psychologically detach, thus not being able to *recover* from work. They suggest that organizations must:

1 encourage employees to take vacations;
2 be aware of the importance of psychological detachment from work; and
3 utilize lunch and micro breaks (for example more flexible, agile ways of working).

It wasn't that long ago that a new initiative came forward: **unlimited annual leave**. Not a restrictive 20 days or similar – as much leave as you wanted. It seemed too good to be true.

This was either born from, or latched on to by, the Silicon Valley giants and was even a part of Sir Richard Branson's Virgin Empire. On the face of it, this looks incredible. As MUCH leave as you like? Wow.

Except it's not all that simple, as proven by this 2018 article from the *Guardian* in 2018.[23] This extract is particularly telling:

> The reality is often quite different. The package is limited to a tiny number of UK workplaces, usually in the technology and professional service sectors. The companies that offer it tend to be demanding and all-consuming workplaces, so taking time off can make employees feel guilty – particularly as it may show their boss and their colleagues that they are not fully committed.

And, if an employee leaves, there's no 'entitlement' arrears of holiday pay to find. If you were cynical, you'd say this was not a perk, but a disguised scam.

And what was most stark was that this was in places where there appeared to be a 'long-hours culture' or a culture of dedication and commitment. Things that would be called presenteeism.

Professor Sir Cary Cooper (Chair of the Board, CIPD and partner at Robertson Cooper) and his business partner Professor Ivan Robertson, have written extensively about presenteeism. Largely this is seen in two areas:

1 attending work when you are really unfit/too ill to do so but feel pressured to attend because of the demands of your work; and
2 a long-hours culture, being logged on and replying to messages when on leave or at home in the evenings.

Both seem to come with a price/cost to people and therefore their employers. In 2009, a piece of research by Robertson Cooper revealed one in four of us had attended work when we were too ill but felt a pressure to attend.[24]

This might seem acceptable, yet the consequences of people with even less energy than normal, distracted by an illness, and with impaired cognitive abilities could be more dangerous to work outcomes, themselves and their colleagues than being absent. Not to mention the fact that unfit people, struggling through, could become more ill, therefore putting themselves in more danger (with a flu developing into pneumonia perhaps) and possibly infecting other colleagues.

Energy management not time management

Many efficiency techniques will advocate this applied working/thinking and then a break/detachment such as the **Pomodoro** technique, which mandates 25 minutes of applied working, followed by anything up to 15 minutes of detachment/break.[25]

Many 'life hackers' swear by this technique yet empirical studies in this area are lacking. No scientific journal articles are found that uphold or refute this technique, apart from a study into short breaks in intense periods of working from the University of Illinois.[26]

Many work-based productivity evangelists support the Pomodoro technique (or an adaptation of it), mainly because of the concept of separating tasks (particularly for knowledge work) into:

a complex, larger pieces of thinking work (such as new ideas, design, analysis and report writing); and

b smaller, routine tasks (such as answering emails, calendar scheduling, booking transportation).

This concept is called **Deep Work**[27] and featured in the work of Cal Newport, Associate Professor at Georgetown University. His premise is to break the day into sections for meetings, the shallow work of admin and emails, social networking and so on, and then protect a period of time for what he calls Deep Work. This is more cognitively challenging, complex, thoughtful work that needs attention, focus and energy; a form of a psychological vacuum, free from distractions, offering the ability to concentrate and channel thoughts into things that need more depth.

When we return to look at what you can do to use and regenerate your own energy reserves, we'll revisit this technique and others.

A safe workplace

We have made workplaces much more physically safe with Health & Safety legislation (though derided in jokes), forcing more compliance with safeguarding us from hazards, dangerous materials, conditions, breaks and more.

From a workplace where family members worked together, to industrial age employers who provided awful working conditions, through the unionized fightback to create fairness of working conditions, to the modern challenges of lean manufacturing and the connected era of knowledge workers, automation and computational power.

Whilst it is laudable that the physical safety attributes of workplaces and working have improved, we've neglected the *psychological and physiological needs* of people and face more complex challenges in creating safety of a different kind.

Instead we have been obsessing about customers, shareholders and the *bottom line*: the economic elements of organizations, businesses and enterprises. We have neglected ourselves and others in pursuit of efficiency and financial targets.

In a workplace where conditions are now (mostly) safe in a physical sense, the psychological aspect has come to prominence. Where once it was coal mine dust, hazardous materials or looking after posture on assembly lines or workbenches, now it is the intense demands placed on workers through targets, always-on for messages or drafting reports, and more generally, a pressurized environment with the threat of being replaced forming an ever-present unspoken threat.

Harvard Business School professor Amy Edmondson has spent the last 20 years researching and reporting on **Psychological Safety** in the workplace. Professor Edmondson's work looks at how coerced many employees are to work either under extreme measurement and constant micro-management of targets, or with an overly aggressive growth strategy that forces them to do unethical things, especially when it comes to selling to customers. Discouraged behaviours are speaking up, challenging, and failure of any sort.

There were exceptions to this. In the case of one organization, the movie studio Pixar,[28] there was a strong sense of psychological safety in the creative writing, designing and production of their stories. Failure was not considered damaging, it was part of the creative process. So people felt able to have a 'punt' on something, to challenge others' ideas knowing they would not be offended; to speak up and offer alternative views.

So, far from people feeling under constant threat of damage through some failure or missed KPI or similar, employees at Pixar were actively encouraged to try things knowing they might not be successful. From such an approach, a winning formula has seen a string of mega-hits for the studio and a reputation that quality comes through every frame, line and image.

Such an environment fosters a range of things such as openness, honesty and compassion – because people will be fragile and vulnerable when they fail. People around them will pick them up and help them fix things, not ignore them, or push them aside for having the audacity to be fallible. Which includes being unwell, having a stressful time with a new child, or a house move, a pet that is ill or a parent that needs care.

Psychological safety means a space to be exposed, unsure, and to be human and have it not work against you in the game of work. It needs leaders to model and create that space; it needs everyone to then step into that space; and it needs people to respond with productive kindness.

With so much energy potentially wasted on worry, anxiety and clear thinking impaired by stress, fixing mistakes is swifter, less risky and behind the *firewall* of the team. Not exposed to customers, or the board, or the investors/public.

Psychological safety is not a pipedream; it is what we need most in the workplaces of the 21st century, with an unstable political environment, a climate emergency and a fragile economy that could fail at any time. **People are frightened** and the last thing they need is a workplace that is harmful.

They need a safehouse.

This is what was revealed when 33,000 people answered questions that formed the results of the 2019 Edelman Trust Barometer.[29] This report tells us who we trust most and least and about what in the modern world. It looks at trust in politics, media, business and not-for-profit organizations (NGOs).

2019's survey made some slight upwards movement to (particularly) NGOs and business. Governments and the media are still ranked lowest on whether people trust them or not. Interestingly, only one in five respondents believed the current working 'system' was good for them and over 55 per cent of the population believe their jobs are at risk through automation.

This provides a lot of insight about people who are in a constant state of anxiety over their jobs and therefore economic independence and comfort. And yet, the trusted relationship between employers and employees scores most highly, proving once again (previous years' surveys also revealed this) that the workplace is a place of relative safety and somewhat a sanctuary from a chaotic *outside* world.

Workplaces make more sense than most institutions and have a lot to offer people in a safety sense. When that relationship is threatened – by poor management and high-stress environments – we can see why the World Health Organization classification of burnout is now a recognized ill-health condition. Too many people are suffering from the same symptoms for this to be a simple by-product of 'working a bit too hard'.

The 2019 report also shared that where people can report a sense of shared action, personal empowerment and job opportunities, it creates higher-energy, safer spaces to work, grow and support others. Indeed, 67 per cent of respondents said that they would be influenced in buying from a company if they knew there was a positive impression about its conduct towards its employees, the community it operates in and the environment more widely. Table 4.1 from the Edelman report 2019 proves a lot of what Professor Amy Edmonson's work on a psychologically safe organization can achieve. Trust at work is strengthened through a new employer–employee contract (albeit not necessarily their legal terms and conditions – more a pledge to each other).

Whilst none of the qualities in this new 'contract' are controversial or even arguable, still too few organizations appear to fully enact these qualities.

We know this is needed in our workplaces; we know it is economically viable to be more humane in how employees are treated at

TABLE 4.1 The new employer–employee 'contract'

Trust: the new employer–employee 'contract'			
1. Lead change	2. Empower employees	3. Start locally	4. CEO/leadership
Be aspirational Address concerns Train the workforce of the future	Give people a voice Create opportunities for shared action Empower people with information	Solve problems at home Improve societal conditions in the local communities in which you operate	Live your values Engage directly Be visible and show a personal commitment, inside and outside the organization

work; and we know Taylorist methods are seriously challenged by the nature of how we work. Yet we see very little progressive action in how work is designed and experienced, with those record rates of illness through workplace stress.

How has it become so hard to sustain a positive balance in our working lives?

And there is now a toll on our social life and hobbies. Caring responsibilities and our community spirit. Missing out on opportunities, choice and influence on things that would help us appreciate the heightened standards of living we've engineered over the last 40 years.

Yes, the workplace is *physically* safer, yet a more trusting and supportive environment is lacking, making it an often unsafe place to be for many of us, psychologically.

This chapter has revealed that it's less likely that your odds are 1 in 20 to experience workplace stress and organization oppression, and that there is more likely a 1 in 3 (33 per cent) chance you are having a tough time at work. It's tougher than it needs to be, and that leads to stress, illness and almost certainly some form of stealthy psychological trauma that could begin to have a strong detrimental impact on your life.

That is, in my humble opinion, way too high a chance that people will suffer through the experience of work; a self-inflicted degradation on life's true ambition and reason for being. This, then, is the crux of this book's challenge: **How can we move on from this plethora of poor practices and misaligned methods, towards something where people genuinely flourish and are not harmed by their work?**

WHAT WE LEARNED FROM THIS CHAPTER

1 People lose energy on cognitive tasks as much as physical tasks and this can lead to bad decisions, mistakes and poor health through workplace pressures. This has an economic and reputational impact of course, but also a humanitarian one. **People being worked to a state of illness is avoidable and should be overcome at all costs.**

2. Not enough attention is paid to the systems that inculcate poor health – it is deemed a personal issue, with work merely reflecting someone's struggles rather than being the instigator of their woes. We need to think more deeply about how we can help people who have distractions and energy-draining life incidents that could cause impairment in the work they do. **A safe space and some focus only on shallow and less significant work whilst heads are cleared could save money and create a safer space for people to be during their work.**

3. Psychological detachment from work is also important and has not been given good weighting in the well-being discussions of late. Whether it's the Pomodoro technique of a short break, the Deep Work philosophy of ring-fenced thinking time, or a vacation or punctuated break from work for a longer time, constant attachment to work is not considered healthy even in the cases of the most eager start-up founder, committed healthcare worker or teacher. **Our mental energy needs replenishing activities or quiet periods in order to optimize the brain when we need it the most.**

4. Psychological safety and presenteeism need a lot more focus than they're currently getting. Such factors are proven to have a huge impact on organizational success and personal well-being. Which in turn helps productivity, creativity and togetherness to face into the challenges faced by modern organizations. **People, culture and change strategies need to incorporate and activate more explicit actions to provide psychological safety for people in the workplace.**

5. Trust and transparency help create more organizations that can be considered safe and therefore committed places to be. **This form of openness is considered a must-have and not a luxury afforded to only the most affluent or established companies.**

6. All of these elements need to be considered in the design of work – the entire premise of this book. That design falls to leaders and, of course, HR and organization design professionals. **We should design in breaks, techniques, help people self-care on energy and mental stamina; we should bring in detachments and safety to avoid the burnout now recognized by the WHO.**

Endnotes

1. Cipd.co.uk
2. CIPD (2019) Rise in stress at work linked to poor management, new research finds. Available from: www.cipd.co.uk/about/media/press/rise-stress-poor-management (archived at https://perma.cc/2WU9-WCHM)
3. CIPD (2019) Health and well-being at work. Available from: www.cipd.co.uk/Images/health-and-well-being-at-work-2019.v1_tcm18-55881.pdf (archived at https://perma.cc/QW89-XXV6)
4. World Health Organization (2019) Burn-out an 'occupational phenomenon': International Classification of Diseases. Available from: www.who.int/mental_health/evidence/burn-out/en/ (archived at https://perma.cc/Q6FY-39MY)
5. NHS (2020) Understanding calories. Available from: www.nhs.uk/live-well/healthy-weight/understanding-calories/ (archived at https://perma.cc/MG9H-6MWT)
6. SA Health (nd) Kilojoules explained. Available from: www.sahealth.sa.gov.au/wps/wcm/connect/public+content/sa+health+internet/healthy+living/healthy+eating/healthy+eating+tips/kilojoules+explained (archived at https://perma.cc/P37N-9RRM)
7. Burgess, L (2018) What percentage of our brain do we use? *Medical News Today*. Available from: www.medicalnewstoday.com/articles/321060.php (archived at https://perma.cc/DZT7-4B49)
8. Mahajan, N (2013) The thinker interview: Jeffrey Pfeffer on human sustainability, *CKGSB Knowledge*. Available from: http://knowledge.ckgsb.edu.cn/2013/04/05/employment/the-thinker-interview-jeffrey-pfeffer-on-human-sustainability/ (archived at https://perma.cc/PE44-GRJR)
9. Fritz, C, Lam C F and Spreitzer, G (2011) It's the little things that matter: an examination of knowledge workers', energy management, *The Academy of Management Perspectives*, 25 (3), pp. 28–39. Available from: https://psycnet.apa.org/record/2011-19569-003 (archived at https://perma.cc/TC3E-AXQ2)
10. Spreitzer, G and Grant, T (2011) Helping students manage their energy: taking their pulse with the energy audit, *Journal of Management Education*. Available from: https://positiveorgs.bus.umich.edu/wp-content/uploads/SpreitzerGrant-StudentEnergy-JrnlMgtEd.pdf (archived at https://perma.cc/5CAM-9537)
11. Earley, C, Wojnaroski, P and Prest, W (1987) Task planning and energy expended: exploration of how goals influence performance, *Journal of Applied Psychology*, 72 (1) pp. 107–44. Available from: https://psycnet.apa.org/record/1987-17299-001 (archived at https://perma.cc/DJ83-R8U2)
12. www.lexico.com/en/definition/taylorism (archived at https://perma.cc/MW79-6DW8)

13 International Health and Safety News (2012) Lack of sleep linked to 274,000 workplace accidents a year. Available from: www.ishn.com/articles/94247-lack-of-sleep-linked-to-274000-workplace-accidents-a-year (archived at https://perma.cc/K4SN-G3YB)

14 Cox, J (2017) British Airways system outage 'caused by IT worker accidentally switching off power supply', *Independent*. Available from: www.independent.co.uk/news/business/news/british-airways-system-outage-it-worker-power-supply-switch-off-accident-flights-delayed-cancelled-a7768581.html (archived at https://perma.cc/GM4W-E4YH)

15 Corfield, G (2017) BA IT systems failure: uninterruptible power supply was interrupted, *The Register*. Available from: www.theregister.co.uk/2017/06/02/british_airways_data_centre_configuration/ (archived at https://perma.cc/LS9T-AHXL)

16 USNRC (nd) Background on the Three Mile Island accident. Available from: www.nrc.gov/reading-rm/doc-collections/fact-sheets/3mile-isle.html (archived at https://perma.cc/34GG-CB9P)

17 Carucci, R (2017) Stress leads to bad decisions: here's how to avoid them, *Harvard Business Review*. Available from: https://hbr.org/2017/08/stress-leads-to-bad-decisions-heres-how-to-avoid-them (archived at https://perma.cc/BAM8-T6NY)

18 Hyppönen, H (2017) fear makes us stupid, *YouTube*. Available from: https://www.youtube.com/watch?v=_ZqImSwYhy8 (archived at https://perma.cc/GT2Z-4VHH)

19 Ampel, B C, Muraven, M and McNay, E C (2018) Mental work requires physical energy: self-control is neither exception nor exceptional, *Frontiers in Psychology*. Available from: https://www.ncbi.nlm.nih.gov/pubmed/30026710 (archived at https://perma.cc/A487-RV2P)

20 Drach-Zahavy, A and Marzuq, N (2013) The weekend matters: exploring when and how nurses best recover from work stress, *Journal of Advanced Nursing*, 69 (3). Available from: https://onlinelibrary.wiley.com/doi/abs/10.1111/j.1365-2648.2012.06033.x (archived at https://perma.cc/W7KM-2AVP)

21 ten Brummelhuis, L and Bakker, A (2012) Staying engaged during the week: the effect of off-job activities on next day work engagement, *Journal of Occupational Health Psychology*, 17 (4), pp. 445–55 https://psycnet.apa.org/record/2012-18555-001 (archived at https://perma.cc/F5NR-2HRS)

22 Fritz, C et al (2013) Embracing work breaks: recovering from work stress, *Organizational Dynamics*, 42, pp. 274–80. Available from: http://thriving.berkeley.edu/sites/default/files/Embracing%20Work%20Breaks%20(Eschleman%20Lecture).pdf (archived at https://perma.cc/KN2H-Y7WK)

23 Spicer, A (2018) The ugly truth about unlimited holidays, *Guardian*, Available from: https://www.theguardian.com/money/shortcuts/2018/jun/05/the-ugly-truth-about-unlimited-holidays (archived at https://perma.cc/CPW6-3JER)

24 Page, L (2009) Presenteeism on the rise as an estimated quarter of UK employees admit to working when ill, *Robertson Cooper*. Available from: www.robertsoncooper.com/blog/presenteeism-on-the-rise-as-an-estimated-quarter-of-uk-employees-admit-to-working-when-ill/ (archived at https://perma.cc/YY4V-A4XL)

25 Francesco Cirillo (nd) The Pomodoro Technique. Available from: https://francescocirillo.com/pages/pomodoro-technique (archived at https://perma.cc/ZLJ8-MH3X)

26 Science Daily (2011) Brief diversions vastly improve focus, researchers find. Available from: www.sciencedaily.com/releases/2011/02/110208131529.htm (archived at https://perma.cc/Y4SB-CRYV)

27 Newport, C (2016) *Deep Work*, Grand Central Publishing. http://www.calnewport.com/books/deep-work/ (archived at https://perma.cc/7X2X-LRKZ)

28 Edmondson, A (2019) Creating psychological safety in the workplace [podcast] *Harvard Business Review*. Available from: https://hbr.org/ideacast/2019/01/creating-psychological-safety-in-the-workplace (archived at https://perma.cc/K3MG-QPDG)

29 2019 Edelman Trust Barometer. Available from: https://www.edelman.com/sites/g/files/aatuss191/files/2019-03/2019_Edelman_Trust_Barometer_Global_Report.pdf?utm_source=website&utm_medium=global_report&utm_campaign=downloads (archived at https://perma.cc/YUA9-5RFA)

05

The 5 x 20 life and the redesign of age

In this chapter, we take a look at a redesign of our lives already well in place – a life of 5 x 20-year cycles.

We're living longer, and quite considerably longer. Being 105 will be commonplace for over 50 per cent of us by 2050.[1] Global average life expectancy increased by 5.5 years between 2000 and 2016, the fastest increase since the 1960s. Combine an ageing population with declining birth rates (mainly in the Western world) and this changes the landscape. In 2018, for the first year on record, people aged 65 and over outnumbered children under five.[2]

By 2050, one in six of us will be over 60, up from one in eleven people in 2019. And that same year should see people over 80 triple to 426 million worldwide.

United Nations global data comparisons[3] show that in 1841, a baby girl was expected to live to just 42 years of age, a boy to 40. **In 2016, a baby girl could expect to reach 83; a boy, 79**.

As we head towards insufficient pension funds (paying people for a longer life post-retirement), many governments' response is longer working lives. The retirement age of 65 (in the UK) will become 68 in 2044, and recent talk in the UK Government was of a further hike to 75.[4]

Lifestyle choices – quality of life, prosperity and wealth, fitness and health – are combined with advances and accessibility to better medical and healthcare provisions. Cancer survival rates have doubled (in the UK[5]) so that 50 per cent of those diagnosed go on to live 10 or more years thereafter.

Whilst some diseases and conditions show an increase – such as Alzheimer's (predicted to rise by 14 per cent in the next five to six years[6]) – we also see newly discovered viruses, some of which become epidemics and force intense and rapid research into treatment and vaccinations, eg HIV and Ebola.

Overall, since the 1990s, we have seen an increase in life expectancy and a subsequent population rise to a predicted 10bn sometime around 2050.

Another first is the rise of 'super-aged'[7] countries; Germany, Japan and Italy will be joined by the Netherlands, France, Sweden, Portugal, Slovenia and Croatia in 2020, and by 2030, Hong Kong, Korea, the United States, the UK and New Zealand, will all have a population where one in five are over 65.

Working lives are therefore longer too. As the number of income-generating younger people are outnumbered by retirees, this puts a burden on governmental funds and services and the funds of wealth managers, with people drawing a pension for longer and needing a wider range of healthcare services.

What does this mean for us not only as a society, but as workers, leaders, owners and energized participants in the world of work?

Moody's (the credit ratings agency) said the global working-age population would grow only half as fast between 2015 and 2030 as during the previous 15 years.[8] It said all countries (except a handful in Africa) would see their working-age populations either decline or grow more slowly over that period.

It forecast in 2015 that this unprecedented pace of population ageing would slow annual global economic growth by 0.4 per cent over the following five years and by 0.9 per cent between 2020 and 2025. In China alone, the current ratio of retired to economically viable working people is 1:6. Yet this will change to 1:2.5 by 2050 – a huge shift in such a short space of time.

This is beyond the reach of pension schemes and more lifestyle and society-level design.

How do we design energizing working systems that accommodate the traditional younger intake and a new range of available, fit and skilled older people?

> The answer may lie in the shift from three phases of life – education, working, retired – to at least five and a philosophy of lifelong learning, self-help, health and wellbeing, and a range of energy-sustaining *portfolio* career options.
>
> Indeed, a recent study in Finland[9] produced the conclusion that we should move the considered 'old age' point for being referred to as 'old' from 65 to 80–85.
>
> Should we be prepared to move the 'magic number' for retirement from 60-something to 70- or even 80-something?
>
> It appears so.

Introduction – happy 200th birthday!

In September 2019, Stanford Professor Stuart Kim had a billion-dollar bet that there is someone alive today who will celebrate their 200th birthday.[10] Whilst the current record is 122-year-old Jeanne Calment (who died in 1997), more people are over 100 years old now than ever before. In the United States, over 70,000 people are recorded as being over 100 years old, compared to 50,000 in 2000[11] – a 44 per cent increase in that category.

One of the more vocal proponents of the extension of life and the definition of ageing is Aubrey de Grey of the SENS Research Foundation.[12] He has long advocated the same theory as Professor Kim, and his early-2000s declarations are now seemingly more viable as we experience the growth of rejuvenation biotechnology techniques such as stem cell research and senolytic therapy (which removes aged cells to allow for rejuvenation through new cells). Biotech is a new form of energy for our physical selves – but what about our mental selves?

Whilst new rejuvenation therapies are aimed at repairing the damage to our physical and mental capabilities brought on by ageing, it is the knock-on impacts to society, how and where we live and work and with whom that come to mind.

The act of reversing the effects of ageing is almost taken as programmable elements of our 'hardware' through genome and biotech advances; it is the 'software' of us that is more complex. Our 'software' is:

- how we think and view ourselves in the world;
- our relationships with others;
- the societal structures we need to adapt to, in order to play a fully functioning and recognized part; and
- the work we do, the workplaces we are part of, and the flow of our careers.

The three-stage model of now

The path of the existing model is something like this:

- childhood, adolescence and education (0–16/22);
- working life (16/22–60/65);
- retirement (60/65–80).

Of course, this overly simplistic model does not take into account parenthood, discovery periods, fighting and adapting to a significant illness, traumatic events like road traffic accidents, being a victim of crime, celebrating a financial windfall and many more.

It is more likely that instead of the one central, working life block, this will be broken down into mini-blocks as we potentially become parents, or tour the globe, or become working specialists. Some blocks are forced upon us, some chosen by us and many occur because we have a range of options previously unavailable to us but now enabled by technological advances and the increase in micro-enterprises and entrepreneurs. But mostly, I'd argue, it's because we will be more capable for longer, with more energized, active minds and bodies.

We will also have to work and *earn* for longer, because our financial models are based on those three stages of life and a demise somewhere prior to our 80s, when in fact many more of us are likely to live some time beyond that – even a further 20 years in many more instances.

What is the five-stage model of the future?

In Lynda Gratton and Andrew Scott's excellent book *The 100-Year Life*[13] they add in three more stages to the working life, linked to Stanford Professor Robert Pogue's phrase 'juvenescence, the state of being youthful, or growing young'. This has a significant impact on our energy – it could be considered a little like the fabled 'fountain of youth', or an elongated version of the less-energizing twilight of our lives.

The three additional stages of Gratton and Scott's book (which split the middle, working block) are:

1 **Explorer** – being able to discover their talents and true purpose in life, aligning values and interests, selecting education, life, love and family pursuits, and finding places and people to work with that reflect those values and changing perspectives on life.

2 **Independent producers** – associated with entrepreneurship, start-ups, side hustles and a range of enterprises that grow, diversify and are a reflection on the ideas and imagination we have as individuals.

3 **Portfolio** – great management thinker Charles Handy coined the phrase 'the portfolio career' in the 1980s, when he predicted the 21st century would see this as a larger norm in our working lives. A range of simultaneous ventures that are aggregated into a person's life *instead* of one job. Featured in an article in 2004,[14] the early signs were that this was beginning to look increasingly accurate. Micro-enterprises, non-executive roles, academic links, part-time roles in a range of companies as well as being independent producers – this stage appears to have once been thought of as the domain of former careerists restructured out of a company (by choice or suggestion) into a varied, multi-faceted portfolio that exploits their experience and wisdom. This is now often a choice for people far younger than the corporate exile and so has become a most desirable approach. It's complex and risky but exciting and rewarding. It effectively combines the traits of the explorer with those of the independent producer into a mixed bag of options and challenges, ideas and start-up scenarios.

It sounds a lot like the 'gigs' way of working we hear so much about now.

The portfolio option in the 100-year life has somewhat rocketed, with the advent of the *slash* or *gig economy*.[15] People who are partly independent producers and partly portfolio workers. In 2017 – arguably at the height of awareness of Uber drivers, Deliveroo riders, warehouse pickers and Task Rabbit fixers and makers – the UK's CIPD produced a report: 'To gig or not to gig'.[16] In that report the gig economy was set against the already-demonized *zero-hours* contract and other alternative forms of contracting people to do work even if that isn't via a job.

Agency work and temporary staffing have been stable aspects of the employment proposition for some time; this new form was built on technology platforms connecting people to work and then reporting on the successful completion of the work and subsequent remuneration.

And with all of this comes scathing criticism of manipulation, exploitation and, to quote, 'the race to the bottom'.[17]

Some called this *Digital Taylorism*;[18] piece work, time-and-motion studied, algorithmic-based work and reward systems. What was interesting for the CIPD, representing human resource professionals, was the demarcation of the legal status of employee, worker and self-employed contractor. This was an area under scrutiny because of the employment and protection rights offered to the employees and to workers, but not to self-employed contractors.

It was all part of the focus on something called *Good Work*.

Not to be confused with working for good causes, this was work that was *good for people*, their families, communities, society and the planet as a whole. Led by the RSA's[19] CEO Matthew Taylor,[20] the British government of the day invited an independent review into the area of Good Work and the emerging alternatives which policy and legislation were not on top of.

The CIPD report and overarching RSA report recommended a range of compliance, regulatory/governance and education actions to bring more understanding, clarity and enforceable action to bear in this twist to the conventional methods of work.

Gig working, independent producers and portfolio workers continue to rise. For example, in the UK alone, the May 2019 data set shows that the number of people who were self-employed in the first calendar quarter of 2019 (January to March) increased by 90,000 to reach a record high of 4.93 million. Between March 2018 and March 2019, the number of self-employed people increased by 180,000.[21]

It appears that two of the three stages in the *100-year life* are increasing and there are no trends or data sets to say that will not continue.

To some people, austerity measures have necessitated the taking on of additional roles to supplement a core job. A 2016 report by indeed.com[22] reported that 89 per cent of those working a second job will continue to do so, indicating that to those in that model of employ, it is not a luxurious, short-term aspect but a continued long-term prospect.

We should feel a little concerned that this is becoming a norm – two jobs could be called a portfolio, but in many cases it is two lower-paid roles stitched together to form a living wage.

The need for an additional dimension to the three new working stages

Gig working and second-job entrapment leads us to think about a fourth element; not necessarily a fourth stage but something that bridges the Explorer–Portfolio range. Something that will probably be more deliberately designed by organizations to take into account the lack of time people have if they are either locked into a demanding full-time role or stitching together a collection of employments (quite literally working then sleeping on repeat in both cases).

In their book, *The 100-Year Life,* Lynda Gratton and Andrew Scott reveal six elements for redesigning corporations:

- expanding the relationship between employer and employee;
- supporting more personal transitions through development programmes/activities;
- shifting practices to a multi-stage life, not just the three stages;

- considering the varying needs of men and women – things like menopause, parenting, etc;
- removing ageist policies and narrative;
- allowing people to experiment and renew, eg with sabbaticals

I agree with these but I am left with a nagging doubt about the effectiveness of these recommendations; they are valiant in attempt but lacking in provocation and exciting allure for company policy makers and decision-taking leaders.

The fourth – additional – dimension to the three working stages (Explorer, Independent Producer and Portfolio) is the element of *organization design* that is more implicit in helping facilitate or host these three working stages and is also linked to wider elements like sustainable business practices, new products and services that enhance the company's success into the future, and being an employer of choice and a highly regarded place of work.

This dimension is the concept we introduced in Chapter 1 – Eudaimonia

An additional dimension: eudaimonia as a business model

An extract from britannica.com[23] helps if you are new to this word:

> Eudaimonia, in Aristotelian ethics, the condition of human flourishing or of living well. The conventional English translation of the ancient Greek term, 'happiness', is unfortunate because eudaimonia, as Aristotle and most other ancient philosophers understood it, does not consist of a state of mind or a feeling of pleasure or contentment, as 'happiness' (as it is commonly used) implies. For Aristotle, eudaimonia is the highest human good…

This additional dimension – and the premise for this entire book – is therefore *to design organizations where people flourish*.

We have seen a huge level of interest in how we, as workers, colleagues and contractors, feel about our work via the *employee engagement* movement. A measure of how our people feel about the work they do and the organization they work for has been with us for some time. Yet the oft-quoted statistic from Gallup's research into this has a twist. Certainly in the United States, the 2018[24] survey into engagement revealed some interesting data:

- 34 per cent of US workers were revealed as engaged, equal to the all-time high on Gallup's previous surveys; and
- 13 per cent were actively disengaged, a new low.

So on that measure, the world of work is headed in a much better direction. But let's not get too excited yet.

The UK Health & Safety Executive report into 2017–2018 absences revealed some shocking statistics that go beyond the engagement survey data:[25]

- 1.4 million working people suffering from a work-related illness;
- 30.7 million working days lost due to work-related illness and workplace injury;
- £15 billion estimated cost of injuries and ill-health from current working conditions (of which £9.7 billion is related to ill-health;
- 44 per cent of all absences are related to workplace stress, not workplace injury.

A majority of absences are about the conditions of work itself, not chronic disease or injury. Such absences are largely about the mismatch between support, expectations, capability, capacity and more – all factors in designing organizations and roles, work routines and reward/support systems.

Who is at fault, then, with creating these undesirable conditions and outcomes?

- **Society?** Sure, but who makes this up and who says society prevents you from doing better things with how work is designed?
- **The markets?** You bet! But again, no one on the FTSE/S&P exchanges forces you to operate in an oppressive and inhumane way.
- **Shareholders?** Again, yes. But they don't make executive decisions on terms and conditions around how you treat your own people.
- **The exec board/leadership?** Definitely, as they do make executive decisions on company culture and focus.

- **HR?** I'd argue yes, as they are closest to the issues and fallout consequences of toxic workplaces, badly designed resource models and inhumane practices in the workplace.
- **Employees/people themselves?** A little unfair, so not really. Often powerless in the face of being dismissed if they 'don't work hard enough', people clearly put up with a lot they shouldn't.

I believe the focus should be on the executive leadership and HR as a combined failure to create those conditions where people, and subsequently the organization, flourish – both in an economic sense but also in a reputational sense.

In August 2019, as I was writing this book, I came across a turn of events linked to this sentiment. The US Business Roundtable (a collection of some of the most powerful companies on the planet) declared the following:[26]

> Businesses play a vital role in the economy by creating jobs, fostering innovation and providing essential goods and services... that underpin economic growth.
>
> While each of our individual companies serves its own corporate purpose, we share a fundamental commitment to all of our stakeholders. We commit to:
>
> - Delivering value to our customers. We will further the tradition of American companies leading the way in meeting or exceeding customer expectations.
> - Investing in our employees. This starts with compensating them fairly and providing important benefits. It also includes supporting them through training and education that help develop new skills for a rapidly changing world. We foster diversity and inclusion, dignity and respect.
> - Dealing fairly and ethically with our suppliers. We are dedicated to serving as good partners to the other companies, large and small, that help us meet our missions.
> - Supporting the communities in which we work. We respect the people in our communities and protect the environment by embracing sustainable practices across our businesses.

- Generating long-term value for shareholders, who provide the capital that allows companies to invest, grow and innovate. We are committed to transparency and effective engagement with shareholders.
- Each of our stakeholders is essential. We commit to deliver value to all of them, for the future success of our companies, our communities and our country.

Whilst the accusations of rhetoric and 'too little too late' sentiments are already circulating on this, this huge departure from the Keynesian 'shareholder value only' model[27] of recent years, is symbolic if nothing else. That the leaders of such *megacorps* are awake to the need to be more than money-making machines (even in being willing to publish this statement) is a significant step towards a more flourishing approach to business.

Of course, it's not the answer. But it is a start of a mindset shift to more equitable approaches to what is meant by value.

Couple this with our earlier look at the New Zealand Prime Minister Jacinda Ardern's declaration at the 2019 World Economic Forum[28] that there will be 'a well-being budget' and we see a different lexicon entering the world of government, away from the obsession with gross domestic product (GDP) and towards a new, more humane way to go about 'the business of business'.

What this then means is action in order to make good on these declarations and intentions.

I believe this can start from the way we design organizations and work so that people flourish not just as employees but in all the dimensions set out in the Business Roundtable declaration. How we do this will feature in later chapters because, as with any good product, we need to know:

1 what the aim is or the problem the product is overcoming;
2 who it is for;
3 in what way they will use this product; and
4 how we design our product to be adaptive to changes in the problem, user community and method of utilization.

Economics and a regenerative model

In order for eudaimonia to become the signature of a more progressive business model, so the economic conditions, parameters and expectations will also need to be changed.

One could easily argue that the reason companies act how they do (in pursuit of profit or operating efficiencies over all else) is the economic model that prevails today. *An economic model designed by everyone therefore owned by no one.* And that presents a more complex model to change.

Whilst there are some fabulous examples of corporate philanthropy, not-for-profit enterprises doing good, cause-related businesses and outliers who operate in a conscientious way about their capital, most of the corporate world is labelled elite and perpetuates inequality – especially of wealth, choice, power and privileges associated with all three in isolation or combination.

In Chapter 8 we will focus on many organizations who, through some of their operating models and a set of principles, give us more than the words of the Business Roundtable's declaration; they already are of this ilk.

The principle of corporate economics is such that profit is the only measure of value, which in itself directs share value, which in turn denotes the company's overall success. Growth, therefore, has become an organizational obsession. Market share dominance is one thing; continued growth is the insatiable need from shareholders, and has directed corporate practice into organization design, work routines, performance-related targets and other expectations.

So what is the alternative? Kate Raworth is quoted as being the 'renegade economist' and has designed a concept called Doughnut Economics[29] which is entirely built around a wider value chain – much like the Business Roundtable's declaration.

Could it be a happy coincidence that we have a potential economic model or is this more about a movement of consciousness towards something more wholesome, equitable and sustainable for the planet?

Raworth's model is bolstered by theories that:

- Progress does not require **constant** growth.
- Growth has solved some problems in the world but has also **created a lot of new ones**.
- Modern society has become **obsessed with growth** – particularly monetary metrics – as the only measure of success, despite residual or consequential impacts to other areas like health and the ecosystem.
- Growth is good, but it's **only a phase**. As eudaimonia is more about long-term flourishing for people, thriving is good for an organization/society.
- We are addicted (financially, politically and socially) to growth and need to provide alternatives as therapeutic interventions, so **regenerative and distributed economies can provide that**.

At the core of this model (hence it being doughnut shaped) is social foundation. What is the social foundation of an enterprise which assures it of not just a profitable sense, but of what good the venture is out to do? Of course this does not have to be charitable.

The outer rim of the doughnut is the ecological ceiling of the planet; how we use natural resources in how we live, eat and drink, travel, create energy, dispose of waste, and produce goods of all varieties.

This outer rim is also a world movement – **Earthovershoot** – which has its own day in July every year.[30] It highlights where we consume more of the planet's natural resources than can be regenerated in a year.

In between are the societal measures, factors and elements that are 'value creating' for society in a range of different ways, not just fiscal. The model shows the interdependencies and complexity of the entirety of our systems, not just the industrialized model – and arguably the markets themselves – we've been used to focusing on since the end of the Second World War.

Conclusion

In Chapter 2 we covered Professor Clare Graves' work on what we now call *Spiral Dynamics* and the awakening sense of self and the whole system we are a part of to become more enlightened and more spiritual.

The regenerative economic model is a financial and ecological addition to the thinking of Spiral Dynamics. What the future, adapted systems we operate in could be like and what the challenges we face really are can be focused on through the combination of a new economic model that tackles the climate emergency and a model of human evolution for spiritual and psychological fulfilment. Not just one built on financial or market growth, profit and fiscally driven operating regimes.

It's a system that encapsulates the entirety of planet Earth and our place within it and the societal frameworks we need and crave.

Equity, balance and regeneration.

Eudaimonia as a business model, then, gives us one true ideology to live to and for; human flourishing as the ultimate measure of a way of being, which we will cover in our closing chapters.

We have seen many attempts at codifying happiness. Indeed, a web search of 'happiness at work' reveals 584,000,000 hits so this is clearly a topic of huge interest. Whilst we are seeing an industry spring up to fill this need, we are at the behest of *productized* versions of happiness still linked to material gain – a hierarchical set-up of privilege and a spirit of consumption.

In the following chapters we will reveal what we truly mean by human flourishing and the energy forces at large within us and around us that may or may not be amplified or suppressed in our modern version of work and living.

We will look at companies who have a flourishing way about them – both economic viability but also regenerative to the environment and, most importantly, to the people who work there.

It feels like a new dawn is upon us.

Political systems that are broken and chaotic; societal structures badly in need of new approaches and how we frame good work, good living and good being are ripe for being adjusted, adapted and acquired to make a difference in a range of ways.

WHAT WE LEARNED FROM THIS CHAPTER

1. People are part of a complex system of macro-level, socio-political, economic and industrialized factors that present us with choices on how to live in a life that is likely to be longer than those of our forefathers. **We must think about designing life and work systems for that longer lifespan**.
2. Paradoxically, those same self-designed systems are presenting us with a range of new challenges both physically and mentally, as we come to grips with a fixation on growth and abundance at the suffering of our spiritually flourishing selves. **We need a more balanced approach to success and measuring achievements beyond financial gain; our work-reward systems would benefit from a broader range of value-added aspects such as time off, sabbaticals and sponsored donations/regenerative activities**.
3. The design of life is no longer about consistency, certainty and predictability. Instead there are more tangents, pivots and options giving us the illusion of choice or the actual chance to make a difference individually, collectively and societally. **We should look at how our organization is designed from the starting point of fluidity, agility and responsiveness**.
4. We have aims, goals and aspirations that may be subject to the conditions we find ourselves in and not so much as a result of what we actually need, believe in or is best for us. Consumerism has become the frame of reference for economic models that in themselves have inculcated a capitalist approach that both enhances levels of living standards, whilst causing suffering disproportionately to regions, individuals, the environment and the biodiversity of our planet. **Whilst this is a huge thing to shift, we can play our part in the economic and ecological ways in which we operate our businesses**.
5. We recognize we have to do something but we feel somewhat helpless to change the machinery of progress whilst helping the engine of capitalism 'rev up' to even greater levels of growth and avarice. **We can start to reduce our consumption of goods and energy; to be more balanced in what we buy and how we live. In turn, our employers can also reduce their carbon footprint and commit to offsetting and regenerative operating policies such as their own clean energy creation**.

> **6** Taking a macro look at the world through ageing, economics and more means a quite baffling set of circumstances. What we realize is that we can create our own response to this by thinking about how we view the lives of the people we work with, what their socio-economic concerns are, what is revealed by new ways of working, and the evidence behind their successes. **We can adapt more locally, closely and design systems that help people get more from their working lives.**
> **7** Eudaimonia as a concept and ideology can become the test for our business model – **at all points across our business, is what we are doing helping people flourish?**

Endnotes

1 Stepler, R (2016) World's centenarian population projected to grow eightfold by 2050, *Pew Research*. Available from: www.pewresearch.org/fact-tank/2016/04/21/worlds-centenarian-population-projected-to-grow-eightfold-by-2050/ (archived at https://perma.cc/2KB3-YULJ)

2 Ritchie, H (2019) The world population is changing: For the first time there are more people over 64 than children younger than 5, *Our World in Data*. Available from: https://ourworldindata.org/population-aged-65-outnumber-children (archived at https://perma.cc/ZD9C-UBGQ)

3 Sanders, L (2018) National life tables, UK: 2014 to 2016, *Office for National Statistics*. Available from: www.ons.gov.uk/peoplepopulationandcommunity/birthsdeathsandmarriages/lifeexpectancies/bulletins/nationallifetablesunitedkingdom/2014to2016 (archived at https://perma.cc/QG4C-2CGU)

4 Batchelor, T (2017) State pension age: millions of people will have to work an extra year before retiring at 68, *Independent*. Available from: www.independent.co.uk/news/uk/politics/state-pension-age-workers-people-extra-year-68-increase-retirement-age-david-gauke-a7849091.html (archived at https://perma.cc/5MSE-VNZD)

5 Cancer Research UK (nd) Cancer survival statistics. Available from: www.cancerresearchuk.org/health-professional/cancer-statistics/survival (archived at https://perma.cc/6DK4-JH6Z)

6 Alzheimer's Association (2019) 2019 Alzheimer's disease facts and figures, *Science Direct*, 15 (3), pp. 321–87. Available from: www.sciencedirect.com/science/article/pii/S1552526019300317 (archived at https://perma.cc/823J-6KGJ)

7 Agediscrimintation.info (2018) Super aged countries: what policy makers can learn about ageing well. Available from: www.agediscrimination.info/news/2018/5/10/super-aged-countries-what-policy-makers-can-learn-about-ageing-well (archived at https://perma.cc/HWK7-GTB5)
8 Moody's (2018) Ageing populations to pressure credit profiles of Japan, Korea over long term. Available from: www.moodys.com/research/Moodys-Ageing-populations-to-pressure-credit-profiles-of-Japan-Korea--PR_390978 (archived at https://perma.cc/H9ZY-5T9Z
9 United Nations (2015) World Population Ageing. Available from: www.un.org/en/development/desa/population/publications/pdf/ageing/WPA2015_Report.pdf (archived at https://perma.cc/X32A-SSX5)
10 Ronson, J (2015) Is there a genetic limit to human longevity? *Inverse*. Available from: www.inverse.com/article/6034-is-there-a-genetic-limit-to-human-longevity (archived at https://perma.cc/8JHC-724C)
11 Fessenden, M (2016) There are now more Americans over age 100 and they're living longer than ever, *Smithsonian Magazine*. Available from: www.smithsonianmag.com/smart-news/there-are-more-americans-over-age-100-now-and-they-are-living-longer-180957914/ (archived at https://perma.cc/RJX6-JEB9)
12 https://www.sens.org/ (archived at https://perma.cc/Q95W-DPPG)
13 Gratton, L and Scott, A (2016) *The 100-Year Life: Living and working in an age of longevity*, Bloomsbury Information. www.100yearlife.com/the-book/ (archived at https://perma.cc/UJA5-59J3)
14 Adler, C (2016) Mix and match, *Guardian*. Available from: www.theguardian.com/money/2006/nov/04/careers.graduates1 (archived at https://perma.cc/PLX3-VNRW)
15 Abaraham, L (2017) Meet the new breed of the gig economy: the slash worker, *and.co*. Available from: www.and.co/blog/future-of-work/meet-the-new-breed-of-the-gig-economy-the-slash-worker/ (archived at https://perma.cc/P5WQ-2LSB)
16 CIPD (2017) To gig or not to gig? Stories from the modern economy. Available from: www.cipd.co.uk/knowledge/work/trends/gig-economy-report (archived at https://perma.cc/MVR6-BF3A)
17 Eltringham, M (2016) Gig economy represents a race to the bottom for many because of client behaviour, *Insight*. Available from: https://workplaceinsight.net/gig-economy-represents-race-bottom-many-client-behaviour/ (archived at https://perma.cc/XWT3-NG3D)
18 Schumpeter (2015) Digital Taylorism, *Economist*. Available at: www.economist.com/business/2015/09/10/digital-taylorism (archived at https://perma.cc/6FE5-3F93)
19 https://www.thersa.org/ (archived at https://perma.cc/4C5A-8R3Q)

20 Taylor, M (2017) Good Work: The Taylor Review of Modern Working Practices, *RSA*. Available from: www.thersa.org/globalassets/pdfs/reports/good-work-taylor-review-into-modern-working-practices.pdf (archived at https://perma.cc/8PNN-2BLQ)

21 Office for National Statistics (2019) Labour market economic commentary May 2019). Available from: www.ons.gov.uk/employmentandlabourmarket/peopleinwork/employmentandemployeetypes/articles/labourmarketeconomiccommentary/may2019 (archived at https://perma.cc/9D29-8C49)

22 Indeed (2016) 89% of people with a second job will continue working double in 2016 [blog]. Available from: http://blog.indeed.com/2016/01/07/people-with-a-second-job-will-continue-working-double/ (archived at https://perma.cc/UW3H-S76P)

23 www.britannica.com/topic/eudaimonia (archived at https://perma.cc/H32T-4YK6)

24 Harter, J (2018) Employee engagement on the rise in the U.S, *Gallup*. Available from: https://news.gallup.com/poll/241649/employee-engagement-rise.aspx?utm_source=link_wwwv9&utm_campaign=item_245786&utm_medium=copy (archived at https://perma.cc/N4SY-9QHS)

25 HSE (2018) The Health and Safety Executive Annual Report and Accounts 2017/18. Available from: www.hse.gov.uk/aboutus/reports/ara-2017-18.pdf (archived at https://perma.cc/649N-N454)

26 https://opportunity.businessroundtable.org/ourcommitment/ (archived at https://perma.cc/F3V6-6B6Z)

27 Stockhammer, E (2006) Shareholder value orientation and the investment-profit puzzle, *Journal of Post Keynesian Economics*, 28 (2) 193–215. Available from: www.researchgate.net/profile/Engelbert_Stockhammer/publication/5172991_Shareholder_value_orientation_and_the_investment-profit_puzzle/links/00b4952efa54be8f10000000.pdf (archived at https://perma.cc/S7FG-C689)

28 Parker, C (2019) New Zealand will have a new 'well-being budget,' says Jacinda Ardern, *World Economic Forum*. Available from: www.weforum.org/agenda/2019/01/new-zealand-s-new-well-being-budget-will-fix-broken-politics-says-jacinda-ardern/ (archived at https://perma.cc/N356-ZXHP)

29 https://www.kateraworth.com/ (archived at https://perma.cc/Q3LQ-5Q8T)

30 https://www.overshootday.org/ (archived at https://perma.cc/MND7-CXS3)

06

20:20 vision

Stimulation to support the redesign of work using human energy principles

In this chapter, we will take a look at a range of forces and energies that we have as human beings with our physical, emotional and spiritual selves.

Many people practise *Zen*, work with *Chakras* and use therapies and approaches labelled as *alternative*. According to the social media site Quora, 20 million people practise yoga daily[1] and a 2016 report described 2 billion people 'doing yoga because it works'.[2]

In a range of circumstances, people discover yoga, meditation and so-called Eastern Mysticism[3] so this aspect of inclusion in our lives appears to be on the rise. Steve Jobs was a famous Zen Buddhist meditator;[4] there are classes and study programmes and practitioners of yoga, QiGong and meditation are part of a growth industry. The yoga industry alone is worth billions (a 2016 report cited $80 billion globally).[5]

Many are sceptical; many scientific studies will both uphold and refute claims of the impact and benefits of yoga and Eastern arts. One supportive piece that comes through a quick web search is a 2016 report citing 13 benefits including better sleep, decreased stress and anxiety, and boosted immune system reactions.[6] Whether we believe them, practise them or doubt them, for many hundreds of years, people have practised gentler, calming exercises in order to heal themselves mentally, physically and, of course, spiritually.

The irony of scientific claims that this is unproven and therefore unreliable sits **right alongside the increasing epidemic of mental**

> **ill-health and stress we referred to in earlier chapters**. And many of the stories we read are of how people recover from such trauma through meditation, mindfulness, yoga, tai chi, reiki healing and, of course, also through coaching, counselling and medical intervention.
>
> So we will take a look at what we can learn by understanding more about Chakras (a particularly well-defined energy map of the human body) and some fascinating research into how this has been channelled into the world of medical and sports science.
>
> Many organizations now offer benefits like on-site yoga classes and corporate membership to health clubs and exercise classes. The precise gains of these are not widely documented, so they fall into the benefits 'packages' and employer brand categories of work, rather than as a fully proven performance enhancement and retention toolkit.
>
> Well-being, though, is big business and a really hot topic, as we've discussed in previous chapters.
>
> So what *are* we talking about when we say meditation, mindfulness, wellness, yoga and Chakras? This chapter will review them for newcomers to this area and give us a business perspective on an ancient practice that just might hold the key to unlocking human potential and balanced ways of being and working.

Overview

To many of us, we have two dimensions to our lives: a personal dimension and a professional dimension. It may sound like this:

- we are at work thinking about **not** being at work; or
- we are not at work and we **are** thinking about work.

It's like the famous *Tao* symbol **Yin Yang** – with the two different polarities that are said to be a part of each human being. In the *taijitu*,[7] in Yin there is a bit of Yang; and in Yang, there is a bit of Yin.

Yin and Yang are opposite but complementary forces and represent a delicate interaction between energies: Yin represents the *feminine principle*, the night, the darkness, the gentle force, and Yang represents the *masculine principle*, the light, warmth, and the active force. Two balancing forces, a lot like work/life balance – a term that is approaching its 50th year of use as a label for competing *and* complementary forces.

Work/life balance

Since the 1970s, work/life balance has been a much-talked-about topic in the world of work. In post-war UK and US economies it was not uncommon for people to work 16 hours per day and in many cases in the United States, 100 hours (in total) per week. A range of work-related legislative acts reduced this to around the 40 hours we've become used to seeing. Or are supposed to be seeing. Indeed, of more relevance to European countries like the UK is the **European Working Time Directive**.[8] Aimed at a maximum of 48 hours per week and associated rest and vacation/holiday time, this is clearly an extension to the realization that no good comes from 'overwork'. The British Medical Association has this at the heart of its policy for medical staff.[9]

Much of the 40-hour construct was to alleviate fatigue on the job for those lifting, sewing, welding, building etc. As recently as 1980, there was a fairly even split between cognitive work and manual work, but the ratio of manual to cognitive work currently sits at 2:1 in favour of cognitive. So in a century of work it's gone from 2:1 in favour of manual to the opposite. In the coming decades, there will be even more disruption and change through digital and robotic automation.

If we are to believe predictions on the shifts coming our way through that digital and robotic automation, we will see even less manual work and the automation of repetitive cognitive work, with those studies giving us a vast range of estimates from 10 per cent to over 50 per cent. Whatever the percentage, a McKinsey report from 2017[10] predicted that 800 million jobs would be lost to some form of automation/technology.

This may ironically be a salvation from low-quality physical and cognitive work that is demanding even through its repetitive nature and volume. Many predict that people will experience a more fulfilling working life with fewer, but more challenging, problems to solve and tasks to complete, giving a sense of greater impact on others' lives through their work.

It may also become the biggest work issue humankind has faced, with millions of people potentially unable to reskill, becoming a hugely disaffected *jobless* class.

There is a growing sense that this is a worry for many people right now, whether the work is in warehousing, road freight, customer service, accountancy, paralegal support, data analysis or taxi driving.

Whilst many may not even admit to it, in the back of their minds is a looming end date to the viability of their work. This will undoubtedly cause some people mild anxieties that may increase as each new story of successful use of driverless vehicles or even higher rates of online retail and automated purchasing in stores, brings home the realization of those jobs disappearing.

On top of this anxiety, we see a natural human reaction to fear and change: focusing down and becoming more closed off and less social – ironically the very thing psychologists say accelerate and amplify the damaging effects of stress. In 2013, psychologist Matthew Liebermann published his research-based findings on the effects of social – and why we're wired to connect.[11] He found it is pre-programmed within us to connect to other people. Therefore, when we are threatened and withdraw into ourselves, it doubles the negative impacts by de-socializing and depriving us of something we have evolved to do: connect and socialize.

On top of this, Columbia University studied working hours and found some statistical correlation between the number of hours we work and the potential damage it can do to us mentally, emotionally and yes, physically.

A study of 80,000 workers revealed over 12.5 hours of **physical inactivity** in any given day. Sedentary living like this was equated to having similar damaging effects to smoking in terms of cutting life expectancy.[12] On top of this, an Australian National University study in 2017 found that anything over 39 hours of work per week is potentially damaging to our health.[13]

So is it any wonder that 25 million people are regularly taking anti-depressant medication??[14] Looking at these conditions we see a cocktail of circumstances that could create even more tension. Lost jobs, more sedentary lifestyles, longer hours, more reliance on artificial stimulants just to get through the day.

Dirty energy is what we have been used to using to compensate for our dip in natural, stimulated energy creation and utilization. Is it any wonder then that more and more of us are turning to alternatives – many of which have been with us for thousands of years (such as narcotic drugs, synthesized stimulants and caffeine, taurine, nicotine and valium)?

Perhaps controversially, this book declares this: *There is no work/life balance, only a balanced life.*

Which brings us onto the Eastern mystic arts and practices.

A balanced life is at the heart of what we call the Eastern mystic arts. Many of us know about them but are sceptical of their effectiveness, instead basing our 'treatment' on scientific, pharmaceutical remedies. Many of us, though, have opened our minds and decided to undertake initiatives to improve our life balance and become more inner/spiritual about ourselves.

So instead of the battles fought to compensate for demanding working schedules through increased benefits like parental leave, flexible working hours and many others,[15] we are seeing employers – and multiple generations of people at work (not just younger people) – placing much more emphasis on a new type of balanced life with wellness at the heart of it, not simply material gain.

Indeed, think tank the New Economics Foundation has committed itself to campaigning for a four-day working week,[16] tackling it from a design perspective. Redesigning the working week expectations from five to four days may not sound much, but many experiments have revealed that this 'additional' day brings more balance, less sedentary ways, more space to think and a general calmness to frenetic ways of being. Happy Ltd[17] tried this and their experiment received mixed reactions, with some people feeling more pressured with the (now less) time to do their work.

So again, this comes to redesign, which we'll cover in later chapters. Yet more interestingly for this chapter, it reveals anxieties that we still persist with the myth that **we can manage time**. We can't. **We can only manage our energy** (within this construct we have created called time).

And managing energy is at the heart of Eastern mystic practices and increasingly is becoming a fusion of Eastern and Western lifestyle choices. People are rightly expressing the desire to improve their energy management (but may call it the ability to live a more balanced, aligned and even more spiritual life), perhaps because we have gradually disconnected from our inner nature and with nature in general. This has led people to live a life with 'autopilot engaged', with the overwhelming pressures of life leading to illnesses coming from mental and emotional/energetic instability and a surge in workplace-related stress as covered earlier in this book.[18]

People appear to realize that *reconnection to self* is the way to achieve a balanced life and in general to gain a deeper understanding of why and how we live our lives the way we do, versus the way we now want to. People are starting to understand how our behaviour has a real impact on our lives and the lives of others, and moreover they are starting to desire to live a more 'aware life'. The word 'woke'[19] applies in this context.

Looking at this scenario, organizations are starting to redesign (albeit in small and sometimes academic ways) to change their models and to adapt to this surging demand and need, hence the growth of the 'benefits' industry, with well-being becoming a key part of the policies and HR systems that many will look for as a sign of a company that has a more balanced way of operating. Many people believe that a balanced, flexible approach to a role in general – along with recognition, learning, prospects and the all-important culture, values and purpose factors – takes us to a more 'spiritual' element to work over purely a transactional one. Maybe 'transcendent' is a little strong for many, but transcendence is becoming more important for some of us.

Material gains, whilst still part of our consumerist society, are being questioned more and more. We are seeing 'slow lifestyles', off-the-grid breaks and 'tiny living' as a post-materialistic view of life from an increasingly disenchanted group of people. Time, experiences and our relationships are becoming more precious to many of us more than cars, boats and luxury homes.

Our struggles to look good, to use our time more productively, and our material gains, are things we do in our *outside* world. How we look to others. What we think, how we look after ourselves and how we nurture our emotional, energetic and spiritual dimensions are our *inside* world. They still have a huge impact on how and if we achieve goals and on our performance and the workplace environment. They are how we feel, which only we can know.

It is the balance – or imbalance – between those *outside* and *inside* worlds that is the cause of many of our 21st-century personal challenges; that and an increasingly unpredictable and volatile world changing more rapidly than we've ever known.

Yes, the systemic element of change has, in itself, *changed*.

We as individuals are forced to change during the restructures to an organization's set-up or way of operating, and we are seeing people feel a sense that the pace of change is more rapid than ever before.

In his book *High-Frequency Change*,[20] author Tom Cheesewright somewhat refutes that, instead referring to the sensation that change is now large waves we notice more, and not smaller ripples we may not.

Is it faster and more relentless? Not necessarily, but it's *more evident* to us, so we see, hear and feel it more, and therefore it seems faster and more relentless.

Change has been how we've developed and we have arguably experienced rapid change before: the discovery of fire, use of tools, language and social structures. All have been huge changes to our way of being. What is interesting about the 21st-century version of change is that it is a further detachment from 'reality' – the world, nature and our sense of community.

According to anthropological approaches, early human beings in the primordial era were linked with the animism and sacredness of nature. Today, modern human society has become more aware of itself yet increasingly detached from nature, moving more towards engineered environments and systems – and even (as we discussed with the 100-year life) resistant to the natural cycle of life and death.

If we asked you:

1 Do you know your true individual nature?
2 When was the last time you felt a deep connection with the energy of nature and felt a part of it?

What would you say? Often it would be when on a vacation, a retreat, as part of an equine-coaching experience[21] or when some traumatic event forced you to reappraise your life. We have normalized an unnatural, machine-like way of being that our energy systems have not been attuned for and maybe never will.

Evolution in how we are physically and psychologically hasn't had the time to reprogramme us for the modern, anxiety-laden lives we now find ourselves living. So we have to redesign that environment or risk more damage to ourselves and negate the scientific and engineered opportunities we have created such as medicines and labour-saving machinery.

So what is human energy and its connection to nature?

The human body consists of *five layers of energy*. The first layer is the *physical body*, which has weight, shape and volume; we can touch it and see it.

But there are four other energy fields surrounding the physical body, and together these five layers, or energy bodies, contain the human energy field. These layers are where our *mental, energetic, spiritual* and *emotional* characteristics are stored.

Why is this so important?

Energy is everything. We, as humans, are made by energy; in science we consider that everything we see and touch is made from energy. The universe is also made from energy. To relate that to being human, we can look at the *source* of things. We are able to deeply understand ourselves and to remove the blocks or resistance stored in the deeper side of our being that may be forced upon us by our modern lifestyles.

From Eastern wisdom to the Western psychological and physics approach

We can trace the beginnings of the teaching of human energy in this way through the 'Vedas'[22] – Indian philosophical poems – (1000 BC). In Sanskrit the word *veda* indicates 'knowledge' and 'wisdom' – and here we find the first hints of yogic philosophy.

In these poems it emerged that people were beginning to research a system to allow human beings to not waste their own energies and to instead find a way to channel them. The spoken word and sense of self gave us the chance to be concerned with identity – 'who am I, really?'– and links back to existentialism, which we covered in Chapter 3.

In this quest for insight into our identity, we can see what we now call the research of the 'inner journey'. Quite literally, all coaching practices and many counselling and therapeutic interventions are framed around this journey metaphor. Past, present and future states play a huge part in that process. And experiences, reactions and feelings are at the heart of how resourceful or helpless people feel in order to balance and restore a sense of control and activation towards remedial action and improvement.

In looking at psychological and physical energy, the practice of yoga teaches that mind and body are the same and unique substance, but two different aspects of *matter*, with different levels of vibration.

The *neuroendocrine system*[23] is considered in yoga to be the most important of all systems. The neuroendocrine system can be defined as the sets of neurons, glands and non-endocrine tissues (such as the gland that produces melatonin, or the sleep hormone), and the neurochemicals, hormones and humoral signals they produce and receive, which function in an integrated manner to collectively regulate a *physiological or behavioural state*.

The science of yoga teaches that in our mind, we have an accumulated memory bank full of impressions and thoughts marked since our birth, which form the foundation of our subconscious mind. It is recognized by Western psychology that certain aspects of our reality are below the level of consciousness.

Carl Gustav Jung was one of the first Western academics to explore these inner frontiers of the mind, this innermost layer called the *unconscious mind.* Jung realized that this is a common part of all human beings at all times and in all places, titled by him as 'collective unconscious'.

The Jungian opera

In 1921 a fundamental study of Jung's research was released, 'The Psychological Types',[24] where he described what he called the four functions of consciousness, divided into two pairs: *sensing and intuition,* or the functions through which facts are learned and the world of factual reality, and *feeling and thinking,* or the functions of judgment and evaluation.

And at the base of Jung's work there was the vision that every human being has a natural predisposition in obtaining and recovering energy. In Jungian work this dichotomy is called *introversion and extroversion,* which refers to our favourite ways to get and focus our own energy either in those *inner* or *outer* worlds.

The 'extroverted' is attuned to the external environment, learns best by discussing with others, likes to get into action, and enjoys solving problems through interaction. The 'introverted', on the other side of this dichotomy, is drawn to contemplation in the inner world, learns best by reflection and enjoys solving problems through individual concentration.

Thinking about the workplace, imagine if an 'introvert' or an 'extrovert' is constantly forced to work in an environment where they are never given the favoured conditions? Are they likely to give their best performance? More so to the point of energy, how much energy will be expended working against their preferences and therefore appearing to perform less well because of being out of balance, rather than incompetence?

We will come back to this practical aspect, but for now let's keep going through the research and further theories.

According to Jung, only one of the functions, as a rule, takes on the role of a leader in people's lives, supported by only one of the other two. In the Western world, it is generally recognized that *thought* is privileged, while *intuition* and *feeling* are less developed or even repressed and relegated to the unconscious, creating an imbalance to a healthy state of the mind and body of the person.

Jung's idea is 'the purpose of an individual's life [...] must be not to suppress or repress, but to get to know the other side of himself, and in this way be able to both enjoy and control the entire range of one's abilities: that is, in the full sense, to know oneself.'

It is the *process of individualization,* which through the integration of the four functions allows us to look at the centre, a sort of fifth faculty, the transcendent function, 'to see, think, feel and intuit the transcendent and act accordingly'. [25] Much as Abraham Maslow described 'self-actualization' in his hierarchy of needs.[26]

In those same years of discovery of the transcendent elements to his work, Jung undertook several journeys to Eastern countries, where he found further confirmation of his vision of human reality and energy.

Modern physics

The US physicist Fritjof Capra, in his famous work the *Tao of Physics*[27] written in 1975 (but still considered contemporary), has the aim of demonstrating that there is a substantial harmony between the spirit of Eastern wisdom and the most recent concepts of Western science. His main concern was, 'Is the concept of knowledge understood in the same way for a Buddhist monk and an American physicist?'

Throughout history it has been found that the human mind is capable of two types of knowledge, that is, two modes of consciousness – rational and intuitive – traditionally combined with science and beliefs.

We have also seen this in business – culture and protocols, process and behaviours, structures and responsive systems.

As already argued by Jung, in the West, intuitive knowledge is not held in high regard, while rational and scientific knowledge is privileged; on the contrary, the Eastern approach is exactly the opposite.

The approach on which Capra puts the accent is the importance of the correspondence between the conception of the world of physicists (Western) and that of the mystics (Eastern). The question, which according to the author is interesting to ask, is not *if this correspondence exists*, more that because it exists, *what meaning it has*. Essentially, the interplay between rational and intuitive, science and beliefs, facts and feelings; tensions we are seeing surface in how we understand our modern world, life and the work we do.

In an attempt to understand the mystery of life, man has followed many different approaches; the way of the scientist and that of the mystic but also those of poets, warriors, artists, preachers, scientists, shamen, politicians, performers and teachers. All of them valid in the context in which they arose, as they are descriptions and representations of reality, but none can give a complete picture of the world.

Capra was talking about managing seemingly competing energies and instead talking of their complementary nature to each other. Balance.

Energy in 'alternative' medicine

According to Chinese medicine, *Qi* (pronounced *Chi*) is the origin of all existence, not only the human one but also of the life of nature and of the entire universe. In the human body, the *Qi* flows along channels connected to each other, the meridians, in all directions, upwards, downwards, inwards and outwards.

The vital energy is collected in all the organs; from the centre of the body it flows towards the external parts and then returns to the starting point. In healthy and vital subjects, the *Qi* energy flows through the whole body in a harmonious and uniform way, providing humans with vital energy both physically and mentally; movement, digestion, but also thought, feeling and sensory perception are the expression of *Qi*.

One example is the Chinese Body Clock, a fascinating version of where our physical and chemical energy goes at certain times of our day. For example, during our 12 noon to 4 pm window, some very different energies are at play with us physiologically; the need to fuel, then absorbing the fuel and thereby experiencing lower energy whilst this is happening. When we look at our working day, it is often in the afternoons where we have to review others' work, sign things off, make judgement calls, finish off the board meeting with key decisions etc.

However, 8 am–12 noon is the time of high energy, clear thinking and good concentration; this is the time to make the best decisions, surely? Take work home and try to do it at 8–9pm? You should be only doing light reading and are probably in need of some love and affection rather than emails or a spreadsheet for a meeting the following day.

None of this is meant to say we should only work between 8 am and noon. But it DOES mean that we might need to pay attention to when we need our peak, optimal cognitive and intuitive power. And that's not often found at 10 at night in a conventional working day!

Whether body clocks or Qi energy, there is a much stronger interest in how we care for ourselves in addition to our physical and mental wellness – our soul and our spirituality are also coming into focus for many of us.

Spirituality

Spirituality is not something remote that we pick up like a radio picks up soundwaves from a broadcast, or like a vapour we inhale, only belonging to a special few people in the world. It comes with the 'human package'. Therefore, it pervades all aspects of life. Psychotherapist Thomas Moore describes the role of spirituality in his book *Care of the Soul*,[28] distinguishing it from soulfulness. Soulfulness is described as *full of, or expressing feelings or emotions*.[29]

Moore describes our spirituality as when we reach consciousness, awareness, and the highest values. In our soulfulness, we experience the most pleasurable and the most exhausting of human experiences and emotions – without one it is difficult if not impossible to truly appreciate the other. These two directions make up the fundamental *vibration* of human life.

We can see this in many of the elements of life Moore covers, as dilemmas we might often face:

- creation–destruction;
- gentleness–aggression;
- solitude–social contact;
- self-love–humility;
- need for approval–no regard for the views of another;
- adrift–anchored;
- openness/freedom–order/limit;
- possessive attachment–dispersion of desire;
- forgiveness–vengeance.

A spiritual point of view is necessary for the soul, something much deeper than our personality and more about our way of *being* in the world, providing the inspiration, and the sense of meaning.

Transcendent states are defined as:[30]

1a: exceeding usual limits: surpassing;

1b: extending or lying beyond the limits of ordinary experience.

In *Kantian* philosophy,[31] being beyond the limits of all possible experience and knowledge:

2: being beyond comprehension;

3: transcending the universe or material existence.

In the broadest sense, spirituality is an aspect of any attempt to approach or attend to the *invisible factors in life* and to transcend the personal, concrete, finite particulars of this world.

Moore says that all humans need to care for the soul by touching upon the spiritual.

Which leads us onto the Chakras – any of several points of physical or spiritual energy in the human body according to yoga philosophy[32] – and a developed understanding of what they symbolize. Of course, you do not need to know about all the Chakras to understand how to be mindful, calm and balance your thinking and doing energies. This explanation is to look at how mind, body and soul are intertwined.

The Chakra system

The Chakra system can be described as the mind/body pathway; the Chakras, according to their location, represent the nervous system's pathways to the spinal cord.

We can compare the Chakra system or inner energy system of the body to the autonomic nervous system. In fact, each Chakra corresponds to a specific nervous plexus, or cluster, of ganglionic neurons along the spinal cord pathway. There is effectively science that aligns to the Chakra systems map of the human body without specifically creating that validation. Chakra systems, of course, pre-date more recent scientific developments based on anatomical research and experiments.

Why would Chakras find their way into a book about redesigning business?

Whilst I doubt we would ever create a *Chief Chakra Officer* role, we can learn a lot more about our individual selves and the reasons we are feeling a certain way about our lives and the work we do.

Let's take mindfulness. The NHS in the UK clearly endorses the practice of mindfulness, witnessed by an article on managing stress and anxiety.[33] Professor Chris Williams (former director of the Oxford Mindfulness Centre) describes it thus:

> mindfulness means knowing directly what is going on inside and outside ourselves, moment by moment.

> It's easy to stop noticing the world around us. It's also easy to lose touch with the way our bodies are feeling and to end up living 'in our heads' – caught up in our thoughts without stopping to notice how those thoughts are driving our emotions and behaviour.
>
> An important part of mindfulness is reconnecting with our bodies and the sensations they experience. This means waking up to the sights, sounds, smells and tastes of the present moment. That might be something as simple as the feel of a banister as we walk upstairs.
>
> Another important part of mindfulness is an awareness of our thoughts and feelings as they happen moment to moment.
>
> It's about allowing ourselves to see the present moment clearly. When we do that, it can positively change the way we see ourselves and our lives.

Being present, in this description, requires a connection with mind, body and yes, soul. Deep feelings and inner narrative about how we feel and what we want to do, connected to how our mind needs to process things and how our body is in that connected triage.

Professor Williams goes on to say:

> Mindfulness isn't the answer to everything, and it's important that our enthusiasm doesn't run ahead of the evidence.
>
> There's encouraging evidence for its use in health, education, prisons and workplaces, but it's important to realize that research is still going on in all of these fields. Once we have the results, we'll be able to see more clearly who mindfulness is most helpful for.

A strong endorsement, even without strong evidence. And a clear understanding of the *outer and inner* aspects of ourselves and of *mind, body and soul*. Mindfulness therefore has a strong endorsement from one of the world's largest and most established healthcare organizations. Mindfulness in business has become a 'thing'. Many people will say they practise it during times of tension or high-stress incidents.

Mindfulness also has a strong foundation in the teachings and practices of those who understand the Chakras. Our Chakras are energy centres that are the control nucleus of various body systems. Even in the Western anatomy model, the autonomic nervous system regulates the activity of various organs and glands in the body.

The ancient *Vedic* wisdom teaches that the evolution of the human being is an inner journey that takes place in the Chakra system, which is a direct route to the energy of the body.

In *Sanskrit*, the ancient, sacred language of India, the word *chakra* means *wheel*. This gives us an insight into the nature of energy, which is in a constant state of flux, and therefore those energy vortices can be in balance or out of balance.

When they are balanced, the exchanges of life force between the creative cosmic source and the individual mind, body and emotions are easy and free. The individual experiences a state of well-being, inner peace and the outer world is handled easily. Joy is the constant background regardless of the outer picture.

Each Chakra is associated with an element of nature, a colour, one of the senses, as well as different physical, mental and emotional dimensions.

The root Chakra: basic trust (red)

This is the first Chakra, whose Sanskrit name is *Muladhara*; in the body it is situated slightly lower than the base of the spine. The evolutionary journey of the human being starts here.

The function of the root Chakra is to connect us to basic trust and to the survival instinct. It is linked to any concern of the physical and material aspects of our life. It gives us the stability to have a solid foundation to our personality, and it is from this centre that we feel a sense of belonging or not belonging. The first Chakra is important in our self-development. If we neglect that area of our inner self, many of our achievements may not last for long.

When this chakra is balanced, people report feeling at home in our world, connected to the people and places around them. They describe an ease in relating to and interacting well with others. They report higher reserves of energy and approach activities with a positive attitude. They describe a sense of trust in their capability to be resourceful whilst feeling grounded.

Imbalance in this Chakra appears to arouse feelings of insecurity, fear and anxiety. There can be a sense of inertia and apathy, and a feeling of not being grounded, as well as being distant.

The sacral Chakra: sexuality and creativity (orange)

The second, or sacral Chakra, in Sanskrit called the *Swadisthana* Chakra, is situated below the pelvic area. It is the depository of our sexual and creative energies. It is our source of inspiration to create or make things happen on many levels, from a creativity point of view as in art, music and poetry or any creative project, but also in the desire for procreation, maternal and paternal instincts. From the other side, from this centre, we experience how self-sufficient we really are, and can influence controlling behaviour in relationships.

When this centre is in balance, people report feelings of openness and being receptive to others, sharing feelings, thoughts and emotions easily; spontaneity and curiosity are also abundant.

Imbalance in this Chakra is reported as leading to sadness, perceiving life as boring and monotonous. There is a fear of being controlled by others or losing self-control.

The solar Chakra: wisdom and power (yellow)

The third Chakra is known as the solar chakra, *Manipura* in Sanskrit, and in the physical body is located around the navel centre. It is considered the source of power and wisdom and where we start to consciously pattern our personality.

When the third Chakra is in balance, people report feeling warm and generous, resilient, optimistic and positive, confident, energetic and skillful.

Imbalance or blockages in this Chakra are reported by people as creating an over-dependence on material gains; there is no trust in anything other than own ability, they can feel aggressive, be manipulative and controlling. People also report the opposite; they become passive, powerless and needy, withdrawing from the challenges and difficulties of life.

The heart Chakra: love and healing (green)

The fourth or heart Chakra, called *Anahata* in Sanskrit, is situated in the middle of the chest at the level of the heart, hence the name. This Chakra is symbolical of a major evolutionary stage for humankind, because from that point onward, the focus changes from the individual self to the group.

When the heart Chakra is balanced, people describe feeling at one with others and the world. There is a free and spontaneous exchange of feelings; they feel more caring, faithful and loving towards everyone. The individual is open to giving and receiving love, sharing of oneself and one's resources unconditionally.

Blockages or dysfunction in this Chakra have people describing feelings of self-centredness, harshness and being demanding. People have described additional feelings of coldness, cruelty and being overprotective, and whilst having passionate feelings, they are more around feeling jealous and possessive.

The throat Chakra: communication (blue)

The fifth Chakra, known as throat Chakra, *Vishuddi* in Sanskrit, is located at the junction between the neck and throat, just between the collarbones. It is considered as the communication centre of the body. The importance of this Chakra is its function as a bridge between the body and the head. This represents symbolically an integration of several aspects of our nature: physical or basic instincts, emotions and feelings together with intellect, memory, reason, cognitive and other mental faculties.

When this Chakra is balanced, people say they can express freely and without fear, knowing when to speak and when to remain silent, and experience a good balance between physical and metaphysical expression. Strong throat Chakra energy gives effective communication skills and leadership abilities as charisma is peculiar to this centre and with such energy a person can inspire others.

Sometimes blocked energy in this Chakra leads one to be shy, introverted and unable to share and express feelings and thoughts openly and freely as there is fear of being judged.

The eyebrow Chakra: awareness (indigo)

The sixth or eyebrow Chakra, *Ajna* Chakra in Sanskrit, is located in the space between the two eyebrows. The significance of this Chakra is that it is the state beyond matter and the physical senses. Through this centre, the human being can perceive the subtle world of spirit.

When this centre is functioning well and it is balanced, the individual has very high idealism and a creative imagination. Imbalance or blockage of this Chakra causes the individual to be full of self-importance, the 'big head' syndrome.

The crown Chakra: spirituality (violet)

The seventh, crown or highest Chakra, *Sahasrara* in Sanskrit, is the peak of the evolutionary journey of humanity. This is the summit of the energy pathway as it ascends along the spinal passage. By the time it reaches the crown Chakra, the different purifying stages of human experience during its journey have caused major changes in the human personality. Actually, this special centre is not considered as part of the material realm. The rare person who reaches such an elevated state of consciousness lives in close communion with the spiritual level, much as Jung described *Transcendence* and Maslow *Self-Actualization*.

In summary

Whilst our Chakras may not seem to have relevance in the world of business, they can teach us a lot about our energies, our mental state of well-being and offer an understanding of why some things just don't seem aligned in our lives, thoughts and state of being.

Thousands of years of teaching have given people a sense of deeper viewpoints on their world and, most importantly, themselves within it. Discovery of this series of models may be shunned in some quarters by the people of business, politics and academia. Yet this state of enlightenment, to others, is their key to unlocking energy sources in a complex, challenging and changing world.

Chakras and HR – a PhD thesis

In 2014, a chance connection resulted in a conversation with PhD student Andronicus Torp – a Dane studying in Bucharest, Romania. It was a fascinating exchange that carried on over following months; it was instrumental in Andronicus becoming Dr Torp and was where I was first introduced to the concept of quantum energy in people. Here is a reproduced summary of Dr Torp's work, shared with his permission:

> **Energy field, Chakras and neuroscience experiment (EPI)** based on the PhD Thesis of Andronicus Torp: Research into an HR assessment method based on the human energy profile, University POLITEHNICA of Bucharest, Doctoral School Entrepreneurship, Business Engineering and Management.

The aim of this research and study was to develop a completely new HR assessment method based on a **Human Energy Profile**.

Earlier in this chapter (and according to William Tiller who wrote the book *Science and Human Transformation: Subtle energies, intentionality and consciousness*[34]) we explored the connection between the energy field of a human being and how that person functions. Instead of looking at psychometric instruments (how we think) there are now opportunities to consider what energy we are emitting to others (and what we are picking up from others). We might call it a 'vibe' – which in essence is short for vibrations, as mentioned around the Chakras.

Is there anything in the 'vibe' we have that can be reliably measured? Can it be used to indicate how much energy people have towards a type of work, role or collaboration? Can we even assess how likely someone is to perform well in a certain task by the vibe they are giving?

Of course not, we'd all say.

Yet we emit electro-magnetic impulses – see this article from *Forbes* magazine.[35] We ARE an electro-magnetic field with atoms and electrons like all things in the universe. So we will be emitting actions and reactions.

And Dr Torp's research was informed by experiments in precisely that – the levels of quantum energy we are emitting and whether, when mapped to Chakras, we can use the measures to predict performance issues, stress and appropriate changes to how people work and what they are working on.

The idea for a proposed HR assessment method is inspired by the book *The Self-Aware Universe* by quantum theory physicist Professor Dr Amit Goswami.[36] In this book, Dr Goswami gives a general introduction to the principles of modern physics and explains how everything in this universe based on Einstein's famous equation, $E=MC2$, can be seen as consisting of energy.

It therefore *should* be possible to make certain assessments about a human being based on that person's energy profile using a tool created to assess the human energy profile, called an EPI – **Electrophotonic Imaging Device** (similar in concept to an electrocardiogram or ECG).

From a theoretical point of view Dr Torp's research is based on:

- energy fields;
- the Chakra system;
- Yin and Yang energies;
- personality traits.

The empirical back-up studies behind the tool are based on:

- performance prediction;
- work improvement;
- employee well-being and development.

Performance prediction

What can measured levels of the quantum energy of human beings tell us about how they will perform in certain roles, circumstances and tasks?

Using the Chakras as a map of human energy sources, pre- and post-performance levels of energy can be taken to look at both potential predictions on levels of performance and reflections on the demands of the task on energy levels. For example, with a low energy level on the heart Chakra in work that involves feeding back to people who have failed assessment tests, we could see this person be cold and overly harsh in criticizing others' efforts. We might want to counter that with some coaching or even allocate someone else with a higher heart-level Chakra to this task.

Work improvement

How do we use the measurements of the human energy profile to improve the work people do and how they apply themselves to their work?

Dr Goswami's work – and the use of a machine that measures the emitting quantum energy of human beings[37] – was able to predict impairing factors to performance based on out-of-line Chakra readings, from the quantum emission of energy.

With athletes (for example in the pre-Glasnost Soviet Union), this machine was used in training routines to detect early onset of injuries such as muscle tears. It was proven to be more accurate than not, when advice to cease training was ignored.

Employee well-being and development

Probably the area with the greatest (potential) use of some form of EPI device that can measure human energy and what is showing as out of line when mapped against Chakras is our own well-being.

In looking at well-being more generally, we can go to the CIPD as one of the biggest bodies in the world supporting better work and working lives. In their factsheet[38] the CIPD gives us this overview:

> Promoting and supporting employee well-being is at the heart of our purpose to champion better work and working lives because an effective workplace well-being programme can deliver mutual benefit to people, organizations, economies and communities. When people are happy and well, businesses can thrive and societies flourish. We believe that work should do more than meet our basic financial needs and contribute to economic growth; it should also improve the quality of our lives by giving us meaning and purpose and contributing to our overall well-being.
>
> The fast-changing world of work and the fluctuating demands it places on employers and employees means that our grasp of health and well-being needs can never stand still. It needs to evolve constantly to understand the impact on people's health and well-being.
>
> At the CIPD, our internal Health and Well-being Champions support and drive change, especially in increasing awareness and understanding of mental health. As well as training line managers in good people management and mental health issues, we hold regular well-being days to promote healthy living. We also offer our staff on-site fitness classes, massages and mindfulness sessions, healthy eating options in our canteen, and an autumn flu vaccination

What is clear from even this opening commentary is that looking after people goes beyond traditional benefits of pay, heating and lighting, protective clothing, devices and codes that ensure safe practices – it also goes into the physical and mental health of people.

Well-being should not be dismissed as a fad – this is a duty of care that is going beyond what the industrial era gave us for workers' rights (often lobbied strongly by unions and research think-tanks). This is a protective covenant that is now part of the *Good Work* deal.

We seem to have acknowledged that working conditions can still be damaging to our health beyond the dangers of operating heavy machinery or cleaning the windows of a skyscraper building in a tiny trolley affixed by ropes and pulleys. Incessant pressure in an accounting firm to deliver a complex set of accounts to a ridiculous deadline shows we are under pressure in the workplace that we have designed or engineered.

A *long-hours* culture and demands is *not* offset by an on-site shower and fresh fruit in the kitchen area. Some leaders seem to think these gestures make it alright to insist on 14–16 hours of work per day.

We may be capable of short stints of this level of exertion, but it is the equivalent of running a marathon, each day, under competitive conditions that even Eliud Kipchoge (and his sub-two-hour marathon achievement in October 2019) would find stressful and more than difficult.

We need a balance of rest, recuperation, thoughtfulness, creativity, distractions, fun, love, laughter and compassionate company alongside any punishing or harsh working conditions. It's difficult to displace pressures if you're on some form of covert military operation or even getting those accounts done to a very tight deadline. But every day, as a norm, this is damaging to us and conflicts with thousands of years of evolutionary marvel in how our body and mind work.

We need to work WITH energy forces and not against them or ignore them or overuse certain elements of our energy.

And whilst we have discovered artificial stimulants (caffeine, taurine, antidepressants, steroids) we are regulating their use with good reason – they may be able to compensate for naturally lacking energy sources in some people's chemistry and biology but they are not to be abused as *performance enhancers*. They can be what I've described as *dirty energy*. Quick fixes, augmented forces and potentially overbearing stimulants that we can become addicted to chemically and psychologically and can cause actual damage to our organs and certainly our energy forces associated with those organs and glands.

In summary

The work of measuring human energy in this way has not been widely publicized (but is mentioned in some journals here[39]); it is based on

Dr Torp's research for his PhD thesis and was shared with me in interview and documentation exchanges.

So, if we have a machine that can measure the emission of quantum energy from humans and detect out-of-line energies that may cause impairment, it could be used to help understand when someone is in peak performance physically and mentally. And it could tell when to rest, recuperate or take on alternative work that is not likely to cause impairment to their mental and physical selves based on the readings only a machine and interpretative analysis can deduct.

It is our theory that this type of factor will become as mainstream as ECGs, heart monitors, glucose level detectors and other forms of scanning the human body.

Will the HR teams of the future be like quantum energy physicists for our workforce? In high-stress roles, certainly. In the mainstream, unlikely. But watch (or sense) this space for further scientific developments that use Eastern mysticism in some bizarre Zen/physics hybrid practice.

We can also see a correlation between the human Chakras energy map and one for an organizational level if we return to the work of the Barrett Values Centre and the consciousness model developed by Richard Barrett.[40] There are three main streams of parallel thought: the *Cyclic Levels of Existence Theory*, the *Consciousness Model*, and *Yogic Chakra Technology*. Perhaps there is something more we should explore at the intersection of Eastern mystic practice, psychological and sociological models for the evolution of collective human endeavour and these levels of consciousness for businesses and organizations.

This model has been used to recentre whole organizations experiencing traumatic change and transformation (and in the case of Iceland an entire nation[41]) to become more aware of the connectivity of a series of energies and the capabilities that come from those energies (see Table 6.1).

Through the synergy between Graves, Beck, Wilber, Laloux, Barrett and the ancient wisdom of Chakras and Tao, we can see an emergent pattern of similar elements: inner and outer world; of thought, actions, dilemmas and competing energy sources. Choices we make and ways of being that are commensurate with a balanced life.

TABLE 6.1 Organizational levels of consciousness

Level	Descriptor
7	**Service** – to humanity
6	**Making a difference** – strategic partnerships & alliances
5	**Internal cohesion** – building internal community
4	**Transformation** – continuous renewal & learning
3	**Self-esteem** – high performance
2	**Relationship** – harmonious relationship
1	**Survival** – financial stability

If we look at human energy levels, known practices like yoga and QiGong which help us balance our energy levels, wellbeing strategies and the introduction of new technologies that can actually measure our energy fields, we could be looking into a whole new way to deploy ourselves, to be deployed by others, and when and how to develop ourselves in tune with our energy states.

It would revolutionize what we work on and how and when we work on things. Yet this technology is largely unknown, Eastern mystical practices are still given little recognition in science and we are now facing that wellness crises this book has already covered.

So I guess until a 'Titan of Technology' creates an EPI app for our smartphones, we may have to rely on yoga, sensing and some enlightened thinking to help us manage our energy with the challenges of the 21st-century world of work.

WHAT WE LEARNED FROM THIS CHAPTER

1 People are also part of a complex physics and biology quantum system. That we have – through long-standing practices mainly from the Eastern parts of the world – developed ways to understand, measure and enhance our quantum energy states (which link to our physiological states) is ignored at our peril. **We don't have to all be yoga practitioners but understanding the connections between our**

spiritual, psychological and physiological selves is an increasingly useful competence, skill and insight to have in navigating a complex, challenging and demanding world.**

2 There are five layers of energy – which are admittedly measurable, yet we don't always have the capability or mechanisms to measure them. Instead, we have to rely on listening and searching within us. **We sense, or feel, a change in us and that might be in raised anxieties. We should follow a deductive trail of search within us about why this is and how we can correct our energy misalignment.**

3 The conditions we create in work are unnatural to us, despite hundreds of years of forced labour, serfdom, industrial production or knowledge work. **We therefore must attune the environment we – especially as leaders – consciously or unconsciously create for our fellow human beings to perform, think, do, and energize themselves about their work.**

4 Eastern mysticism is not just for the society drop-outs or trendy parents of suburban life. We are looking seriously at an epidemic of ill-health and premature demise through self-inflicted working and living regimes. **We need more balance and Eastern mystic arts provide that in abundance.**

5 We can describe ourselves as a compassionate employer through the introduction of more focus on well-being. And like in the previous chapter's reflection on New Zealand Prime Minister Jacinda Ardern's declaration, **we should measure the impact of well-being initiatives and practices as much as we do outputs and profit margins.**

6 We have a duty of care to ourselves AND to each other. We can inspire others to self-care and we must start with an understanding of what caring for ourselves really is. Many of the Eastern arts have answers to which we are not yet even able to formulate the questions. **We must move from denial, to awareness, to action, to aggregation and to wider dissemination.**

We need a wellness revolution to counter workplace stress evolution.

Endnotes

1 Quora (2018) How many people do yoga worldwide? Available from: www.quora.com/How-many-people-do-yoga-worldwide (archived at https://perma.cc/6CAW-XWHD)
2 UN News (2016) 2 billion people practise yoga 'because it works'. Available from: https://news.un.org/en/audio/2016/06/614172 (archived at https://perma.cc/2RF4-9FRR)
3 www.merriam-webster.com/dictionary/mysticism (archived at https://perma.cc/RNF5-2PAZ)
4 Baer, D (2015) Here's how Zen meditation changed Steve Jobs' life and sparked a design revolution, *Business Insider*. Available from: www.businessinsider.com/steve-jobs-zen-meditation-buddhism-2015-1?r=US&IR=T (archived at https://perma.cc/H97T-2U5Q)
5 Delaney, B (2017) The yoga industry is booming – but does it make you a better person? *Guardian*. Available from: www.theguardian.com/lifeandstyle/2017/sep/17/yoga-better-person-lifestyle-exercise (archived at https://perma.cc/G38M-T4Z3)
6 Link, R (2017) 13 benefits of yoga that are supported by science, *Healthline*. Available from: www.healthline.com/nutrition/13-benefits-of-yoga (archived at https://perma.cc/PHZ4-JLY2)
7 www.definitions.net/definition/taijitu (archived at https://perma.cc/YU6U-QTH6)
8 European Commission (nd) Working conditions – working time directive. Available from: https://ec.europa.eu/social/main.jsp?catId=706&langId=en&intPageId=205 (archived at https://perma.cc/NA4W-BNV5)
9 BMA (2017) What is the European Working Time Directive? Available from: www.bma.org.uk/advice/employment/working-hours/ewtd (archived at https://perma.cc/E3MU-J5UL)
10 Manyika, J et al (2017) Jobs lost, jobs gained: what the future of work will mean for jobs, skills, and wages, *McKinsey*. Available from: www.mckinsey.com/featured-insights/future-of-work/jobs-lost-jobs-gained-what-the-future-of-work-will-mean-for-jobs-skills-and-wages (archived at https://perma.cc/QXK9-7WNB)
11 Smith, E (2013) Social connection makes a better brain, *The Atlantic*. Available from: www.theatlantic.com/health/archive/2013/10/social-connection-makes-a-better-brain/280934/ (archived at https://perma.cc/FZ73-MM78)
12 Diaz, K et al (2017) Patterns of sedentary behavior and mortality in U.S. middle-aged and older adults: a national cohort study, *Annals of Internal Medicine*. Available from: https://annals.org/aim/article-abstract/2653704/patterns-sedentary-behavior-mortality-u-s-middle-aged-older-adults (archived at https://perma.cc/4UZ9-UU2N)

13　Australian National University (2017) A healthy work limit is 39 hours per week. Available from: www.anu.edu.au/news/all-news/a-healthy-work-limit-is-39-hours-per-week (archived at https://perma.cc/C3VB-L9QD)

14　Australian Pharmaceutical Association (2018) Many people taking antidepressants discover they cannot quit. Available from: www.pharmacist.com/article/many-people-taking-antidepressants-discover-they-cannot-quit (archived at https://perma.cc/MU5E-T8HM)

15　Webber, A (2018) Employers offering health and wellbeing benefits on the rise, *Occupational Health and Wellbeing*. Available from: www.personneltoday.com/hr/employers-offering-health-wellbeing-benefits-rise/ (archived at https://perma.cc/97AL-MLT3)

16　Martin, A (2019) A shorter working week is in reach, *New Economics Foundation*. Available from: https://neweconomics.org/2019/02/a-shorter-working-week-is-in-reach (archived at https://perma.cc/K2W8-5FAR)

17　Stewart, H (2019) A four day week? Let's start with a four day August, *Happy*. Available from: www.happy.co.uk/blogs/a-four-day-week-let-s-start-with-a-four-day-august/ (archived at https://perma.cc/72M2-7U34)

18　Health and Safety Executive (2019) Work-related stress, anxiety or depression statistics in Great Britain, 2019. Available from: www.hse.gov.uk/statistics/causdis/stress.pdf (archived at https://perma.cc/P9HN-MPHJ)

19　www.merriam-webster.com/words-at-play/woke-meaning-origin (archived at https://perma.cc/HJS8-Q25A)

20　Cheesewright, T (2019) *High Frequency Change: Why we feel like change happens faster now, and what to do about it*, LID Publishing. Available from: https://tomcheesewright.com/high-frequency-change/ (archived at https://perma.cc/D4GY-UYCK)

21　Wadhurst, G (2012) Equine-assisted coaching? Hold your horses, *Guardian*. Available from: www.theguardian.com/money/2012/may/25/equine-assisted-coaching-horses (archived at https://perma.cc/ZKH9-SMF3)

22　www.ancient.eu/The_Vedas/ (archived at https://perma.cc/7NXH-AXRP)

23　www.sciencedirect.com/topics/agricultural-and-biological-sciences/neuroendocrine-system (archived at https://perma.cc/W7ES-XGBT)

24　https://psychologia.co/jung-personality-types/ (archived at https://perma.cc/9BRL-WCGT)

25　www.cgjungpage.org/learn/resources/jung-s-psychology/852-introduction-to-jungs-psychology (archived at https://perma.cc/QMX5-JH9T)

26　McLeod, S (2018) Maslow's Hierarchy of Needs, *Simply Psychology*. Available from: www.simplypsychology.org/maslow.html (archived at https://perma.cc/YHA9-FRWU)

27　Capra, F (1975) *The Tao of Physics*, Shambhala Publications. https://conscioused.org/books/the-tao-of-physics-fritjof-capra-review-summary (archived at https://perma.cc/G8RT-GVN9)

28 Moore, T (1992) *Care of the Soul*, Harper Collins. http://thomasmooresoul.com/ (archived at https://perma.cc/UBK7-YJH7)
29 www.merriam-webster.com/dictionary/soulful (archived at https://perma.cc/W28N-YLKW)
30 www.merriam-webster.com/dictionary/transcendent (archived at https://perma.cc/D58W-H72G)
31 www.britannica.com/topic/Kantianism (archived at https://perma.cc/2QH6-4KFH)
32 www.merriam-webster.com/dictionary/chakras (archived at https://perma.cc/DAB5-536X)
33 www.nhs.uk/conditions/stress-anxiety-depression/mindfulness/ (archived at https://perma.cc/6LSA-V9YK)
34 Tiller, W (1997) *Science and Human Transformation: Subtle energies, intentionality and consciousness*, Pavior Publishing
35 Quora (2017) How the human body creates electromagnetic fields, *Forbes*. Available from: www.forbes.com/sites/quora/2017/11/03/how-the-human-body-creates-electromagnetic-fields/#cb2683156eae (archived at https://perma.cc/H5Y6-HVTB)
36 www.amitgoswami.org/ (archived at https://perma.cc/JKZ2-NN9J)
37 Ball, P (2017) The strange linke between the human mind and quantum physics, *BBC Earth*. Available from: www.bbc.com/earth/story/20170215-the-strange-link-between-the-human-mind-and-quantum-physics (archived at https://perma.cc/KWZ6-QTWS)
38 CIPD (2019) Well-being at work. Available from: www.cipd.co.uk/knowledge/culture/well-being/factsheet (archived at https://perma.cc/D8YH-HCQU)
39 Narayanan, C, Korotov, K and Srinivasan, T (2018) Bioenergy and its implication for yoga therapy, *International Journal of Yoga*, **11** (2) pp. 157–65. Available from: www.ncbi.nlm.nih.gov/pmc/articles/PMC5934952/ (archived at https://perma.cc/J2F9-XWUE)
40 www.valuescentre.com/barrett-model/ (archived at https://perma.cc/2BBX-KSWL)
41 https://richardbarrettblog.net/tag/governance/ (archived at https://perma.cc/8YZV-HA7Y)

07

The 20 misuses of energy in the workplace

In this chapter, we explore the ways in which some organizations and workplaces have become tortuous, toxic and soul-destroying places to be and why.

What is baffling to many of us is that the elements of a highly regarded, high-performing organization are well known. Research has, for many years now, urged workplaces to become engaging places, not just about demanding toil. We've seen statistic after statistic show that a place of work where people are looked after by their managers, and thereby the entire organization, equates to a sustainably successful organization, and one whose value is not simply vested in brand or products but in the people who make up the workforce.

So why do people who run organizations continue to create – or perpetuate – such toxic working conditions? Is it that ignorance is bliss, or a willful creation of an oppressive environment?

In this chapter we will explore these reasons including the view, still held by many, that the more you take the heat off the workforce, the more there will be slacking off. There is also an inability by some to trust people to perform without some form of punitive measures to keep everyone focused.

However, we also examine how this mode of operating is now increasingly questioned as dehumanizing and devaluing people and is suggested to be avoided at all costs. The advent of social technologies has

> given people a voice and a chance to call out such toxic culture. Glassdoor.com reviews are the workplace equivalent of Trip Advisor or Yelp for hotels and restaurants. Places where mistreatment and unfair approaches are experienced can be anonymously reported on and given a 'buyer beware' approach to working there.

Misuses #1–5: cult workplaces

There are many times when lecturing students yet to take their energy to the workplace that I ask the question: *Who would you want to work for and why?*

The answers are:

- Apple
- Google
- Facebook
- Virgin Group

And rarely any others (although some answers are to create a unicorn start-up[1] or be a YouTuber).

The *why* question is normally responded to with, 'They're a cool-sounding workplace – lots of benefits and career advancement/diversity of choice.' When I then ask if they've ever met anyone who works at those companies or have any other experience of them, the answer is no. Every time.

So these have become **cult workplaces**. What I mean by a cult workplace is one with an over-attachment to work, an obsessive nature to working and a sense of pseudo-brainwashing in coerced *belonging*.

I make no suggestion that these places don't have lots of good aspects in being a place to work. Glassdoor.co.uk reviews of Google show a 4.4 rating overall (out of 5). Glassdoor will tell you this is a good rating, especially for a company where there are 12,000 reviews. Apple has 4.0 and 16,000 reviews; Virgin Group (a varied and disparate business with Media, airlines (Atlantic), banking (Money), fitness

(Active), Holidays, and Care) varies between a low of 2.5 and a high of 3.8. Facebook comes in a little better at 4.4 for 4,000 reviews. There is a clear disparity between students' perceptions of some of these companies and the actual working experience shown through these reviews.

Do these back up the thoughts of those students? Some do – the tech giants Google and Facebook for example. And perhaps the charismatic Sir Richard Branson could account for the views of the students over Glassdoor reviewers.

In 2014, a story broke[2] that some Google employees had no fixed abode or home and were living either on their Mountain View campus or in their cars/vans in the car park.

Now this may be considered a very savvy perk of no-rental living, but in reality it was people who were never 'escaping' their workplace (parking lot or office space living).

Douglas Rushkoff, a well-known American writer, looked deeper into this, especially when he heard of unrest, with residents of places near to Google HQ in California protesting at increased rent and property prices. This was due to the influx of engineers and designers on high-salary roles. His research culminated in the book *Throwing Rocks at the Google Bus*.[3] In it, he takes a wider look at the advent of the 'Titans of Tech' to look more intensely into the phenomenon that is working in and around the Silicon Valley technology industry.

Whilst Rushkoff is balanced with his writing and doesn't demonize or overly sensationalize Google at all, he doesn't pull any punches on how the advent of such HUGE technology companies has distorted the benefits many felt the World Wide Web would bring, following Tim Berners-Lee's vision for an open space for all to share, connect and learn.

Rushkoff went to great lengths to describe how even the Google Bus of the title was a well-intended deployment of lower carbon emissions (saving 29,000 tonnes of carbon[4]) from a range of employees who might otherwise have driven separate cars to the campus but instead all travelled in shuttle buses laid on by the company. Yet they were attacked by California residents as a manifestation of the company responsible for raising living costs and making housing unaffordable.

Such incidents led to more scrutiny of the benefits Google offered to their employees – why *did* so many people want to work there? Why would a tiny group of employees choose to live at their place of work? Is Google one of the first companies ever where people were obsessive, overly attached to their work – a **cult workplace?**

If indeed Google and others (any organization where people seem to be obsessed with their employer) are cult workplaces, is there anything wrong with that?

A cult is defined as:[5]

- a religion regarded as unorthodox or spurious;
- great devotion to a person, idea, object, movement, or work (such as a film or book).

I would suggest elements of this second aspect form my definition of a cult workplace: a fixation, obsession and over-attachment to work. Where you only identify through being that worker, with very little that looks like a balanced life.

Management school INSEAD published an article by Manfried Kets de Vries (a renowned management thinker and author), 'Is Your Organization a Cult?'[6] In his writing he covers this by describing a range of factors that make it a cult:

- Cults create a feel of magic in the existence of the organization and magical powers in the founders or the source of the organization.
- A propagated set of ideologies and values where dissenters are swiftly castigated and punished.
- A charismatic leader with whom employees can easily identify and an emotional attachment to the firm that overrides all other aspects of their lives.
- An us-vs-them paranoia about the outside world.

That the students I speak to talk glowingly of companies they have no experience of, speaks to some of this image and perception (idolization of people like Steve Jobs, Elon Musk, Sir Richard Branson, Mark Zuckerberg, and a pseudo-romantic view of being a Googler or working at Snap, Twitter or Tesla).

So Kets de Vries makes a strong case that there is an imbalance in this kind of workplace. On the one hand they create fierce loyalty, commitment to the cause, unwavering belief in the mission and things normally associated with high-performing workplaces where people are incredibly engaged. On the other hand, a leader who has unquestioned authority over the direction of the company and how it operates, with anyone who dares question things punished for daring to do so.

So how do we balance a cult workplace with a good one?

Figure 7.1 shows my interpretation of a model we suggest helps you identify if you are in danger of becoming a cult workplace.

There is a focus on customers for all organizations but there is a difference between love and respect and obsession. Cult workplaces heat up the intensity of this focus to beyond boiling point.

Cult workplaces swoon over their community (and anyone else's community). People who will talk about them even if they're not

FIGURE 7.1 The cult workplace design

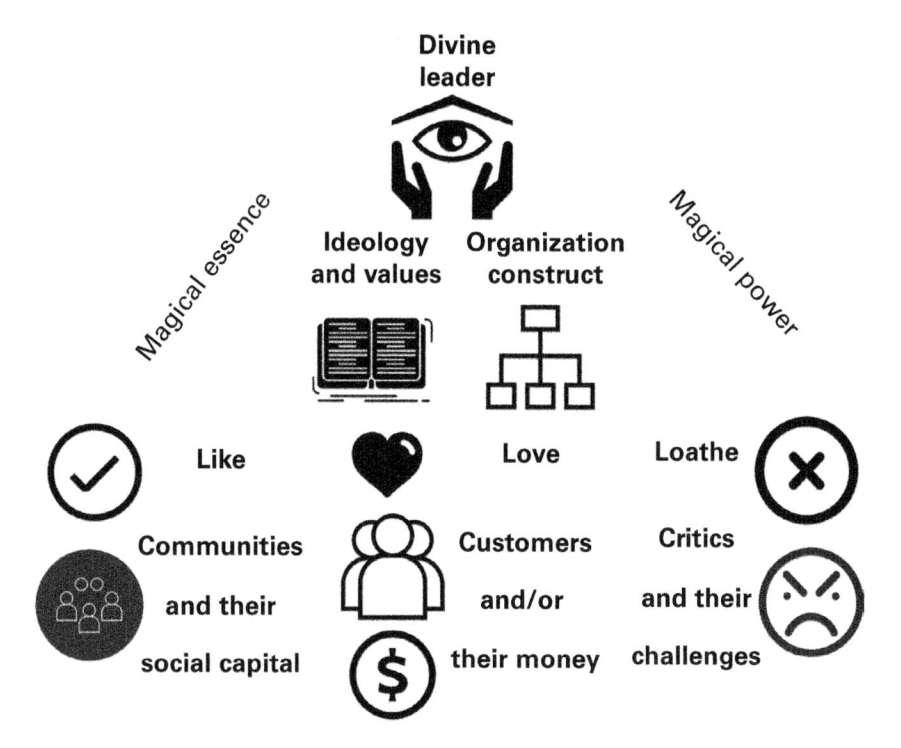

- Divine leader
- Ideology and values
- Organization construct
- Magical essence
- Magical power
- Like — Communities and their social capital
- Love — Customers and/or their money
- Loathe — Critics and their challenges

customers but admire the company and what it does and purportedly stands for. This social capital is also leveraged by arranging culture or discovery tours so others can see how they do what they do.

I believe that cult workplaces detest any form of criticism, whether from ex-employees or any social media traffic, and may respond through threats of litigation or by completely ignoring the comments; criticism appears not to be taken with any humility or intent to explore or act. Cult workplaces may internally dismiss criticism as jealousy or attempts to demean their good intentions; even testifying to political inquiries is seen as a chance to promote the vision, mission and values of the company.

In looking at recent failures such as WeWork, there was a sense that the company had a magical essence and power that was only challenged at times of financial scrutiny. This appears to be the only time when the hard facts of financing, ecological operating practices, supersized bills for supersized perks for employees and upwardly spiralling pay rates matter.

What are the downsides of being a cult workplace?

Some may think that this kind of loyalty, commitment, identification and affection has to be the thing every company/organization wants, surely?

It depends on how much of this is 'management' controlling how employees behave and even what they think. It can be a confusing sensation – whether a place is committed and loyal or a cult and an obsession.

For example, an employee of an oft-cited financial institution in Scandinavia once said to me, 'We only recruit through referral and even then, it's a series of micro-interviews/conversations with a selection of existing employees. If there's a consensus that you're the right kind of person to uphold our values and enhance our organization, you're offered a deal.'

He continued, 'When I asked them about what it was like to work here, I kept getting the same answers. All positives, but almost identical answers. I began to think this is more like a cult. After the fifth conversation I just realized that we have an employer here who really is consistent, caring and credible.' He was offered the deal, and hasn't regretted it for a second. It is NOT a cult workplace, it's just a human-centred place of work that many believe holds the blueprint for successful enterprise in the 21st century.

Our first five misuses of energy in the workplace, therefore, are centred on the Cult Workplace and its non-sustainable and imbalanced use of human energy and organization design:

1 **An over-attachment to work**. It's like everyone is the start-up CEO giving their all but in a well-established business. It's exhausting and links to our previous identification of peak work and the undue stress we are finding ourselves put under.

2 **An-over identification of self with the brand**. Being hard-working and committed is one thing; defining yourself entirely because you're an engineer, designer, marketeer or team leader at *Megacorp Inc* is another. Whilst this may seem like a buzz of energy to start with, it can blur the lines between what you are energized by and what the company wants you to be energized by.

3 **Indoctrinated values are the wrong kind of energy force**. In some examples, corporate values have gone being from nice defining statements of intent and ways of being that energize people by inspiring them, to statements that may coerce, force or even shame people to behave in a certain way. Values ought to inspire you to be your best, not be seen as strict measures that you are fearful of – that is not good use of energy.

4 **Brutal openness**. It's one thing to be honest and sharing; it's another when over-sharing or forcing people to reveal intimate information about their lives outside of work they'd rather not share becomes brutal. It is potentially psychologically traumatic, and certainly an energy drain when you are coerced into revealing things you'd rather not. There is a line between life and work that means you shouldn't have to reveal something that doesn't impact on your work or working relationships. Many of us deal with a range of personal issues and we can detach from them whilst at work (sometimes the one thing that makes sense in our lives). Accepting some things will need

to be shared (that are impacting on your performance or behaviours at work), there should be a safe, compassionate and understanding environment to do so, not making people feel obligated to reveal things in pursuit of 'openness'. We may not be ready, or could be overly sensitive about the issue and need professional help.

5 **Management by panopticon.** There have been reported instances where people are willingly given an implant and chipped to track their every move; have sensors attached to work devices and have sleep and health monitored by their wristbands. That's *Digital Taylorism* (forensic scrutiny and very strict management of people's time and focus/application) and a borderline invasion of privacy. A cult workplace may insist or strongly encourage this to be the norm. How much energy you have when 'on duty' is probably fine to share with your employer; outside of that, it's dangerous ground for both parties.

This is not an exhaustive list. It is meant to be a little extreme and even shock some people into thinking 'Have I created a cult?' or 'Am I part of a cult?'

In Manfred Kets de Vries' *HBR* article[7] his closing line is the ultimate litmus test: *When a culture ceases to embrace diversity and dissent, it becomes a cult.*

Be careful out there folks.

Misuses #6–10: scare-ups

There's a phenomenon in the world of work – scale. We seem to have created the next 'wannabe' for all aspiring youngsters who used to want to be a film star or a pop icon. They now aspire to be a YouTuber or to create a start-up tech company and build a billion-dollar app.

Fuelled by the stories of Zuckerberg and Musk (and before them Jobs and Gates) this has become the new dream; to set up a digital technology company that acquires a value of billions, sell it, and become an investor, philanthropist or socialite. Or all three.

WhatsApp is the story that most would know – a 2009 start-up messaging application for the booming smartphone market. It quickly became the world's most used messaging platform and was eventually wholly acquired by Facebook in 2014 for US $19bn. At the time, it had an engineering staff of 35 for over 900 million users.[8]

So becoming a start-up CEO is one thing, but getting past start-up and into scale-up is a whole different dimension; let's not forget that the vast majority of start-ups fail – 90 per cent according to this 2015 *Forbes* article[9] and 70 per cent in an updated version in 2019.[10]

Singularity University[11] is at the heart of the interest in scaling enterprises and next-generation technological advancement. It describes itself as 'a global learning and innovation community using exponential technologies to tackle the world's biggest challenges and build a better future for all.' In 2015, Salim Ismail, with Michael Malone and Yuri Van Geest, published *Exponential Organizations*[12] which charted the rise of some of the fastest growth machines in recent business history: Amazon Web Services, AirBnB, TED, Waze, Kickstarter, DIYDrones, Quirky, Coyote Logistics, Tangerine Bank, Uber. In addition, other reported stories are of Spotify, Etsy, Netflix, Shopify, GitHub, Tesla, Snap, Zoom, Indiegogo and Valve.

Whilst this book has codified the components of a lot of the fastest-growing enterprises we've ever seen, the failure rate is our balancing measure. Still, some CEOs get the start-up going, acquire customers via sales, and then have to take the big decision to scale. This can be a scary aspect of a business, and is why this set of dysfunctions is framed around the *scare-ups* of the business world.

Having personal experience of business founders in this position, and hearing stories from others, there is a pattern and this next set of dysfunctions describes some common pitfalls and energy losses.

Let's take a fable-like approach to this and introduce you to a fictional representative of this phenomenon in the shape of a scaling tech company: CAInine.

Jed is the founder and CEO of CAInine, an AI-based dog-walking and training app that uses GPS technology to track your dog's movement, calories in and out, provides a monitor to talk to your dog even when you're not at home, and a link to your veterinary records via an implanted chip and an app on your smart device.

CAInine started with Jed and his college friends Anya and Zeke. The three of them have shares, with Jed holding 34 per cent and Anya and Zeke with 33 per cent each (giving Jed a tiny lead share as CEO and founder). They have received some financing to get going from a local investor and the initial app and hardware production have been well received by the dog-crazy public of Toronto where the company is based.

A large technology company is interested in funding their next stage – to go to a worldwide market – which will take the company staff from the three founders and six engineers/designers to 180 people across the globe handling sales, distribution, production, marketing, customer support and partnerships.

Jed is happy to lead this expansion and will focus on building a bigger board, local leadership and reporting to investors. He hires a Head of Talent from Amsterdam, as they will have a huge presence in Europe, someone recommended to him by his new investing tech company.

The Head of Talent is new to this level of role but has great potential. Quickly exhausting their network, they instruct local recruitment agents to find people to a hastily assembled set of job specifications. Market salaries are high in some areas so there are some balances to be made between very experienced hires who cost a lot, and high potentials with less experience but who cost less to hire and pay.

Sales leads are prioritized and in key territories across the globe, people are hired and start building a series of orders. Engineers are harder to hire, and there is a struggle in Toronto and Amsterdam as there is such competition for the roles. So the company sets up a team in Mumbai to build a new engineering team there.

Marketing is slow to start and whilst there are new orders to process, the localized web presence, support infrastructure, local sales regulations and partnerships are not made. Order times stretch and customers cancel. The sales team are frustrated by their lack of marketing support and some leave for other roles.

The engineering team are up and running in Mumbai but there is a difficult working transition to the Toronto team (now asked to be their managers) with the time difference and them having to let go of their coding duties (things they all love doing). The Toronto engineering team get dissatisfied and most of them leave.

The Head of Talent, somewhat overwhelmed by the scale of the new role, is signed off with stress-related absence and things start to grind to a halt. Jed is summoned to the tech company HQ and further investment is frozen until things start to settle down. Anya is trying to hold things together but Zeke is now unhappy and wants to sell his shares and leave.

With their 'runway' burned, and insufficient customer orders to sustain revenue projections, Jed and Anya offer to sell their entire stakes to the investor company who buy them out for a fraction of what they once thought the company was worth.

An unhappy end to a promising venture.

This is fictional but based on real experiences and many people will recognize this catalogue of events that creates a scary version of the future. The energy given and subsequently wasted in this venture is a story told 1,000 times per week with research[13] showing that the reason for over a quarter of failures lies with having the **wrong people in post**.

Our next five misuses then are:

6 **Overly rapid expansion to key roles.** Compromising on skills, behaviours and values.

7 **CEO grip too loose or too tight.** Being overly focused on internal reporting and not on making sure expansion was sustainable and sensibly planned.

8 **Cultural misalignment.** A culture of togetherness, flexibility, cohesion and support is necessary so the right hires, expectations and collaborative working would ensure things are more aligned and assured by this cultural cohesion.

9 **Token or superficial demonstration of a purpose and set of values.** We accept people have a variety of values yet the company having a strong set of aligned values people believe in provides comfort, security and certainty.

10 Dramas and crises as a norm. A lack of a strategy, gameplan and processes catches up with leaders really quickly. Snap decisions show a lack of planning and appreciation of flow. Energies can get lost and burn out quickly when constantly fire-fighting.

All of these scary instances are avoidable and a waste of the energy, things that negated CAInine – a reasonably successful local venture with the potential to scale. Energies were lost by being overly rapid in decisions and actions; superficial and distracted when energies would have been better utilized with some upfront planning, clarity and certainty of roles for the crucial initial set of hires (like a Head of OD and a Lead Engineer figure).

Lost energy, lost capital and lost opportunity. Not all start-ups scale well, and some (like WhatsApp) scale ridiculously well. There is no secret recipe to go from start-up to scale-up. There are books on the subject, like Eric Ries' famous *Lean Startup*[14] and Reid Hoffman's *Blitzscaling*[15] and yet still the failure rates are high and start-up to scale-up is still the most scary aspect of running a new enterprise. Energy alignment could be a missing component to the success of new ventures.

Misuses #11–15: faux trendy

There is no doubt that in the world of business, we see trends that are not only about customer buying habits, but about great service offers and fast-selling products that create new markets. These are the **value propositions** that help companies achieve good revenue sales and please shareholders.

There is another factor now emerging that also help define successful enterprises: **their employer brand**. Now as much a thing as the product brand, it seems that every company wants to be cool, desirable and on-trend with other companies who have that reputation and social capital. As a result of open access to a range of information sources on the web for reviewing customer experiences, so has the rise of LinkedIn, Glassdoor.com and social media created a need to present the company as **an employer of choice**. Again, the UK's CIPD helps us with a definition[16] that includes the following:

> the way in which organizations differentiate themselves in the labour market, enabling them to recruit, retain and engage the right people. A strong employer brand helps businesses compete for the best talent and establish credibility. It should connect with an organization's values and must run consistently through its approach to people management.

It's not just a recruitment marketing tool – it runs consistently through the company's approach to people management.

This is also encapsulated by the term *employee experience (or EX)* which has come from the realization that there are multiple perspectives, experiences, touchpoints and events that lead a company to set out its values, brand and offer not just at hiring stage, but throughout the employee's stages of working, developing, progressing, adapting and even leaving the company.

With so much emphasis now on these elements, many organizations are now keener than ever to tell you what working with them is like. McKinsey's famed War for Talent in 1997[17] gave the sense that the key power was no longer in the hiring employer but in the (prospective) employee. Key talented people had to choose you, rather it being simply the employer's choice who to hire.

We now find ourselves as employers having to compete not *just* on salary, location or career prospects but on culture, values, inclusion, flexible working, purpose, benefits and corporate social responsibility. Companies are now committing energy and resources to how they are presented to the outside world and that there is as much consistency in that proposition as possible – or else they are only a Glassdoor.com review away from having to address some issues of incongruence with messaging and actual experience.

Another example of how organizations are focusing on employer branding is snappy straplines that define their purpose (like *TED – Ideas Worth Spreading*); imagery that is inclusive and welcomes people from a range of demographics and a set of values that describe how you are as a company.

Patagonia, a sporting and outdoor apparel retailer with headquarters in the United States, is one of the most admired companies on the planet. Their values set[18] includes building the best product (as you might expect) but also:

Cause no unnecessary harm
We know that our business activity – from lighting stores to dyeing shirts – is part of the problem. We work steadily to change our business practices and share what we've learned. But we recognize that this is not enough. We seek not only to do less harm, but more good.

Use business to protect nature
The challenges we face as a society require leadership. Once we identify a problem, we act. We embrace risk and act to protect and restore the stability, integrity and beauty of the web of life.

Not bound by convention
Our success – and much of the fun – lies in developing new ways to do things.

Of course, these aren't a set of values that everyone will be energized by, but it is safe to say that those who do choose to apply for work at Patagonia (and are chosen by the company, obviously) put huge stock on these values; they provide constant guidance, stimulation and energy towards what matters to them and to helping sustain a purposeful and profitable business.

What appears to have happened in the business world is an understanding that values matter and many organizations are now 'leveraging' their employer brand and crafting finely tuned mission and vision statements that have the strongest appeal.

The use of a company's purpose with an extravagant feel to it has a term: **purpose washing**. And some commentators in public relations and the media are strong on calling out inconsistencies between what a company sells and does and how it portrays itself. *Conflated* is a word used often about companies using virtuous words but with less virtuous actions.

This all adds up to companies that could be trying to create energy and stimulus through being *faux trendy*; imitations, fakery, falsehoods or, at best, desperate attempts to jump on bandwagons and convince people there is a 'right-on' nature to the company.

But what are the signs of a company trying – perhaps with good intent – to be a little more human-centred, progressive and dynamic versus those who are faking it?

Our next five dysfunctions then are:

11 **Purpose washing.** As defined – the incongruence between what the company's stated purpose is and the actual products and services they provide. *Fuelling the social fabric of togetherness for party-goers?* Or an alcoholic drinks producer? Beware conflation and if you feel it, sense it and see it, raise it with whoever you feel could influence a better, truer version of your purpose. Purpose – true and articulate – is a great energy source for people who believe in this spirit of the enterprise.

12 **Bandwagon jumpers.** You can spot this one a mile off. We've got fake grass carpet, deck chairs in our internal beach area, sleep pods, ping-pong tables, a free bar every Friday. Whilst these are not in themselves the wrong thing to do, inflicting them on people without consultation or looking at what people truly need would see you as jumping on the bandwagon of trendy things to have in an office. You might still end up with some of these, but involve people, look at the benefits things like this bring and what it says about your culture and togetherness. Some of this could appear to create energy but it could also be a little spike in energy that is hard to sustain and come across as tokenistic if not managed carefully.

13 **Look like a catwalk show – work like a sweatshop.** All elegant and demure, stylish and sophisticated on the outside, and yet inside the company it's run like a boot camp every day. Over-glamourizing will catch you out in the end as the Glassdoor reviews, tweets and blogs that will be your undoing pile up. Overwork is exhausting for people and depletes energy constantly with no regenerative qualities. Looking different to prospective investors or employees can have a demoralizing effect on existing employees who are more confused with this fake 'shop window'.

14 **Lip-service engagement.** Relying on your pulse app for social engagement at work to let you know how people feel is laudable but not the only way to assess what's needed and also could set you up to fail if you don't respond, act and take note of what's really mattering to your people. Surveying is only the beginning and failing to notice what is important and enter into dialogue or act on suggestions is going to result in lost energy/commitment.

15 **Inauthentic leadership.** Groucho Marx is credited as saying, 'The secret of life is honesty and fair dealing. If you can fake that, you've got it made.'[19] So it can be with authentic leadership. Pretending you care about your people and their needs will lose loyalty, innovation, togetherness and vital human energy. Showing interest in people, what is important to them and being seen to have employees' interests at heart engenders a spirit of belief and dedication that is difficult to otherwise incentivize even with bonuses, perks and beneficial policies.

The opposite of this comes in the shape of the late Southwest Airlines CEO Herb Kelleher, in Barry-Wehmiller's CEO Bob Chapman, CEO of the Nike Foundation Maria Eitel, Patagonia's founder Yvon Chouinard, Impact's founder Ray Anderson and Patachou Foundation's CEO Martha Hoover; all represent those inspiring figures who set the course for the organization and inspire those vital colleagues on the journey to play their part.

Being on-trend or with the times is fine – of course, it's energizing to work with a company that has a progressive and in-tune feel to it. However, fake it and give it a tokenistic, superficial feel and it could backfire.

Misuses #16–20: living museums

Possibly the most recognizable of all the misuse categories, many organizations are this: living museums. While the decorations and tools may be 21st century, the mindset, ways of being and structures hark back to industrialized institutions, an homage to the 20th century and even the 19th.

A 2018 article from *Forbes*[20] somewhat proves that point. Its four main characteristics of overcoming an outdated workplace were (in summary):

a recognize a work/life blend and be more sympathetic to people's outside-work challenges;

b be more flexible to generate more creativity;

c ditch dress codes and be more relaxed about attire;

d introduce brain-breaks and stimulation through physical activities.

Dress codes? Having a life outside of work? A break from brain-processing activities? Not exactly cutting-edge practices. It does explain the largely untouched charter of expectations, conditions and systems at play in many workplaces and that they literally are an throwback to a supposedly bygone era.

What stops organizations from moving with the times? Is it company traditions, organizational rituals and people in leading positions who come from that era of formality and stiffness? Perhaps. Whatever the reasons, there are thankfully a growing number of noticeable shifts to more progressive and flexible ways. ING Bank, for example, are now famed for their agile approaches whilst still being a highly regarded financial institution. Their YouTube video showcasing how they work in this way has over 60,000 views as of the end of 2019.[21]

This video alone shows the opposite of a living museum – different technology, seating, processes, language and a more energizing way to work. It talks to a different structure, approaches to getting things done, making decisions and all in the setting of a more flexible, fluid and progressive approach to using space.

But how can we spot if we are working in a living museum? And can we change it?

Of course, is the answer; maybe steadily but things like space and furniture can be rearranged and made to feel more dynamic and flexible, which is a start.

Our final five misuses then are:

16 **An ever-increasing process stack.** When no one cleanses or purges processes inside the company walls, things just stack up and you either create digital portals to handle the same request for a travel permit or even worse, additional processes are introduced because of the introduction of new technology (authorization protocols for example). Outdate, energy-zapping processes hamper an organization's effectiveness and give people the impression that bureaucracy rules and innovation is a disturbance in that forcefield. A process tsar could clean things up regularly and be included in revamping outdated processes and removing those no longer adding value to anyone.

17 **Failed change and transformation projects.** Remember that programme to move us all into video-only meetings? How about that travel portal that was supposed to give us easier ways to purchase and track our expenses for travelling on company business? And weren't we supposed to be having all our Finance queries answered by a chatbot?

We may not realize it but signalling a big change or transformation ought to be backed up by delivering the intended benefits and improvements the programmes set out to do – or at least communicate what adaptations have been made or had to be made to the ambitions set out in an all-company declaration. Failed transformational programmes and change initiatives only add to the feeling that the museum is still alive, perhaps with improved *digital signage*.

18 **Underdeveloped potential.** A difficult one to spot unless you're one of those feeling underdeveloped. An organization that is not looking to try out new things, give people chances to learn in new environments and situations, and generally create more fluidity by rotating people to develop expertise as part of structured learning programmes, will have a very static, stuck and undynamic feel to it. Developing people is a sign of investment, an enabler of more flexibility, and a chance for people to prove themselves in a range of settings. Deliberately developmental organizations (DDOs) were the subject of the book *An Everyone Culture*,[22] which set out

to demonstrate just how much energy was created by having a very strong culture of helping people learn and develop to find their best place, be most fulfilled and add the most value.

19 **Hidden social loafers.**[23] In larger organizations – but not restricted to those of super size – people find themselves in positions where they can somewhat coast or, as French Professor Max Ringelmann's experiments revealed, *socially loaf*. This social psychology concept is when, in a group setting, some people work less hard than if they were working on something alone. Somewhat masked in the group context, people can put less effort in, not exceed, tick over – whatever the phrase. Inside living museums there are normally plenty of places that social loafing, and even absence, can exist (witnessed by an example from 2016 of someone off sick for six years before it was noticed[24]). This is not meant to be a reason to publicly display all the work people do all the time; however, collective and open team set-ups, leaders who care and people who are energized by their work will help prevent the conditions for social loafing to occur.

20 **Rites of passage to promotion and influence.** There is something wonderful about loyalty and long service to an employer that signifies that there is something lasting and good about a company that people would wish to spend 10+ years working there. What that doesn't necessarily mean is that lengthy tenure equates to automatic promotion based on years' service, seniority and privileges on decision making because of experience, or being the crucial consultation point of key aspects of the company because you've been around for a long time. Showing an adaptive spirit and approach, shifting and changing with what the company needs into the future, nurturing and bringing on new, fresh talent and perspectives AND sticking with the company for 10+ years are what would symbolize loyalty and responsiveness to need. Lots of narrative about 'how it was better when…' and an overly nostalgic view on the company may be nice as part of the heritage of the company, but could be a symbol of being more living museum than viable sustainable organization fit for the then, now and the future.

There are bound to be more than these 20 misuses, and I've restricted it to this number based around the four archetypes of organizational characterization (again there will be more) that I feel are misusing human energy in the world of work because of their overriding damaging or inattentive systems and designed flaws.

So whether this is your organization being a borderline **cult** – well-intended but an overly conditioned way of being; whether it is because you are **scaling** in a way that is burning human energy and any venture capital you have; or you are so keen to match the true pioneers in the world of work that you are becoming a parody of new thinking by falling into the **faux trendy** trap; or that you're holding on for dear life to a past model and have become a **living museum** – these archetypes are urging us to do something different and, that wonderful word with little definition but we all get it: **better**.

We need better-designed systems and our final two chapters will help us achieve that. There are few or no solutions in this chapter as we are setting out the parameters where there is an almost criminal waste of human energy at work in a range of circumstances that we can address.

You may or may not recognize some of these 20 dysfunctions and you may be a hybrid of all four archetypes and more. This chapter is not an exhaustive list or a fully fledged scientific research study and these are the conclusions of that. They are representative of areas where we burn, misuse and certainly waste human energy; wasteful not just in optimal performance from people but in systems that are purporting to be optimal when in fact they're stagnant, insincere and even harmful. Cultures are created on the systems that we design and how people behave in them (and of course, where there isn't design, how behaviours then shape the culture and the systems – not always for positive or a greater good).

WHAT WE LEARNED FROM THIS CHAPTER

1 People can have good intentions to create energized workplaces but these can be harmful if not inclusive, open, clear, well-designed, constantly tuned and genuine versions of the best environments for people to flourish. **Those of us who believe we need some shift in**

culture or design should look at evidence, include others and create a compelling case to make adjustments that benefit people, the enterprise and ultimately the long-term effectiveness and positive outcomes for customers, community and planet.

2   There may be 20 dysfunctions, 200 or 2,000. Perhaps we get the dysfunctions we tolerate in ourselves and the system we work in. As Maya Angelou is quoted as saying, 'If you don't like something, change it. If you can't change it, change your attitude.'[25] **We can all identify our own and the system we work in, and look to name the dysfunctions, look at their cause and how to overcome them via positive action with others to make the changes.**

3   Four archetypes (or metaphors) are suggested here: Cults, Scare-ups, Faux Trendy and Living Museums, when in reality there are many, many more variations. **Whatever metaphor we might use, our organization has a character that may or may not be making best use of our human energy. If it is wasteful of this precious resource, we will need to redesign and develop into a more appropriate, positive and inclusive metaphor.**

Endnotes

1   Campos, J (2019) What's a unicorn start-up? *European Innovation Academy*. Available from: www.inacademy.eu/blog/whats-a-unicorn-startup-company/ (archived at https://perma.cc/33YE-K7US)

2   Sparkes, M (2014) Google staff shun homes and live in car park, *Telegraph*. Available from: www.telegraph.co.uk/technology/google/11089188/Google-staff-shun-homes-and-live-in-car-park.html (archived at https://perma.cc/S2WA-UUFL)

3   Rushkoff, D (2016) *Throwing Rocks at the Google Bus: How growth became the enemy of prosperity*, Portfolio. https://rushkoff.com/books/throwing-rocks-at-the-google-bus/ (archived at https://perma.cc/A374-PXCS)

4   Thornhill, J (2016) Review: Throwing Rocks at the Google Bus, *Financial Times*. Available from: www.ft.com/content/a4e7cda0-deda-11e5-b072-006d8d362ba3 (archived at https://perma.cc/7WQ4-6JKB)

5   https://www.merriam-webster.com/dictionary/cult (archived at https://perma.cc/J449-4DVN)

6 Kets de Vries, M (2018) Is your organization a cult? *Insead Knowledge*. Available from: https://knowledge.insead.edu/blog/insead-blog/is-your-organisation-a-cult-10371 (archived at https://perma.cc/GBA2-S5QN)

7 Kets de Vries, M (2019) Is your corporate culture cultish? *Harvard Business Review*. Available from: https://hbr.org/2019/05/is-your-corporate-culture-cultish (archived at https://perma.cc/4P82-8G9N)

8 Olsen, P (2014) Facebook closes $19bn WhatsApp deal, *Forbes*. Available from: www.forbes.com/sites/parmyolson/2014/10/06/facebook-closes-19-billion-whatsapp-deal/#368acc425c66 (archived at https://perma.cc/9NH8-FL98)

9 Patel, N (2015) 90% of startups fail: here's what you need to know about the 10%, *Forbes*. Available from: www.forbes.com/sites/neilpatel/2015/01/16/90-of-startups-will-fail-heres-what-you-need-to-know-about-the-10/#259a93306679 (archived at https://perma.cc/BR5N-NLMY)

10 Lee Yohn, D (2019) Why startups fail, *Forbes*. Available from: www.forbes.com/sites/deniselyohn/2019/05/01/why-start-ups-fail/#30db735c28a5 (archived at https://perma.cc/B54U-WT9L)

11 https://su.org/ (archived at https://perma.cc/8EAJ-WYWS)

12 Ismail, S, Malone, M and van Geest, Y (2014) *Exponential Organizations: Why new organizations are ten times better, faster, and cheaper than yours (and what to do about it)*, Diversion Publishing. www.openexo.com/exponential-organizations-book (archived at https://perma.cc/PA5H-BRL2)

13 Sweetwood, M (2018) Infographic: the 20 most common reasons startups fail and how to avoid them, *Entrepreneur*. Available from: www.entrepreneur.com/article/307724 (archived at https://perma.cc/MC5B-U5YX)

14 Reis, E (2011) *The Lean Startup: How today's entrepreneurs use continuous innovation to create radically successful businesses*, Currency. https://leanstartup.co/ (archived at https://perma.cc/ZVP6-4TTN)

15 Hoffmanm R and Yeh, C (2018) *Blitzscaling: The lightning-fast path to building massively valuable companies*, Currency. www.blitzscaling.com/ (archived at https://perma.cc/NU93-RNUC)

16 CIPD (2019) Employer Brand. Available from: www.cipd.co.uk/knowledge/fundamentals/people/recruitment/brand-factsheet (archived at https://perma.cc/8JVU-EY86)

17 People Insight (2019) Employee experience vs employee engagement: what's the difference? [blog] Available from: https://peopleinsight.co.uk/employee-experience-vs-engagement/ (archived at https://perma.cc/FCT2-GC79)

18 Patagonia's Mission Statement (nd) Available from: www.patagonia.com/company-info.html (archived at https://perma.cc/7UUQ-LTAA)

19 www.goodreads.com/quotes/3090-the-secret-of-life-is-honesty-and-fair-dealing-if (archived at https://perma.cc/LFW2-PGBD)

20 Kurter, H (2018) The 4 outdated workplace rules employers still grip onto, *Forbes*. Available from: www.forbes.com/sites/heidilynnekurter/2018/11/19/the-4-outdated-workplace-rules-employers-still-grip-onto/#6f603988122e (archived at https://perma.cc/SX7S-MCF5)
21 ING (2017) Our Agile Way of Working, *YouTube* [video] Available from: https://www.youtube.com/watch?v=D3iu2kfZ3w4 (archived at https://perma.cc/U4AW-ZSU5)
22 Kegan, R and Lahey, L (2016) *An Everyone Culture: Becoming a deliberately developmental organization*, Harvard Business Review Press. https://store.hbr.org/product/an-everyone-culture-becoming-a-deliberately-developmental-organization/14259 (archived at https://perma.cc/3FYX-BYNF)
23 http://www.businessdictionary.com/definition/social-loafing.html (archived at https://perma.cc/3Y4T-FMSY)
24 BBC News (2016) Spanish civil servant off work unnoticed for six years. Available from: www.bbc.co.uk/news/world-europe-35557725 (archived at https://perma.cc/747Q-K6P6)
25 www.quotationspage.com/quote/37547.html (archived at https://perma.cc/B97G-HG7G)

08

The 2020 list of energized workplaces

In this chapter we will discuss examples where the *people factor* is not a platitude, it is the real driving force behind organizational success and there appears to be an approach to **design organizations where people flourish**.

These stories do not come from extensive visits or interviews. Many books that do contain case studies are comprehensive and detailed expositions of how a company operates. In some of the most lauded organizations, there are still less than positive Glassdoor.com reviews, and even personal experiences of current and ex-employees that tell a different story.

In my opinion, the worlds of business literature and conferences are littered with stories that sound ideal and perhaps over glamorized, so are probably just as flawed as places we have all worked in. Which is why the research for this aspect of this book was not based on adding to the carbon footprint and jetting across the world to spend time on well-rehearsed culture tours and focus groups. It was desk-based research looking into the range of organizations who, in my opinion, have human interests at the heart of their business, who are designed for more people-centric practices and are viable, successful businesses in their own right. Different in their sectors, constructs or ways of operating, there is no single entity that is yet the archetypal *energized workplace*.

I explore sectors from a wide sphere: from technology to education; from healthcare to retail and the supermarkets. These are organizations that stood

> out, appeared to be designed to bring out the best from their people in ways that put their well-being before profit and market share, yet yield good economic return and reputation.
>
> There are some terrific organizations that we know about (and many more besides that we don't) who appear to already make good decisions about the energy of their people. They may or may not be aware of their optimizing and regenerative ways of using that energy and being fair to people in that exchange, but nonetheless they demonstrate a designed approach that is fair, inspiring and sustainable.
>
> Not all of the referenced companies would be admired by everyone who reads this book; there are even ex-employees who will report them as having been a less than energizing experience. Which somewhat proves the point about trying to involve everyone in designing their most energized environment – even if they are not 100 per cent energized by the things the organization is setting out to stimulate, reward and support.
>
> These organizations are doing their best to create their versions of the energized workplace. Hopefully they will also inspire you to create yours.

In researching organizations and their case studies, stories and narratives, several archetypes came through. In presenting these stories, the archetypes give you some indication of their philosophy, starting point, business model, sector considerations and operating systems.

Self-managed organizations

These companies have made as a key point 'freedom' and empowerment to employees. In this type of organization 'trust' is the main value for employees and their managers, and it leads to having self-direction and accountability. Whilst many self-managed companies operate differently, they tend to have similarities in decentralized decision making, non-hierarchical structures, and open information sharing. Employees are responsible for their own work allocation and time and there is no need to have any kind of 'control' from senior members and managers. This alone seemed to be a feature that created energy: people having control over themselves.

CASE STUDY
Cyberclick

Barcelona: online marketing

Cyberclick put their people first and this message is extremely prominent on their website. Their main three values are:[1]

1. **Admire people** (Humility and respect are two crucial elements for every personal and professional achievement.).
2. **Always find a better way** (We always want to go the extra mile. Here at Cyberclick, we have a mentality of 'always learning' and 'always testing'.)
3. **Customer experience freaks** (We don't limit ourselves to just meet the expectations of our clients, we go above and beyond.)

There are no work allocation roles – people work on what they want and set the goals themselves. They measure their happiness through a short daily survey which used to be anonymous, but because of such high levels of trust, the employees removed this filter. The scores are discussed on a weekly basis, and if an unhappy score shows up, it will be discussed immediately and only when it is resolved is 'work' resumed.

Where they speak about joining their team (28 of them) on their website, they state that they don't keep track of work hours or vacation time; and it's not just a salary, but about YOU. They appear very human-centric.

Whilst recognizing this is a controversial area with some negative examples in other companies, Cyberclick choice to give employees unlimited vacation time appears to be a genuine empowering feature.

In their blog post[2] they say:

> Far from the usual paternalism found in many companies, employees feel that they are once again the master of their own time and that their colleagues trust them to manage it responsibly. Being able to decide your own free days facilitates individuals to be able to reconcile personal and work life.

And more, as:

> Unlimited vacations result in greater satisfaction and well-being at work. And here we come to the crux of the question of how your company could benefit: an individual who feels empowered, who believes that their employer trusts them and can adapt work to his life and not the other way around, will be a happy and satisfied employee. In the end, these positive emotions will also have a positive impact on your work.

The company is not just about unlimited vacations but see this as an example of how they operate – in freedom, openness, and with togetherness. As CEO David Tomas says:

> Corporate culture can be manufactured by design or by default. This can emerge organically, without any control, and is the sum of all the employees or the company could have designed it. But it is ideal to define internally, choosing values that represent the unique personality of the entity.

In order to create the Cyberclick culture, a mixture of emergent behaviours are mixed with deliberate intentional aspects. Self-management does not mean you leave everything to chance, more that people agree on some parameters and principles which give others the confidence to be self-managed and to allow that emergence and iterative way of being to shape things. There is energy in allowing this discovery with all people in the company and the participative nature of shaping things around us.

Cyberclick pay a lot of attention to energy through their in-work leisure activities. Some people would think that a football table, lego building and a climbing wall are all gimmicks. And in some places, they are. At Cyberclick they are an offer to employees to recharge, socialize, take a break and be physically engaged in something other than a computer keyboard.

Cyberclick became a WorldBlu™ certified culture in 2019 and several videos on their website showcase that culture. WorldBlu exists to create more cultures of freedom, democracy and inclusion in the workplace and has an assessment tool and range of supportive approaches to help companies become Freedom-Centred Workplaces.

On the basis of this, **Cyberclick are really pushing themselves to be an Energized Workplace.**

Rewarding organizations

Another form of energy is the seeking, recognition, giving and appreciation of rewards. Of course, reward appears in ALL organizations in the form of pay and pensions, and a range of additional benefits and recognition schemes. It would be difficult to find companies on any stock exchange or even a micro business venture that didn't have an approach to reward.

There are different elements to those companies who use reward not just as compensation, but as a **stimulation and energizing element**. They focus on the rewards they give to their employees as a key aspect of a people-centric company culture; they want to help people feel engaged with what they do, who they work with and feel part of a community. They believe in the fact that you can have fun at work. This doesn't mean you are slacking off from working, but actually being energized so you can work in a better, more balanced way.

CASE STUDY
SomeOne

London, Sydney, Berlin, New York and Hong Kong: branding practice

SomeOne was voted 'best studio in the world' (2018) having grown from six people to 50 in the last decade.

When SomeOne started 15 years ago, they set out three objectives:

1 do great work;
2 make enough money;
3 have fun!

They state that:[3]

> If at any point we found that one of these aspects was missing from the practice, we'd know things were going askew and that we'd need to make adjustments. It's served us well, and while doing great work doesn't always mean we make life easy for ourselves, it's been a sure-fire way of attracting more great projects.

- They take 'the business of having fun seriously' and don't want to be like traditional companies who just add a compulsory Christmas night out onto the annual work calendar.
- They have an annual summer getaway for all employees (#SomeSummerParty19). It is an all-expenses-paid, three-day trip to Ibiza.

Many people look at companies of this ilk and sense they are too much fun and not enough business. Yet this company is a classic creative agency with a large range of blue-chip clients. They seem fiercely proud of their energized way to reward people, to have empowered and non-hierarchical ways of working, and have won awards for their work.

Their Glassdoor.com public profile has seven very positive reviews and one very negative. You could say this was someone who didn't align at all with the high-spirited culture SomeOne has created.

Whether you agree with annual parties as a recognition and bonding gesture or a generally more fun approach to work, this company has set its stall out to be **an Energized Workplace**.

CASE STUDY
BrewDog

Globally, HQ in Ellon, Scotland: breweries/bars/hotels

BrewDog was founded in 2007 in a small Scottish town by two craft beer enthusiasts. The company has grown rapidly due to injections of cash and the brand filling a gap in the market for good craft beer – 'beer for punks'.

BrewDog is undoubtedly a well-known global brand, arguably one of the most successful (of numerous) craft brewers. It is still at the forefront of people's minds with regards to beer, thanks in part to its memorable brand and some outlandish publicity stunts.

They are likely an attractive place to work for employees for the following reasons:

- BrewDog are passionate about two things – their beer and their people.
- They state on their website that by 2020 they want to be the best company to work for in the UK.[4]
- Staff benefits include being a living wage employer, enhanced maternity and paternity, private health care, pension contribution, Unicorn fund (10 per cent of profits to charities voted by employees), childcare vouchers, life assurance, staff discount (25–50 per cent off products), Cicerone training (world leader in beer education) for all employees, education support fund (for employees training to benefit their roles), a gym membership, dog years (see below) and pawternity leave (see below).
- Dog years: 'At many companies, you get a gold watch or impersonal voucher to mark a long service milestone, but as you've probably realized... we are anything but a normal place to work. So, make it to five years at BrewDog and we will reward staff with a four-week paid sabbatical, and another every five years on. At 10 years' service, we'll also pay for you to attend the Copenhagen Beer Celebration – all expenses paid!'[5]

- Pawternity leave: 'We know that welcoming a four-legged arrival to the family is a big commitment. Gaining trust, housetraining and working out routines takes time so we have decided to make things easy by offering Puppy Leave. It's like Parental Leave, but with more throwing of sticks. Take on a new dog (either puppy or a rescue dog) and our staff can have a week away from work to start that lifetime's bond. We also allow dogs in our offices so they'll never be too far away!' Their approach to pawternity is pretty radical!

Again, Glassdoor.com reviews can create a sobering aspect to this array of benefits. Clearly, if you're a beer enthusiast all of the above are appealing. Some reviews are less inspired about this and more scathing of culture, decisions and the entry-level roles, proving how hard it is to scale and take care of things that matter at all levels.

Overall, the brand and its enthused approach to providing a range of rewards and benefits that are in themselves quirky will appeal to many as **an Energized Workplace**.

Open value organizations

An open organization values transparency, inclusivity, adaptability, collaboration, and community. Every company has its own culture, so no two open organizations look the same. But opening up the way your organization works can lead to greater team alignment and achieving shared goals.

CASE STUDY
Red Hat

Globally (35 countries), HQ in Raleigh, North Carolina: enterprise open source technology solutions

The company refers to its employees as *Red Hatters* and their growth in scale and offering is due, they say, to being a '100 per cent open' company. Openness is key to their culture of innovation.

- Jim Whitehurst, their CEO, states: 'I wasn't the person brought in to clean up the chaos, I was the person brought in to scale this more organic way of working. To put it simply, I was brought in to create a context for people to do their best work.'[6]

- The openness embodied by Red Hatters benefits their customers also. Red Hatters are encouraged to debate (leading to more ideas and interesting outcomes), are empowered to act on decisions made, are committed to open source technology and all have a shared belief binding them together, thus improving knowledge for customers.
- With this open culture, they massively value creativity – everyone is encouraged to innovate and challenge conventions.
- Their #RedHatOpenStudio hashtag conjures up debate and input on Twitter from creatives; it is really engaging and highlights the high-quality work Red Hat do (animations, for example).
- In October 2019, they ranked number three on Forbes' World's Best Employers List (behind Alphabet and Microsoft). This was their first time on the list, and part of the reason they were acquired by IBM for $34 billion in the summer of 2019.
- Red Hat made it on to the Best Workplaces for Parents List in 2018 (United States).
- They currently employ about 13,000 associates, with about 25 per cent of the workforce working remotely.
- Delisa Alexander, Red Hat's Chief People Officer (since 2011) defines open leadership within the organization and what these types of leaders embody: 'They tend to have a growth mindset where they think everyone has something special to contribute. Everyone has something unique they can offer. And that a leader's role, whether it's a manager or a team lead or technical lead, their role is to act in an inclusive way. And a way that really brings out that individual's strengths and helps them to contribute their unique talents.'[7]

In his book *The Open Organization*[8] Jim Whitehurst it is clear from the contributions that Red Hat is centred on participation and wasn't Jim's book – but he acted as a mouthpiece for the company. Operating decentralized open source software as your product perhaps helps become a decentralized operating platform as a company of people. Yet this required attention, focus and inclusion in order to create that 'all-in' feel.

Having over 1,600 reviews on Glassdoor and an overall 4/5 rating with a 93 per cent approval of Jim as CEO is a good indication that the philosophy of openness and inclusion is a significant feature of the company and therefore a factor in **Red Hat being an Energized Workplace**.

Personal growth-focused organizations

Some companies strongly believe that only by starting with an individual's development and growth can a company truly and sustainably grow.

There are views that the attainment of 'self-actualized' states of being comes from increasing our own level of consciousness through development, enlightenment and evolution. Becoming more self-aware, an individual can gain more freedom of choice, awareness of opportunities and clarity on what they want from life. This can then be set against an aligned point of view

Peter Senge famously described the Learning Organization in his book *The Fifth Discipline*.[9] This is an organization that in and of itself, learns and adapts to what it needs in order to provide relevant, sustainable, in-demand services and products and a good place to work and grow for the people who are employed there. Personal Mastery and Team Learning are two core elements of Senge's work and link to learning activity at individual levels, collective levels and help drive an organizational-level culture of learning.

CASE STUDY
Mindvalley

Global, HQ Malaysia: educators in fulfilling, happy lives, eLearning, social media, events, mentoring

Mindvalley state: 'Being human is more than just what our broken education system makes it out to be. We teach the world the art of truly living extraordinary, fulfilling, happy lives.'[10]

Mindvalley have an admirable ambition and belief that they can help shape the future of humanity by shaping the future of education, with their mission being 'to create personal transformation that raises human consciousness'.

They have 300 employees across over 59 countries, all of whom are extremely passionate about personal growth.

- They describe their unique culture and wellness models in a range of their seminars, learning content and models.
- They are a regular on the WorldBlu[11] list for most freedom-centred cultures – 11 consecutive years (to 2018).

- They embrace fresh talent (hiring for potential and talent rather than to specific roles) with the average age of employees being 24.
- Flexible working is normal – where and when people work is their choice linked to their goals and the team's needs.
- They celebrate success – each week Vishen (CEO) asks employees for a report of their achievements. He collates the information and presents it in an 'Awesomeness Report' which is shared with all employees.
- Five of the maximum 45 hours a week employees are expected to work must be spent learning.
- Every month, 10 per cent of the company's profits get distributed to employees, not in stock options, but via their salaries. Employees are each given 100 points to give to any number of their peers who they think are deserving of a bonus.
- Mindvalley has set up a culture to suit those with a youthful zeal. This is a key factor in the 2020 workplace as we will see that employees born between 1980 and 2000 will comprise half of the global workforce and the approaches of more open feedback, purpose-led self-directed work and constant learning and reinvention are stated as facets of the 2020 workforce and beyond.

With such an emphasis on positivity and happiness, learning and growing, **Mindvalley feels like a very Energized Workplace**.

CASE STUDY

Wegmans

Rochester, NY, USA: supermarket chain

A surprise inclusion in 2018's US Best Companies to Work For index, this family-owned, 100+-year-old supermarket defies the odds of corporate giants who pay really well and stack their offer of employment with a range of perks and benefits, and instead relies on looking after people and supporting them in a range of other ways.

Wegmans is built on:

- **Great managers**. Ninety-three per cent of employees surveyed said that 'management is honest and ethical in its business practices'. Ninety-six per cent said they had 'great bosses' and 97 per cent claimed to benefit from 'great communication'.[12]

- **Positive culture and working environment**. Ninety-eight per cent of workers called the workplace a 'great atmosphere', while 95 per cent said the facilities contribute to a good working environment. Additionally, rewards programmes provide praise, thanks, and recognition for 'work anniversaries, developmental goals, and acts of service for helping others'. They even allow employees to reward colleagues for 'living company values', with $5 coupons for prepared foods at the store.

- **A listening ear** and bias for action. Wegmans claims to invest in various programmes that put employees' ideas into action, encouraging workers to contribute to decisions that improve their work and benefit the company.

- **Flexible scheduling**. Employees praise the flexibility they have in finding the right schedule, and the company offers telecommuting for certain positions.

- **Necessary tools and resources**. Ninety-six per cent of those surveyed said they are given the resources and equipment to do their jobs. 'We believe this makes our work more fun and more meaningful, whether a cashier, chef, accountant, or baker', said the company in an official statement.

- **Employee development**. The company invests more than $50 million annually in training and development, which includes providing management trainee and leadership development programmes, department universities, workshops, and certification programmes. Wegmans also offered $5 million in tuition assistance in 2016. (Employees aren't obliged to return to Wegmans after graduation, although many do.)

- **Perks**. Wegmans offers health insurance for qualifying part-time employees, 100 per cent company-paid health coverage for dependents (for full-time employees), and fairly generous paid time off benefits.

- **Social initiatives**. Ninety-five per cent said they feel good about the ways the company contributes to the community. (Wegmans donated more than $6.5 million to philanthropic causes in 2016.)

With this full stack of supportive, community-based, people-centric practices, it's safe to say that **people would describe Wegman's as an Energized Workplace**.

Well-being organizations

Well-being is a key element now in most company strategies larger or smaller in size. It is recognized that absence management (a rather ugly 20th-century term) is outdated and instead of monitoring absence, creating a culture of wellness is a primary aim so that people can look after themselves and when things become tough on people's health, the company can support them.

There are many organizations that have the feel of this energy, such as:

- **Happy Ltd**[13] in London, where you get to choose your manager as the person who can help you develop and use your energy in an environment of self-management, learning and wellbeing.
- **Matt Black Systems**,[14] a small company in the South of England (Poole, Dorset), again with self-management and autonomy as a mode of operation and belief. They describe their system as creating an approach that 'demolishes internal barriers and allows our staff to take control of (and responsibility for) every unit from start to finish.' Individualized commitment, collective endeavour and high quality are the trademarks of this energized culture.
- **Interface**[15] has one of the most endearing and energizing stories of a humble company doing great things beyond normal comprehension. Using plastics that could damage the environment, rewoven into high-grade carpet tiles, is only part of founder Ray Anderson's story. After his death, his legacy of innovative, inclusive ecologically sound practice has made Interface one of the greenest companies on the planet, and one where people only tell of their love of working there. It's a truly regenerating company and an energized place to work, with people's love of ecologically sound products and practice making a real difference in areas like removing plastics from the ocean and creating systems of commerce and trade in developing regions.
- **REI**[16] is one of the USA's most loved recreational equipment providers and, it turns out, also one of its best employers, set up as a co-operative. Their website tells the story of their origin: 'We

began as a community of climbers in search of quality outdoor gear. Now, 78 years and nearly 150 stores later, our community of more than 16 million members is still united in the belief that an outdoor life is a life well lived.' Regularly on the list of best North American employers, their co-operative business model, shared values over profit, and *REI Yay* days provide an energetic workplace not just for those who love the outdoors.

In summary

We have looked at 10 companies who are not without shortcomings, challenges and not to everyone's liking. But nevertheless, they have an energized feel to the way they are setting up their culture and way of operating.

There are many more that people come across and indices like the Times Best Companies to Work For[17] in the UK, the Top Employers Institute,[18] Glassdoor's Best Companies to Work For[19] and Fortune Best Companies to Work For[20] all provide rankings for those employers who, subject to criteria, can demonstrate an employee experience that has many features like well-being, flexibility, development, support and assistance schemes, social mobility opportunities for those from under-privileged backgrounds, community involvement, charitable donations and more. People's experiences of working in such companies may not feel the same as the ones projected in the award submissions but largely, they appear to be providing a range of options for their people to flourish.

However, there is probably no single organization that is the exemplar of the Energized Workplace for us to study, decode and set out as an archetype for others to follow. In the days of FW Taylor's theory of scientific management, that was also the case and continues to be. The interplay of organizations with people is a complex, ever-shifting relationship, just as in society, communities and even in friendships and loving family relationships.

Attempting to set out the most energizing of working environments that stimulate – reward, recognition, inspiration, comfort, development and fulfilment – is something as perplexing as perhaps life itself. It doesn't mean we shouldn't try or celebrate organizations who are trying.

These 10 companies have their own operating environments, people with differing needs, demands from clients and customers, operate in different communities, use different models for financing, distributing and investing income, and have different views even of success.

However, they are – as all organizations are – powered by people and the energy they give to their work. Designing so that people flourish and their energy is sustainably managed and responsively regenerated is one of the challenges of our, and any, time.

Endnotes

1 www.cyberclick.es/en/about (archived at https://perma.cc/X7QB-2T52)
2 www.cyberclick.es/numericalblogen/unlimited-vacations-how-could-your-company-benefit (archived at https://perma.cc/3KDR-4J8Z)
3 https://the-dots.com/projects/someone-summer-party-349205 (archived at https://perma.cc/MV9T-7ZX6)
4 www.brewdog.com/uk/ (archived at https://perma.cc/XT3E-YGWJ)
5 www.brewdog.com/uk/community/culture (archived at https://perma.cc/6UYK-T23X)
6 www.redhat.com/en/about/our-culture (archived at https://perma.cc/UNR9-X2NF)
7 www.redhat.com/en/about/company/leadership?source=searchresultlisting (archived at https://perma.cc/DL79-4J69)
8 www.redhat.com/en/explore/the-open-organization-book (archived at https://perma.cc/DZH5-58ZP)
9 Senge, P (2006) *The Fifth Discipline*, Random House. www.penguinrandomhouse.com/books/163984/the-fifth-discipline-by-peter-m-senge/ (archived at https://perma.cc/47JU-NGBT)
10 https://webinars.mindvalley.com/mvcom/about/?utm_source=google (archived at https://perma.cc/SE5F-RR46)
11 www.worldblu.com/mindvalley (archived at https://perma.cc/83GC-ZQAR)

12 Bariso, J (2017) How a family-owned supermarket chain became one of the best places to work in America, *Inc*. Available from: www.inc.com/justin-bariso/how-a-family-owned-supermarket-chain-became-one-of-the-best-places-to-work-in-am.html (archived at https://perma.cc/6QPZ-2B7P)
13 www.happy.co.uk/about-us/ (archived at https://perma.cc/U9ZH-A9BV)
14 www.mattblacksystems.com/about-us/ (archived at https://perma.cc/BWG8-AX74)
15 www.interface.com/US/en-US/sustainability/our-history-en_US (archived at https://perma.cc/S5N5-RWGL)
16 https://rei.jobs/careers/MicroSiteCulture (archived at https://perma.cc/J297-7EVD)
17 www.b.co.uk/the-lists/ (archived at https://perma.cc/BAZ5-2JXR)
18 www.top-employers.com/en-GB/ (archived at https://perma.cc/A7FJ-UC9E)
19 www.glassdoor.com/blog/best-places-to-work-2019/ (archived at https://perma.cc/GB4C-P5FH)
20 https://fortune.com/best-companies/ (archived at https://perma.cc/JD4C-EY9K)

09

20 minutes per day to energize yourself

In this penultimate chapter, we look into what we can all do as individuals to be more aware, attuned and active in understanding our energy.

In looking at how we can help people, we look at the concept of *Quotients*. *Intelligence Quotient* (IQ[1]) has been with us for a long time – intelligence tests that show how we can solve puzzles and use our creative mind to show how much of a genius we are (or not). *Emotional Quotient* (EQ[2]) has been with us since the 1990s and is often seen as a complement to intellect; it looks at how we relate to others and manage our emotional state, and is built around understanding and using self-awareness, self-regulation, motivation, empathy and social skills.

What neither IQ nor EQ measure is the energy we have or use in either being intellectually or emotionally competent. Which is where NQ (eNergy Quotient) may come in.

Energy – in our human physiological self – is an obvious one. We know when our muscles ache, when our back is sore, and when our breathing is deeper and more laboured, that we are tired. But what about mental or spiritual energy? We may have a headache, be unable to concentrate and be easily distracted. These are likely signs we are emotionally and mentally lacking in energy.

Spiritual energy is another matter altogether, and as we covered in Chapter 6, there is a lot to it, but also a lot of scepticism that we have the right ways to measure, generate and regenerate spiritual energy. For some it is recognized faiths and to others it's about nature and factors which stoke their passions like injustice, animal welfare or poverty.

> However we define it, we are animated by things like a sense of purpose, a feeling of transcendence about things greater than ourselves, and a sense of belonging to either movements, traditions or philosophies.
>
> In this chapter, we will look at some self-care approaches to be applied in the workplace and how to understand, design and utilize our energy better even for 20 minutes per day.
>
> As with all changes in the world it starts with you, so welcome to your eNergy Quotient – or NQ.

NQ element 1: SO – source energy

Where do we get our spiritual or psychological energy from? And how can we adjust it, utilize it and regenerate it?

In many ways this is a question that has taxed human beings since the concept of consciousness was discovered by early scholars and philosophers, although it took many thousands of years for philosopher Descartes to come up with *Cogito, ergo sum* (I think, therefore I am).

Whatever defined our emergence into becoming thinking and spiritually aware beings, we have – for as long as we can remember – found a source within us. An energy that is stirred when we are animated by challenges, curiosity and things that matter to us. Some are animated by thrills and danger, some by fun and hedonistic activities, some by intellectual stimulation and others by belonging, fairness and helping others.

So what is your source?

Before we look at four elements of what we believe help define your source we can look at another eastern philosophical tool – the concept of *Ikigai*[3] from Japan: *Iki* meaning life and *gai* meaning value.

Represented in Figure 9.1, it is now considered to be a most helpful tool to bring in that balanced life we mentioned in Chapter 6.

Distinguishing vocation, passion, mission and profession is a helpful code to those who are energized by distinct but related elements in their life.

A researcher into currently incurable diseases may be animated by a past experience of a loved one with that disease. Their energy

FIGURE 9.1 Ikigai

What you love				
What you're good at	Passion	Ikigai	Mission	What the world needs
	Profession		Vocation	
What you can be paid for				

to devote themselves to their work becomes a passion, a mission and happens to manifest itself in a vocation and professional arena with funded research into the cause, cessation and cure of that disease.

However, if there was a sudden loss of funding, that one key element would make the vocation a harder one to practise as continued study and membership of bodies costs time, effort and money. The passion and mission would still be there but it would make their own life more difficult without professional support through a salary and operational costs to be covered.

Taking the Ikigai principles and applying them to yourself could be a most useful way of career planning, identifying development activities and checking your own sense of balance in:

- what you are good at doing (which may or may not relate to what you are actually doing in some form of paid employment);
- what you really feel you'd like or love to do (again, that may or may not be what you are actually in paid employ doing);
- whether what you do is something the world needs (the value you are creating for others); and
- how you could be financially compensated for that work you do or want to do (either in line with, less than or more than what you currently earn through your work).

Of course, it could also be a good tool for people in choosing what and where they want to work before they enter into the labour market. This is also covered in a personal adaptation of the Business Model Canvas[4] called **Business Model You**.[5,6]

It explores your energy from the context of:

1. how you help (where you add value);
2. who you are and what you have (beliefs, attitudes, skills and energy);
3. what you do (how your energy is expended);
4. who you help (the beneficiary of your energy and value);
5. how they know you (and how you deliver value through your energy);
6. how you interact (and share your energy in doing what you do with them);
7. who helps you (and ends up sharing their energy with you);
8. what you give (energy, skills, knowledge);
9. what you get (energy, skills, knowledge).

What both of these tools are attempting to do is match energies and resources.

Our source is best defined by the areas of passion, mission, vocation and professionalization, in many distinct areas but all related to our source – our energy that some might describe as their *calling*.

We are, in essence, looking for a sustainable balance in the four elements of the Ikigai or the nine elements of Business Model You.

NQ element 2: SU – sustainable energy

Whether we are in a self-employed entrepreneur model, a small enterprise or a huge organization, we have a 'source' and so does the enterprise we work with or for.

We are one human being that is part of a system (even if we are a solo entrepreneur we are likely to be working with or for other people). And that system has a source. Some may call it a purpose but it is the centre of the reason the company exists: to solve problems, create something, service something, most likely something that other people need. As management thinker Peter Drucker once said:[7] 'The purpose of a business is to create and keep a customer.'

The source is that dream of a once-solo entrepreneur founder of the company, who created the product or service that people wanted and then scaled the organization into a huge multinational entity. The product line may have been adapted and expanded but the source is likely to be the same: to provide the purpose for continuing to exist (and of course, in a capitalist free-market world, one that delights shareholders and stock exchanges equally), yet still be an entity that has a heritage and a future – thereby being sustainable.

Sustainability has a strong connection to the environment (even before the phrase Climate Emergency was coined). Corporate social responsibility (CSR) became an additional element as we first encountered pollution, ecological disasters like chemical, oil and nuclear spills, and ethical use of materials and natural resources.

There is also a sustainable version of you.

Alongside the environmental aspects of individual behaviours, being sustainable also means taking into consideration **your own energy**. Not wasting it but preserving it where possible and using it wisely and in balance with your ability to regenerate it.

We know we get energy from what we eat and drink so there is a nutrition aspect of sustainability, as for a human body to 'perform' well it is necessary to follow a healthy nutrition plan. Indeed, many organizations now recognize the impact of a good diet and their own canteens and meal services will have a strong healthy set of food options.

There are other elements of the working aspects of life that can help create a more sustainable you:

- making people aware of burnout and other stress-related symptoms;
- organizing healing activities (eg mindfulness and meditation sessions, well-being workshops etc);

- organizations should push the individual to not work overtime (if it is not strictly needed), create a healthy atmosphere in the workplace, invite the individual to take holidays etc);
- breaks, some form of physical movement and resting periods are much more useful to you completing a strong and high-impact day.

In terms of sustainability at an individual level, we have developed a reflective log for your experiences, highs and lows in energy, successful recharging activities, sleep patterns, regenerative activities that boost energy and so on (see Figure 9.2).

Either draw the grid in a notebook and write your responses to the questions, or enter details into a spreadsheet. Keeping this journal will help you identify things, people, circumstances and generally be more attentive to your energy levels.

Once patterns start emerging for regular drains or boosts to your energy during the day, you can become more proactive in managing your energy levels and understanding how you can channel yourself to tackle the big challenges of the day and when and how to recharge and boost your energy levels.

FIGURE 9.2 NQ reflective journal

Date:	Your NQ reflective journal
How would you describe your mood today? What was your greatest accomplishment today?	
When were my energy peaks today? What created them?	When were my energy slumps today? What caused them?
What other surge(s) or sparks did I get?	What drained me today?
How did I recharge today?	What stopped me replenishing my energy supply?

Of course, there will be times when it feels like you've been hijacked by others and there will be little chance for you to exert control over when, how and where your energy is deployed. Finding the right time, place and even words to use to excuse yourself or take yourself somewhere to think, be calm and focus may only need 10 minutes in any given day. 'Comfort breaks' has become a choice phrase to explain the need to visit the bathroom, so it can also be a cover-all for a thinking, pausing, reflecting, breathing break to just be a little calmer and kinder to yourself.

Alongside this, an energy map will help you look at the tasks you are facing today or this week (see Figure 9.3), where the size of the circle reflects the amount of time you will have to spent on the task/activity.

'Sustainable me' isn't about clichés like bounce-backability or the pseudo-athletics of resilience. This is you, taking note of where your energy is, how it's used, gained and lost, and what you can do to manage the way you deal with your day and subsequently your week.

Recording things and mapping out your day and week could be just the consciousness you need to bring yourself a better understanding of how you navigate what is otherwise a blur of activities and constant demands.

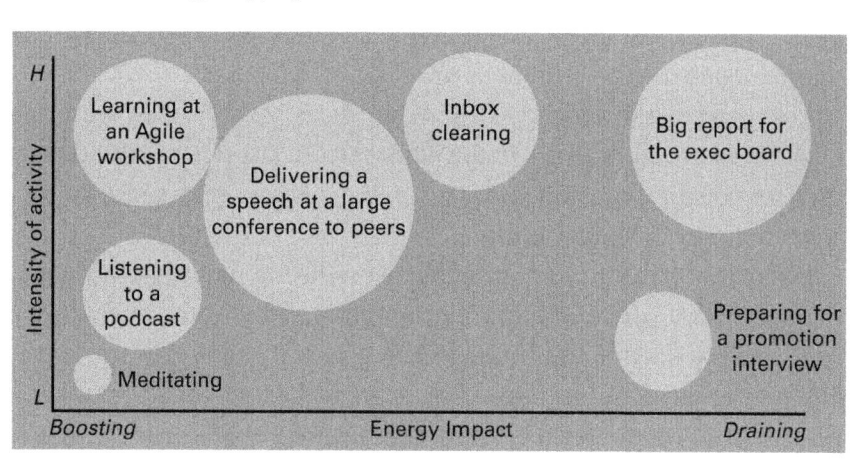

FIGURE 9.3 Energy mapping

NQ element 3: IN – introspective energy

Internalizing things is often regarded as a bad thing to do. We are encouraged to 'let it out', and with good reason in many cases. Externalizing things can make a huge difference.

We've already established just how strong an impact work can have on our very being, so the **balanced life** mantra comes to mind for this element: the impact the organization has on our 'inner energy'.

Introspection starts by a connection (or re-connection) to our inner dialogue. Listening to ourselves, and allowing ourselves space to think, to put words to our feelings and describe our comfort, discomfort, confusion, clarity and conjecture. It is also about accepting and being open about what we find when we dive deeper into *ourselves* and to act on the signals that our bodies and minds are giving.

And of course, we can and do ignore our inner dialogue. After all, what does our inner self know about the needs and demands we're encountering from others? And we can hardly excuse ourselves from a really demanding challenge quite forcibly presented to us by our boss 'because my inner dialogue said I need to slow down a bit' can we?

In Chapter 4 we revealed how our brain is our most used muscle, consuming over 20 per cent of our calories in the process of thinking. As a muscle, our brain requires exercise just as our other muscles need it, and meditation is one way that may help to train this muscle and teach our mind to regulate itself. Sitting in silence, paying attention to the breath, leads over time to the development of clarity and calmness and a clearer thought process.

You may be thinking, 'Do I have to meditate?' or 'Can we bring meditation or mindfulness in the workplace?' The point is not the act itself of 'meditating' but how what happens in that space allows connection to the inner world.

It's also possible to sustain meditation during daily activities, and not only when sitting still in a certain place. Attention can be drawn to the movement of the body, to the physical sensations, or to the flow of thoughts and feelings. This is defined as 'presence', or awareness. And of course we can bring that into the workplace; if we are 'present' and 'centred' during our daily tasks we will definitely perform at higher level.

And then we could slow down and try the precious gift of observing, feeling, taking care of ourselves and learning the art of listening to that infinite and silent space that is within us which is going to help us to connect with others in a respectful and healthy way.

NQ element 4: PL – self-system interplay

The interplay between two or more things (or people) is the effect on each or reaction to each other. Self-system (also referred to as self-dynamism) was a personality concept created by Harry S Sullivan,[8] which he believed served to minimize the tension of anxiety. The self-system was defined as a unique collection of experiences that was used to describe one's own self.

Self-system as a major structure in personality development that could appear as early as six months of age. The positive reinforcement a child receives during mid-infancy will not only prompt the development of the self-system, but also act as preparation for living in wider society.

In order for the self-system to develop, Sullivan affirmed that 'good me' and 'bad me' personifications must first form. These personifications are organized perceptions that are accounts of certain experiences.

The 'good me' personification consists of experiences that are rewarded, where a child would sense a noticeable decrease of anxiety. The 'bad me' personification on the other hand consists of experiences that are punished and cause greater anxiety to a child. These personifications then fuse into what Sullivan called the **self-system**.

The self-system revolves around the ideas of perception, evaluation, and regulatory behaviour. Since this concept is associated with the self, it was often compared to Sigmund Freud's ego construct; Freudian analysts were concerned about the self-system, claiming that it was equivalent to the ego.

Once we step as employees into the social construct that is an organization, we also bring our whole self, which includes our inner self-system. For some time, we have to orient ourselves, know who to trust and befriend and perform well so that we can be secure in our employ.

It is important to understand how we work *at work*. It helps us enormously if we understand how we work and function as individuals and how we will operate in the systems used in our place of work.

If we know our self-system is defined by kind thoughts of others, by wanting to help people, and we are recruited to a role that chases people in debt to repay, we may find our inner system and the demands of the job are incongruent and we are experiencing exhaustion tensions between our inner and outer systems.

It is finding the right formula of inner and outer energies that will help create a more satisfying working experience and that begins with a deeper understanding of our self-system and the other systems we work within.

NQ element 5: PU – purpose: yours and the organization's

In Chapter 7 we introduced the phrase *purpose washing*, which described how some organizations are jumping on the popular view that organizations with a virtuous purpose are very appealing to job seekers who are very talented and have lots of potential.

Having a purpose of your own may seem like a rather overly grandiose thing, yet ambitions, plans and a general direction in life aren't just for the super privileged (though having privileges clearly helps any ambitions come to reality).

Having a sense of 'what am I here for' is part of our Ikigai or source. Finding work and an employer where there is a synergy between your purpose and that of the organization is a truly forceful match.

When we are driven from that higher purpose, this seems to make more sense; you understand the 'why', feel totally involved, engaged and even inspired by work.

The merits of knowing what your purpose **is** will at least help you know what you're looking for. Or, in the case of Marvin Gaye, finding something different once your employer has helped you develop.

Using the Ikigai approach we can start to define the things we want to do because we enjoy them, we're good at them and/or we can get paid for them. Our purpose sits somewhere in the middle of our passion, or mission and our vocation.

Developing your inner self; unity with others; service to others and expressing your full potential are all at the heart of a self/systems belonging equation to work out your meaning and how that is manifested in the work the you do and the environment you do it in.

NQ element 6: PR – the promise (aka the deal) between employee and employer

We have an uncanny knack of not realizing how good we've got things. There are many examples of companies who are inclusive, supportive and far from toxic, but this doesn't mean people won't find things to be unhappy about or criticize.

There has been much thinking about the concept of an employee value proposition (EVP).[9] So much so that research from HR consulting firm Willis Towers Watson[10] revealed that people are five times more likely to be highly engaged if their organization has an effective EVP (which could translate into better performance, retention, lower recruitment and dispute resolution costs and creation of greater value from customers). This is often referred to as **the deal** between employer and employee. In return for work, commitment, adaptability and a series of behaviours consistent with the organization's values and strategic intent, employees get a salary, development and a range of other benefits and rewards.

In Chapter 4 we covered another part of the 'deal' in the provision of *psychological safety*: how comfortable people are in speaking up about behaviours that are counter to the organization's values and expectations.

There may be times where the deal is questioned. Where people feel underappreciated, overworked, isolated, overwhelmed, stale, stuck or a combination or cluster of these emotions. The deal, at this time, feels very unfair and neglected. This is a de-energizing state to be in.

Instead of letting this state fester, or feel like an additional burden, there is a chance to reflect and remind ourselves of the state of the deal. A simple + / - list of factors will show how many of the good things we're overlooking and taking for granted. It will also give us a chance to feel more conviction in raising our concerns if we can demonstrate a fair and balanced perspective on things. It may even be that we have a very different perspective as we have been a little over-focused on things that are challenging us.

A more reflective, balanced and factual take on things can help us realize how severe or not something is.

It could be that the deal with our employer is a good one, and the current tension is with teammates. Perhaps a feeling that there isn't a fair split of responsibilities and allocated work. This would need some correcting and is either something the team leader can help recalibrate, or that the team themselves can work out. Indeed, it may be that the team have never agreed a way of working together or behaving. So a 're-contracting' exercise is useful to stabilize people on expectations, fair allocation of work and appreciation of each other's work contributing to success. Famous self-managed company Morning Star from California uses a *colleague letter of understanding*[11] approach which clarifies the work of teams without the need for managerial representation, intervention or supervision.

The promises we make to ourselves, our team and ultimately our employer, need to form a fair and valued exchange between all elements and if not, the deal needs some recalibrating.

Workplace promises can be broken but often are just left unattended and forgotten about. Reminding ourselves of the deal and even striking a fresh version gives us some invigorated energy or, at least, removes friction-creating distractions and doubts.

NQ element 7: FL – flow, deep work and understanding your optimized self

American-Hungarian Professor of Psychology Mihaly Csikszent-mihalyi[12] is perhaps most famous for his concept of *flow*:[13]

> a state in which people are so involved in an activity that nothing else seems to matter; the experience is so enjoyable that people will continue to do it even at great cost, for the sheer sake of doing it.

Linked to theories of happiness being a fluctuating state, his work has influenced a range of theories, practices and understanding of the perplexing state of abundance and higher living standards, yet plummeting levels of reported happiness.

Flow is described in eight characteristics:

- total concentration on the task you have in front of you;
- clear definition of the goal and reward for this work (including getting immediate feedback from others);
- normal sensations of time (moving on too fast or too slowly) are transformed;
- you are intrinsically rewarded by the experience;
- there is a feel of effortlessness and ease to the work – it flows;
- there is a positive, charging tension between the challenge and your level of skill/competence and experiences;
- actions and awareness come together so there is a feel of a loss of self-consciousness;
- you feel totally in control of the task.

Easy, right?

Not at all. This is something we might occasionally experience and yet, being aware that this is the state of flow (in short, enough pressure and enough skills/belief) is likely to increase our chances of being in this state.

What many people would attest to, is that the first characteristic of flow (total concentration) is harder and harder in a wired, always-on world, with heightened expectations of speed of response and action.

The answer to this comes in the shape of a concept of deep work[14] from computer science professor and author Cal Newport. Deep work is essentially a human energy tool and is *the ability to focus without distraction on a cognitively demanding task.*

In essence, there are two categories for work: deep and shallow work (see Figure 9.4).

FIGURE 9.4 Deep work and shallow work

Deep work	Shallow work
The 'Flow' state; high intensity and stimulus – pressure vs accomplishment.	The illusion of productivity fuelled by others' expectations
Harder but yields better work!	Busyness as a proxy for productivity
Examples: *Complex problems;* *New products and services;* *Breakthrough solutions;* *Research, analysis, deductions;* *Innovation and new precedents.*	Examples: *Answering/sending email;* *Inbox management;* *Answering repetitive queries;* *Organizing calendars;* *Excessive meetings.*

In looking at how we are energized, these two states require different energies from us:

Deep work is focused, attentive, thoughtful, creative, challenging and immersive.

Shallow work is at a very surface level of thought, short bursts of higher-volume tasks and still occupying, immersive and time-consuming.

This issue comes when trying to undertake deep work with a shallow mindset and vice versa.

Many people who have advocated 'time management strategies' have attempted to give us some balance over this, with four-box grids of importance and urgency. We've never had as many productivity guides, gurus and gimmicks and yet that heightened sense of being productive seems to have made us even more paranoid about any lack of productive time.

This is explained by those who have created the **Take Back Your Time**[15] movement, which 'seeks to challenge the epidemic of overwork, over-scheduling and time famine… that threatens our health, our relationships, our communities, and our environment.' It seems I'm not the only one to be worried about peak work.

What deep work and flow have in common in helping us is a sense of control of decisions on how we can and want to work, so we can be productive, feel good about our accomplishments and not feel bad about rest; off-the-grid activities, procrastination and being comfortable being a little bit bored now and then. Being in a constant flow state might be as exhausting as pursuing it. We need a lot more variety when it comes to stimulus, focus and contemplation.

NQ element 8: VA – variety: the spice of life or a life of space?

What deep work and the flow state are teaching us is that we are likely to be more energized when we feel we have control over the circumstances we find ourselves in.

One of the critical energies we have is being stimulated and whilst doing the same thing over and over again (a big influence in FW Taylor's theories we mentioned before) in a workplace, it's easy to understand how we would lose concentration and drift, affecting our output and quality. Management was introduced to provide a supervisory stimulation to counter that machine-like repetition.

Variety therefore appears to be a naturally occurring state of attention, thought, awareness, challenge and a break from a repetitive norm. Quite why so many jobs are still filled with huge volumes of processing is now a little enigmatic when we understand how easily bored, distracted and unmotivated we might become. As highly mechanistic and algorithmic work may be further automated, roles might be designed with the variety that people will now need in mind.

However, many roles – such as a supermarket checkout operative or hotel reception clerk – may seem repetitive and doing the same task, but each customer is a potential interaction, a social exchange and a variation.

Variety is therefore a potentially under-utilized aspect of those time-management methods we are now inundated with. **Timeboxing**[16] is one such technique; it introduces boxed segments to days which can introduce a range of varieties to your work, hobbies or study.

Used in the energizing Agile Project[17] methodology, timeboxing looks at a task or challenge and invites you to think about how to apportion time to the task to then box it in your schedule, journal or calendar.

But how long should something take? When visiting Menlo Innovations[18] in 2016 and attending their culture tour, I found the method I'd been looking for.

Work is allocated to one of these timeboxed values:

TABLE 9.1 Timeboxed values for assessing how long work will take to complete

0.25	0.5	1	2
4	8	16	32
64	132	246	Hours

An email might take only five minutes to review and answer, yet once you then file the message and make a note on the customer record that this has been agreed you're probably nearer 10 minutes. So if you estimate the task 'agree with client X date for delivery of initial brand guidelines' you're not far off if you allocated 0.25 of an hour to it.

A collaborative effort with colleagues to design the brand logo might be given 16 hours' work. So with four of you in that room, you have four hours each to create something or you split the work and timebox it thus:

TABLE 9.2 Compiled efforts used in timeboxing

A one-hour sketching session with four of you. So that's **4 hours** gone into the task already.	A 30-minute discussion to agree the best sketches (so another **2 hours**).
Two of the team need two hours each to design logos in some software (**4 hours = 10 in total so far**).	Leaving the team with **6 hours** to make the decision and finalize the brand to send to the client plus make amendments the client wants.

Next time you know this can be done a little quicker, so you'd choose eight hours and reduce the sketching time.

Timeboxing isn't just about measuring tasks and being efficient, it's helping you introduce variety into your day by allowing you to timebox learning, breaks, reading, research, meditation, planning and other activities we have to fit in the normal run of every working day.

That's one way to plan for variety and see how inspiring, energizing and challenging your day might be. Another important aspect, though, is taking breaks from work. Planning days or weeks where you are on vacation and do no such timeboxing, and amble through days being spontaneous, present and more random about your time and energy is also important.

NQ elements 9–12: The Edge – DI (Discovery), RE (Relationships), LE (Learning), and IN (Innovation)

In my TEDx talk of 2018[19] I introduced the concept of **The Edge**. It was where I described a metaphorical place at the edge of an organization's boundaries where people could find energizing activities and approaches to help them with their burdensome working life.

The concept was already documented via the work of Alberts & Hayes in their 2003 work *Power to the Edge*.[20] When studying command and control mechanisms of leadership in the information age, their conclusion was that increased decision making and accountability was better pushed to the edge of the organization, not centralized too far away from the point of need: relevance and insight.

At times of great emergency, speed and pressure, centralizing all decisions can cause failure, loss and damage. When the need to act is paramount in such circumstances, a lack of practice in being cohesive, aligned and yet rapid and clear hampers people in doing this. When times are good, centralized decision making can be seen as the cause of this control and others may see no need for any dispersal of accountability, authority and application. 'Let's flag it up to those in the power positions', or even worse, 'I won't say anything because they must know about this and will act accordingly'. This may result in something like the bystander effect[21] (somewhat).

The Edge concept aligns to the four remaining elements of our NQ (and arguably others of the 12) to start to build a way of being, operating, and doing things that means more self-designed responsibility, accountability, decisions, control and therefore being in a place of influence and, yes, Flow.

We have to be energized to learn

Learning about ourselves (in some of the ways we've described earlier in this book), about our immediate and wider environment, about our colleagues, collaborators and customers, and about our processes, protocols and performance capabilities that we will need if we want to be more autonomous, accountable and *actualized* in our work.

We have to be energized to discover

We may well enter into some uncertain territory, with things we have no experience of or skill for. Being curious, vigilant and attentive to things means we are no longer simply processing the things on our job description but being more aware and in tune with things around us so that we are more knowing. This has a huge impact on energy. It can be exciting and overwhelming in equal measure. Our curiosity needs fuelling in order to bring more discovery-based approaches and energy to our 'game'.

We have to be energized about innovation

This does not mean we suddenly have to become Ada Lovelace, Elon Musk or even Nikola Tesla. We have to start to use the power and energy in being excited about identifying new things we can introduce, do, *hacks* we can make to our routines and processes. An innovative element does not mean you have to create bold and totally new things, but be inspired by your learning and discovery to experiment, try new things and use the data, evidence and insight that comes from them to act your way into a new way of being.

We have to be energized and attentive to and from our relationships

Perhaps the most obvious form of energy boost or depletion is other people around us. *Drains*, *Mood Hoovers* and *Vampires* seem to suck the life out of people, places and situations. But *Radiators*[22] bring sunshine, positivity and energy to situations and others. It isn't just in this situation but it is the attention, warmth, sincerity, giving, receiving, help, support, conversation, listening and belief that other people give and get from you and you from them.

The Edge (as a concept) means you might have to timebox activities to fit into your working day to spend time with people, learn about them and their work, discover new things about your company and the work it does, and innovate with people around improvement and decisions that bring more value to your work and that of others.

The Edge and these four elements (plus the other eight in the NQ table of elements) will help you become more in control of your energy; more aware of where you need boosts and where you are drained by things and others.

The Edge is where you can move from the cage of an overly defined job, to more interesting parts of your working life.

In summary

Knowing our source, being sustainable about energy through understanding and using more introspection, and the interplay of us with others and systems form the foundation of our elements of NQ.

Having a strong sense of purpose, being aware and acting on the promises you make to yourself, others and they to you, and working in a flow state and with variety will help you build on the inner confidence and clarity you create.

FIGURE 9.5   20 minutes per day on one of your NQ (eNergy Quotient) elements

DIscovery	RElationships	LEarning	INnovation
VAriety	FLow	PRomise	PUrpose
SOurce	SUstainable	INtrospective	InterPLay

And The Edge – the top of the elemental table for NQ – helps you be energized about the things you've put into place that give you a solid foundation to who you are and what you want from your work and that balanced life (see Figure 9.5).

Twenty minutes per day is our recommended MVP – in this case *Minimum Viable Practice*. Work on what gives you the most energy and what you are drawn to. Link it to the second part of your practice and so on. No science. Just will, curiosity and your energy.

Only you are the vessel of your own energy and only you can be the one to create the shifts you want and need to bring more energy to your working and more balanced life.

Endnotes

1. www.sciencedaily.com/terms/intelligence_quotient.htm (archived at https://perma.cc/TQA7-P9KP)
2. https://psychcentral.com/lib/what-is-emotional-intelligence-eq/ (archived at https://perma.cc/R8XJ-2EZP)
3. http://theviewinside.me/what-is-your-ikigai/ (archived at https://perma.cc/SE5D-KCTE)
4. Strategyzer (nd) Business model canvas. Available from: www.strategyzer.com/canvas/business-model-canvas (archived at https://perma.cc/W859-LNLZ)
5. Creatlr (nd) Personal business model canvas. Available from: www.creatlr.com/template/R0ouCCnO5mzKWdYpW7Rmsf/personal-business-model-canvas/ (archived at https://perma.cc/2H8G-59RM)

6 BusinessModelYou.com – The Personal Business Model Canvas is a derivative work from BusinessModelGeneration.com. This template is licensed under Creative Commons Attribution-ShareAlike 3.0 Unported. To view a copy or read more, visit http://creativecommons.org/licenses/by-sa/3.0/ (archived at https://perma.cc/2NCS-V5TE)

7 Stern, S (2011) the importance of creating and keeping a customer, *Financial Times*. Available from: www.ft.com/content/88803a36-f108-11e0-b56f-00144feab49a (archived at https://perma.cc/V6TX-FZ85)

8 https://dictionary.apa.org/interpersonal-theory (archived at https://perma.cc/EB62-DJ38)

9 PM Insight (2016) How to build a better employer value proposition. Available from: https://pminsight.cipd.co.uk/how-to-build-a-better-employer-value-proposition (archived at https://perma.cc/VDD3-79GJ)

10 www.willistowerswatson.com/en-US/Insights/all-insights#sort=%40fdate13762%20descending (archived at https://perma.cc/MNB9-H4LW)

11 Pim (2017) Morning Star's success story: no bosses, no titles, no structural hierarchy, *Corporate Rebels*. Available from: https://corporate-rebels.com/morning-star/ (archived at https://perma.cc/XT5Z-5FZ4)

12 www.cgu.edu/people/mihaly-csikszentmihalyi/ (archived at https://perma.cc/4RDY-Q74L)

13 Oppland, M (2019) 8 ways to create flow according to Mihaly Csikszentmihalyi, *Positive Psychology*. Available from: https://positivepsychology.com/mihaly-csikszentmihalyi-father-of-flow/ (archived at https://perma.cc/92PS-G2B6)

14 Newport, C (2016) *Deep Work: Rules for focused success in a distracted world*, Grand central Publishing. www.calnewport.com/books/deep-work/ (archived at https://perma.cc/F3MQ-7VXE)

15 www.takebackyourtime.org/ (archived at https://perma.cc/S5TY-8Z8X)

16 Zao-Sanders, M (2018) How timeboxing works and why it will make you more productive, *Harvard Business Review*. Available from: https://hbr.org/2018/12/how-timeboxing-works-and-why-it-will-make-you-more-productive (archived at https://perma.cc/LCP5-4VBW)

17 Sacolick, I (2018) What is agile methodology? Modern software development explained, *InfoWorld*. Available from: www.infoworld.com/article/3237508/what-is-agile-methodology-modern-software-development-explained.html (archived at https://perma.cc/4UVE-KK32)

18 https://menloinnovations.com/ (archived at https://perma.cc/S27L-WYBS)

19 Timms, P (2018) The Edge – people powered design [video] *TED*. Available from: www.ted.com/talks/perry_timms_the_edge_people_powered_design (archived at https://perma.cc/VEB9-J7K6)

20 Hayes, R and Albers, D (2003) *Power to the Edge*, Cforty Onesr Cooperative Research. http://www.dodccrp.org/files/Alberts_Power.pdf (archived at https://perma.cc/7VVA-H9ZN)
21 www.psychologytoday.com/gb/basics/bystander-effect (archived at https://perma.cc/RV4J-4ULM)
22 Pylas, S (2016) Are you a radiator or a drain online? *Huffington Post*. Available from: www.huffingtonpost.co.uk/sarah-pylas/radiator-or-drain_b_7630554.html (archived at https://perma.cc/QN5R-Y6GB)

10

Tools for the next 20 years

In this final chapter, we wrap up all that has gone before in this book and set out how we can truly deliver the subtitle – **designing organizations where people flourish**.

Not everyone will have the chance to wave their models, schemas, flowcharts and revised role profiles at their most senior HR professional or CEO and declare, 'Here's our future blueprint, let's put it together'. However, organization design can no longer be a specialized task for a group of practitioners without the appreciation of their operational, marketing, research, financial, legal, safety, facilities and governance colleagues. **This chapter urges us ALL to be organization designers**.

This is not an attempt to dilute such a powerful and specialized aspect of organizational development and human resource management. It is a genuine attempt to give this function, role, specialism, craft, science and even artform the prominence it deserves. Those exemplary professionals and leaders already steeped in and revered for organization design need some help despite their own and their collective brilliance.

When we say organization design to most people, they will default to the chart with boxes and lines. When we say 'let's learn to drive', an instructor doesn't just show you the route they'll take you on today. A complex set of operational, functional, procedural, legal, moral, social, cognitive and intuitive factors are at play, just as they are in organizational life.

Organization design is not building some roads and putting some signs up and expecting it to all work. It is complex traffic flow management, maintenance, emergency handling, future planning and balancing a delicate ecosystem of behaviours, norms, exceptions and outcomes.

> Whilst not an entire book dedicated to organization design, this chapter will look at ways we can truly look at designing with humans in mind; not just machines, cogs and tuning but a sophisticated interplay between variable but mostly brilliant human behaviours and applied endeavours and a system that aggregates, channels and makes the most of the amazing energy we have as sentient, physical and spiritual beings.
>
> Is *Eudaimonia* a pipedream? A nirvana or utopia we will never achieve? Or can an organization truly be designed so that its people flourish? In this chapter we'll make our best attempts at predicting how this could become one of the greatest design feats of the next 20 years.

What is organization design?

I could have written this entire book about this subject but that wouldn't have addressed the reasons why only a chapter is needed here for this fascinating and often unheralded aspect of the world of work.

Our friends at the CIPD describe organization design (OD) as:[1]

> the review of what the company wants and needs, an analysis of the gap between its current state and where it wants to be in future, and the design of organizational practices that will bridge that gap. It's a fundamental, wide-reaching, future-focused activity that often requires a review of the entire organization and its context to decide what does and doesn't work. It will therefore usually involve a holistic review of everything from systems, structures, people practices, rewards, performance measures, policies, processes, culture and the wider environment.

A largely specialized, niche and even a little mysterious aspect of a human resources function, OD is also found in change, performance and even operational functions. It is also considered a subset of organization development (also abbreviated to OD). Some use ODD (organization design & development) as a catch-all term for both areas. The difference between design and development is covered in the CIPD's excellent overview:

The key difference between organization design and organization development is the scale of the issue(s) and the solutions required to resolve them. If they are relatively self-contained and local in their impact, then an organization development approach is more suitable.

However, if success in one area is inextricably linked to practice elsewhere, and a variety of mechanisms need re-aligning, then a larger-scale organization design activity would ensure that changes fit with each other.

In Chapter 2 we looked at organization development and the convulsive and overly regular *restructure* fad that HR seemed to have landed itself with throughout the early 2000s and to this day. It is very much an exemplar of an organizational tension in the 21st century – constant tinkering with a 20th-century fixed-structure mindset using a fluid approach to adjust to changing needs and circumstances. Much of the restructuring obsession in senior leaders is perhaps down to being trapped within those two mental models and use of energy: consistency and certainty craved by leaders and their teams in handling complex business issues and workflow; and the shifts, adaptations and responsive needed for markets, consumers and employees, insight and data analysis, optimization and more.

We could take a highly topical organization design brief of now: we need a digital transformation to use the latest in cutting-edge technologies, which will need some organization redesign.

This is one of the 2010s' most prominent stimuli to change. Whether it is artificial intelligence, social technologies, cloud or *knowledge management*, CEOs and boards across the world are clamouring for an advantage, edge or optimal performance by better leveraging emerging digital technologies.

Often the 'solutions' are already in mind: use of cloud-based data storage and retrieval over internally hosted and extensive networked servers hosting applications, data and platforms that enable the organization to conduct its business. This is transforming the use of digital tools. Once the cloud is implemented, there is unlikely to be a return to internally hosted data storage and application 'hosting'. It is hardly a fundamental review of how structures are organized;

people's roles are set to deliver the necessary work that creates the value of the organization.

It is using the same vehicle to travel but with more supercharged elements and in-car entertainment, instead of asking 'is this even the best vehicle for our future journeys?' An organization design approach will start from the point of what is the intended destination and how best can we get there via the most appropriate vehicular format?

We may be a high-performance two-seater sports car now, but for our future we need to be a sports utility vehicle (SUV). We need more luggage space, passenger comfort and safety; still with performance and luxury, but with a more practical configuration for driver and passengers whilst being kinder to the environment on fuel consumption, yet with the build quality and reliability needed. And we must still turn heads and be a continuance of our brand, reputation and prestige.

Less a *Porsche Carrera* as we were when we were a start-up, and more a Porsche *Cayenne Hybrid* to take us into a more versatile future.

Organization design will make sense of what we are now (or have become) and will help design in all the features needed to make the right choices for the design of what we will need to be.

Included in that is of course the structural side of the organization's set-up but more the essence, the flow of work, decisions, inclusion, leading roles, intelligence and insight, progression, governance, compliance, safety, rigour, adaptability and with it the culture, forces of togetherness through purpose, values and mission and the utilization of the most important feature of any organization, **its people and their energies**. Energies that lead to the work being done that services the value the organization is looking to create for its customers, stakeholders, partners, suppliers and, increasingly, its community and the environment.

The energy of people is – at the moment – a rarely defined or design consideration. Skills, aptitudes, capabilities, future potential, experience, expertise, knowledge, craft, location, seniority and even reputation/social capital[2] all feature highly. And rightly so – these are often known entities and will be valuable data points in looking at the all-important functioning of any redesigned organization.

Why would we design an organization around people's energies and if we did, how would we know them and what difference would that make?

A pretty crucial and fundamental question to ask. As we've explored in previous chapters, people's spirit, emotions, preferences and as a result their energies are often aligned to, but exclusively indicated by, their experience, expertise and execution on the job. We still design an organization largely around this.

A person = 40 or so hours of work per week, with a variety of skills within that defined by their role and position in the company and attached to a functional unit or division. We are not always taking into account whether they would be happier and better utilized:

1. by a different working routine of 10, 20 or 30 hours per week;
2. in regularized routines of work or a random and more challenging selection of their own workload;
3. as part of a close-knit, highly collaborative team or as part of a practice which is made up of solo experts very focused on their specialist skills and knowledge;
4. in changing, complex project environments with a new collection of people with every venture or established in a wider pool on more conventional work stacks;
5. in lead roles and responsibilities which help bring others into a situation to deliver needed outcomes or being lead and working more peer-to-peer;
6. internally, location based or externally, remotely based.

Of course, some roles and types of work are needed on-site (looking after patients in healthcare and counselling vulnerable adults, for example) as well as some off-site customer sales and support representatives.

The crucial organization design considerations aren't just fixed to the 40-hour, present, commoditized employee. Ways of handling:

- flow of work and decisions;
- use of tools and technologies;
- capabilities and support; and
- conducive environments

are all considerations of organization then role design that start with a macro version of the organization and end up in a micro version with roles and people considerations.

There are examples of organization design facilitated from the people/energy perspective.

The writing on the wall story

As a consulting advisor, I was asked by a client to help with organization design in a small but influential company in a challenging sector. The history of the organization was important: formerly a governmental organization, highly regulated and yet highly innovative. With regulation and a more open-market model to their service, they became a wholly independent, self-financing venture. This required a radical organization design for the new ways to generate income without receiving government funding.

Many considerations had already been thought through about the people the organization had both from its former government days and its now more entrepreneurial present and future. Yet there was a design issue. The former silos of the old government model were no longer serving it well. There was tension between new, highly skilled and innovative commercial product creators, and the incumbent leaders of the functions. Yet there was expertise, contacts, reputation and yes, energy in those leaders who had not been recruited to be commercial giants, but experts in their fields.

Redundancies could have been one consideration; redesign the functions, remove the now obsolete leaders, replace them with commercially minded new leaders and re-establish the design based on these functions. That was considered but discarded as too risky. Risky because the leaders had strong networks, relationships, credibility and market reputation that any new leaders would be unlikely to match. So it was felt necessary to redesign their roles to maximize that skill and experience (and yes, energy – these people were good at this and clearly loved the work) whilst not forcing them to becoming agile scrum masters for the new innovation teams (which they hadn't been hired for and didn't appear to have any energy for on current experience).

So our brief was to redesign the organization to optimize the skills and energies of those in place NOW and thereby create value in those respective roles which would make the organization economically viable, add value in a highly competitive market, and enhance their reputation in that market with their new design, products and services and relationships with the market providers, suppliers and consumers.

The *'writing on the wall'* element came from only a day's work in a large room with white-board-type walls that could be written on with markers. An extensive mapping exercise showed the current state of the organization in its flow, structure, skills and energies.

This was on the left side of the wall space.

On the right side were the future needs of the organization, with the people and the structure that could deliver that need. It became clear that the existing hierarchical and functional silos were not going to serve the organization's needs. We needed something more radical but also pertinent to the skills and energy people had for a type of work, and the optimal shape, space and flow that would facilitate that.

The final organization design (without names in boxes but looking at functional, professional expertise) looked like Figure 10.1.

This is hybrid of a flatter, non-hierarchical model favoured by digital and design companies and a series of outward-facing lead roles that built relationships and leveraged external networks, expertise, lead practices and professional areas. Less line management and more professional development, lead generation and expertise acquisition.

The results were presented to slightly dubious executives but a helpfully enthusiastic CEO made sure the decision was made to trial

FIGURE 10.1 Organization design example

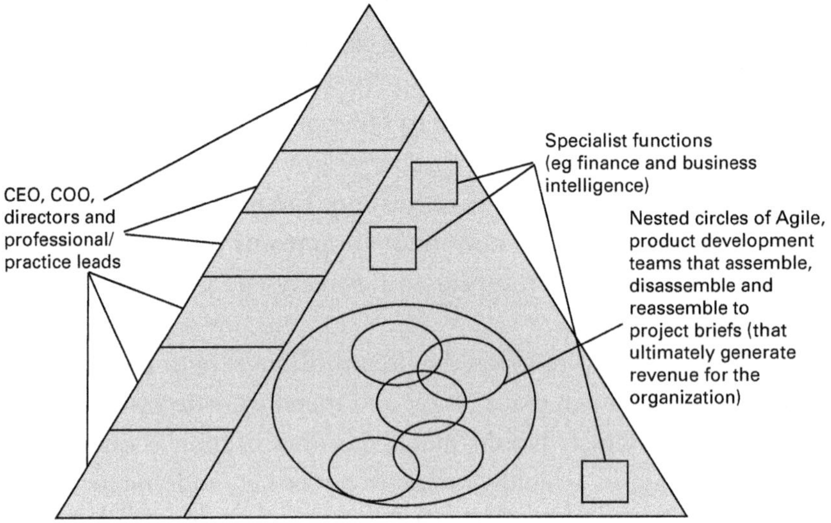

CEO, COO, directors and professional/practice leads

Specialist functions (eg finance and business intelligence)

Nested circles of Agile, product development teams that assemble, disassemble and reassemble to project briefs (that ultimately generate revenue for the organization)

this design. Reward, governance, duty of care and HR and performance management systems were adjusted to facilitate this model and communication and engagement activities implemented so that people could shape their new roles.

One year on, a review of the model proved its success: energized people, clear on their role (that they designed) and a move away from the wrong shapes, flows, energies and activities towards a realigned mixture of empowerment, clarity and connectedness. Arguably scalable and built for succession, the design elements are now owned by the entire organization and not just within HR.

Your story

You may work in a tiny micro-enterprise, a large conglomerate or somewhere in between. You may know about organization design or be an enthusiastic novice. What this one story proves is that the organization is a model of how people are, where their energies are and how best to unleash that in the most appropriate way.

In creating your 'writing on the wall' story, you could take the same approach – a huge wall space to draw, write and model everything about your company. If it's a complex 120,000-person organization that might mean a lot of wall space.

There is a process but also a number of ways to scale and adapt that process. Let's start at the beginning.

Stage 1: Know what you already have

This sounds a little trite. I mentioned in Chapter 2 a number of different elements of organizational life that end up as folklore, myths, untouchable practices and how that can be unhelpful in optimizing people's energy.

A large-scale map of the organization is essential to understand not just its structure but its energy flow. The diagram in the writing on the wall story was for 180 people.

Many 120,000-strong organizations are made up of units of 100–200 people so you could start with the whole and take a more forensic view of the smaller units you have. You can link them all later like an architect will design a series of houses and make it into an estate of homes, shops, roads and so on.

The first stage looks something like this:

> **Know what you already have around:**
> - People and their roles/responsibilities, skills, experience, power/influence;
> - Their relationships to others – internal to team; across the organization, outside of the organization;
> - Purpose of the work they do, the flow of that work and decisions they make as part of their work;
> - Tools, policies and processes people need and use;
> - Metrics and performance standards that define success at individual and collective levels;
> - Knowledge and information people need, use and create.

Stage 2: Draft what you need to be/become

This is a somewhat obvious but also tricky element. Having an aspiration 'to leverage more emerging digital technology' is too vague – leverage is a pseudo-verb and more of an adjective; it doesn't really describe the doing. The same would go for 'update to newer technology' or similar.

So the need to be/become should be a lot clearer in order to chart the desired shape, form, manner and approach that the redesigned organization will be like **and what that will deliver**.

We do see this in use in the Agile methodology's 'Product Story',[3] a clear and yet brief summary that communicates the organization's strategy and the high-level goals the organization will achieve/deliver. In the 'writing on the wall' example we had to shift from government grants that supplied the necessary revenue to full-cost recovery alongside two other key factors:

1 not to lose expertise and strong networking presence whilst amplifying the need to generate revenue; and
2 organizing to fully utilize the innovation and commercial skills of the product developers

This stage can be represented thus:

> Describe the best vision you can around:
>
> - The problems and challenges faced by the organization that necessitates a review of the design and what the new design will need to deliver (expressed as goals or outcomes);
> - The opportunities and new, additional elements to services, products and solutions (similarly expressed as goals or outcomes);
> - What additional skills, competencies, behaviours and attitudes people will need to acquire and use;
> - Differences in relationships with others – internal and external;
> - Specific adaptations to the work they do, the flow of it and different decisions they will be expected to make;
> - New tools, policies and processes needed for this adapted work and way of working;
> - Estimated metrics and perfomance standards that help define goals at individual and collective levels;
> - What additional knowledge and information people would need, where they might get it, use it and create it.

At this point, where people are in the organization is not relevant. We can map people in later. What is relevant is how you create the 'work stacks' that will need to be delivered. In our case study, we knew we needed an internal finance function, an internal recruitment function and an internal business intelligence function – the rest was subject to whatever we could imagine. So we modelled the organization; not its entire structure, but we modelled it in boxes, arrows and flow of information.

Stacks is an interesting concept that is used in the technology world for information storage and use. In computing, a stack is a data structure used to store a collection of objects. Individual items can be added and stored in a stack using a push operation. Objects can be retrieved using a pop operation, which removes an item from the stack.[4]

We can also use this approach to define our business in the same way. First identified by ESADE Business School Professor Ivan Bofarull,[5] this approach to defining a business model by such information stacks is a handy way to describe the various functions, process and factors that make up a business model. They can influence everything from how files are stored and created to things that the business delivers that create value.

An example of a business model represented as stacks is the adaption of the PTHR[6] Business Model shown in Figure 10.2.

FIGURE 10.2 Stacks model

Stack 1: Principles	Stack 2: Processes	Stack 3: Strategy
Our way of being and our operating system	Use of tools, technologies, protocols and systems.	Our aspirations; growth plans and impact assessment of our work.

Stack 4: Marketing	Stack 5: Events	Stack 6: Consulting
Communication channels and awareness of our brand	Keynotes and podcasts; round tables, hosting and curating	Our core product: bespoke, tailored and responsive advisory support.

Stack 7: Products and content	Stack 8: Partnerships and agency
Customer products and services and the content we create that supports and enable them.	Partner organisations in delivering to our customers including our supply chain and service partners.

It shows how the elements of the way a business operates and can be set out, and how the process, storage and use of information can be guided by the use of stacks. There is more than simply processing of information using this model, and more about how to represent the energies that are needed to bring each stack into play.

For example, a client approaches the company to use its consultancy services to build a fresh employer brand. The client has a history of having some animal-tested products as part of its customer offer. The company principles state that this would be a compromise of ethics and values that the people who work for the company wish to uphold. So rather than simply looking at the revenue that work could bring, this decision is shaped by Stack 1 (Principles) and declined.

The client then comes back stating they have identified their last supplier who uses animal testing and removed them from their offer so they are now animal-test free and want *even more* to work with this company. Stack 1 (Principles) is clear and so then Stack 2 (Processes) and Stack 6 (Consulting) comes into play.

A video production partner is needed for this work, so Stack 8 is used and Stack 3 is updated as this client is in a new market for the company; Stack 4 (Marketing) will be used to share the (anonymized) case study of the work in this area and a standard offer is then built following this work using Stack 7 (Products & Content).

Whilst this may seem very high level, it can certainly help to bring a fledgling, adapted business model to life and provide enough representation that others can see how work will flow.

This leads to our next stage.

Stage 3: Model your organization not your structure

> Research alternatives and sketch out your model, **not** your structure:
>
> - There are a range of alternatives to the traditional, divisional demarcation of roles and responsibilities inside the organization; structured around geographical, functional, product/service speciality, even a micro-enterprise model. Looking into many of the options will help you understand existing frames you can use and adapt.

> - Consider creating models that sit just above the micro (individual) level and more at the meso (team) level and build them, first aggregating them into the macro, organization-level model. You don't have to build the house first, you can design each room you know you need and then put them together!
> - Meso-level models may be different within (existing or proposed) functions or unit. So the question is then: can a division tolerate that variety of models and functions, or is this an indication it should sielsewhere and perhaps even be independent of its former host' division?
> - Models can be designed and then workflow rolled through them like a series of scenarios. Where work is instigated, received, decided upon, actioned, knowledge stored and used again, shaping processes and reviewed for efficiency and effectiveness. Any technological automation planned will be addressed within this stage of the modelling process.

Modelling the organization in this way will then allow us to map our existing people, their skills, and likely best place to be in the new model. However, that's only the functional aspect where many organizations would end their design process, and go into consultation and conversations about how to make this happen.

This does not address the topic (fully) around energy.

Stage 4: Mapping people's energy to develop a state of flourishing

With our approach being led by *Eudaimonia as a business model concept*, we take an additional step which may still result in us consulting others but is more about the energy side of this book. It's not just what are people **capable** of but what work do they **do/want to do** that brings them to life.

If we are designing based on competence and so on, what are we considering about their preferred style, location, construct and approach of the work being proposed in the new model that will either generate/use/regenerate or simply deplete their energy?

In our case study, we knew the product development teams wanted (and needed) to be nimble, experimental, rapid, adaptive and free to try out crazy concepts before launching a bona fide product/service that would generate revenue. We also knew their incumbent leadership team were not energized by this crazy, chaotic and somewhat dangerous approach, preferring instead more linear, predictable ways of developing solutions. This was a big energy mismatch.

Instead, we designed to keep the two energies not just apart but complementary, where one could see the benefit in the other's energy being used in certain ways. As a result, people flourished from not having their energies twisted into forced compliance but instead channelled into things they knew they were good at, could add value and yes, needed some adaptation.

In Chapter 9 we talked at length about the personal energizing approaches through knowing one's Source, going to the Edge and more.

> How people are inspired and intrinsically motivated to do their best work:
>
> - **Rate the +/– energies of the work.** The flow and variety of work will give you an indication of the tasks, activities, communication and decision making that is needed. This will form into work stacks which starts to look like it needs teams and specialists to tackle the work. Rating the work stack on complexity, variety, volume and any other factor you feel represents the necessary energies this work would need from the people doing the work. If you are not familiar with this work, you can invite others to help you rate this on an energy-based scale.
>
> - **High-level assessment of the energy match of people to the work.** Without knowing what specific people are energized about, crafting an energy-based version of the model is as useful as creating the competence/skills-based version of what is needed to process the work as once you then map who is available to do the work you can make an initial assessment on whether they are energized by what is needed for this area of work.
>
> - **More detailed analysis of the energy needs/match.** You may consult others not just on proposed changes to a team or division they are currently working on, but alos on the energies this work is expected to need and generate. At an individual level, completing their Energy Quotient self-assessment may help clarify whether there is a good match between modelled intent and individual energy, and adjust accordingly. Recognizing that perhaps matching everyone's personal energy preferences or needs may be a tall order, a eudaimonia approach sets out to see everyone flourish so some persistence and ingenuity may be required.

Stage 5: Fusing the model with the energies, skills and work stacks into a structure

> A representation of where people are in the overall schema:
>
> - The recommended divisions, units or directorates that are a sensible way to apportion key functional elements and their work stacks.
>   *Note. you do not have to put people in hierachical boxes, you can show it as linked circles or other shapes.*

> - The numbers of people to effectively deliver on the work in those stacks and the recommended structure at a team-type level.
> - The roles, competencies and energies people will nedd/demonstrate in those teams and with that work.
> - Alignment, levels and seniority for decision making and duty of care to others etc.
> - Revises metrics and performance standards that define success at individual and collective levels.
> - Knowledge and information people need, use and create.

What may also be needed is a range of other information such as quality standards and a range of flexible working processes and policies that may be a departure from existing working norms. These should not be underestimated as crucial enablers of any business model that is setting out to create a flourishing environment for its people *as well as* effective and efficient running of the organization's key value creation for its customers and stakeholders.

It is perhaps symbolic that the structure is the final piece in the puzzle that is the organization design. Many experiences have this as the first or even the only stage in the organization design process.

There is also a (secret) sixth stage: the levels of comfort in leaders adopting this new design.

Greatly influenced by UK-based global consulting firm the Bridge Partnership,[7] there is a definite need to inquire of the leaders how they feel about this redesign and their comfort in taking on new areas of work, people's energies as well as their competences and behaviours and the flow of work in this new model/schema. This is not an invitation for them to overwrite or reject any of the principles in the redesign but to explore what they are the most and least comfortable about and why.

This is part of the Bridge Partnership's approach to creating value through their own consulting model, which is one I greatly admire and use (with their permission) in my own work in this area. It reveals a lot about stated ambition and actual levels of comfort, aspirational goals and levels of comfort in them and their teams in achieving this, and generally creates more dialogue than interference or stand-offs.

Our organization design process for a eudaimonic business model

Stage 1: Know what you already have – **map out your existing energies.**

Stage 2: Draft what you need to be/become – **map out your future energies.**

Stage 3: Model your organization not your structure – **your future energies' 'current'.**

Stage 4: Mapping people's energy – **your future energies' channels and sustainable approaches.**

Stage 5: Fusing the model and energies into a structure – **your future energies' circuitry.**

Stage 6: Levels of comfort your leaders have about your model, energies and structure – **your key users of the organization's energy.**

This should help us design organizations where people flourish and create an energized workplace.

In closing

Human energy is a complex thing. As we have seen throughout history, people have wondered at how we create not only the energy to live, breathe, run and just function, but the wonders of the mind, of how we feel and our energies of a spiritual and often incomprehensible nature.

We hear of superhuman feats of endurance, application and intelligence. Of course, alongside this, incomprehensible damage, destruction and the loathsome ways some people behave prove we have that constant battle between enlightenment and ignorance.

A more compassionate, considerate and comforting place of work is fast emerging as a need in that turbulent world. Where once we toiled and it was dangerous and harsh, now the world outside of work has become more dangerous and harsher and a place of work is our safehouse.

Without over glamourizing work, when we have that job/career/role that fulfils us, so our life seems to follow suit. Sometimes when the work collapses in on us, so does our life. Of course, we also know that work can become so dominant it interferes with life and causes that to collapse.

Balancing work and life is hard, and our intention is to create **a balanced life**. Some of that balance will be easier to create if more workplaces focus beyond financial gains and efficiencies and into places where people flourish *and* deliver those gains/efficiencies.

We have designed some harmful ways of being at work; of course, work is not devoid of the societal influences of the time and is very much a reflection of societal norms including injustices. We are, perhaps, at our most scientifically enlightened (through psychological studies, understanding the brain and our complex social interactions) and yet we are appearing somewhat stuck in a frame of reference built for less enlightened times.

Through Clare Graves' pioneering work in the 1950s and 1960s we now understand more that just knowing about better ways to be and live does not automatically mean the systems that deliver them are a natural evolution. We can be incredibly retrograde when we choose or need to be and our energies become channelled in very different ways to those we would expect of a progressive species.

Through Richard Barrett's values work, we can see how recovery comes from more than systems and numbers – it comes from spirit and soul. Energy-creating belief systems have perhaps always charged us – into war with other societies and ideologies and, of course, into collaboration with those who believe in the same things we do.

With the ancient wisdom of Chakras and QiGong we have early attempts to measure and code our energy sources and our developing psychological, physical and spiritual systems, even though there may not be recognized sciences that can prove this is a 'reality' in the way we now trust ECGs and X-rays.

With Organization Design (OD) we have a discipline that exists and could be strengthened to become less 'just' within HR and more a practice that leaders and many others within organizations are capable of using. Expertise in OD will still be valued and practitioners need not fear the loss of control or professional practice. They should be delighted by more interest and active participation in a craft that is at present largely undervalued.

With personal understanding of our energy – and how this is impacted upon by working environments – comes a sense of more control and influence in how to bring the regenerative and right kinds of energy in to balance and eradicate those of constant depletion, exhaustion, stress, anxiety and fear. We need help to achieve this of course, but a better personal understanding by our colleagues and leaders of our energies and use of them in the workplace will see a healthier approach at work.

Attitudes and systems are hard things to shift, which is why all parts of the system and all attitudes at play within that system will need to be somehow addressed. No one function, profession or leader is likely to 'lead the charge'; a combined approach is needed and this book advocates that inclusive and wide-ranging approach. Yet it does start with the design, with our understanding of our energy and making adjustments to our lives accordingly, in combination with roles, an organization's expectations and systems and those of our colleagues and leaders, partners and collaborators.

What this book *really* calls for is a recognition that human energy by nature is a precious, fierce yet delicate force. But it can be channelled, regenerated and applied in even the most mechanical setting with the right conditions. Over 200 years of industry have somewhat proved that but at a cost. We haven't re-tuned the engines of organizations to be cleaner, and the green energy of human beings is a fitting metaphor as we look to reduce our dependence on dirty combustion energy and move towards using electric and renewable forms of power.

It is not yet proven beyond doubt that if your people are flourishing in their work, your business will be viable and successful. Yet is seems incomprehensible to think otherwise. If your people are unhappy, shattered, shackled and anxious yet you are still performing well as an organization in financial terms, that is too great a cost to humanity and should start to become a thing of a bygone era. The Business Roundtable declaration of 'beyond shareholders' may still seem to be a mere rhetorical statement to many of us, but it nonetheless symbolizes a view that more than profit is essential to be truly considered a sustainable, successful enterprise.

Whilst we can look at 2019 as a banner year for the declaration of a climate emergency, there are clear signs that we have to take the environmental impacts more seriously in how we operate our businesses and run our lives. Volunteer firefighters risking their lives in the Australian bushfires are not doing so because it lines their pockets with riches but because they are energized by providing a life- and ecology-saving service. Ocean clean-up entrepreneurs are not likely doing it because of the revenue involved in recovering plastic, but because they are energized by their disgust at our abuse of the natural world.

We have more people than ever on the planet, who are discovering new things and living longer in doing so. On the one hand, this is a huge problem for the planet to sustain but on the other hand, there are more people to point towards the problems the human race has created that led us to declare the climate emergency in the first place. You may not agree with the tactics of Extinction Rebellion[8] but you know their message is about bringing attention to what we can do to stop our own and the planet's destruction.

What can redesigned organizations do to help us with such huge problems?

They can start to create more fulfilled, enlightened and capable people, which is a great platform to build from. A platform to allow us all to come together and reverse our damage, regenerate our ecological systems, and restore our own balance with nature, life and our own inner thoughts, desires, wishes and feelings. A world where more people flourish starts with workplaces designed for that aim.

It seems fitting to end with a quote from good friend, inspiration and business leader who introduced me to the concept of Eudaimonia in the first place – Matthew Gonnering of Widen Inc,[9] based in Madison, Wisconsin:

> My purpose is to live the eudaimonious life and help others do the same. I have reframed my role as Chief Eudaimonia Officer to remind us of our moral obligations. I still fulfill traditional CEO responsibilities but with a philosophical perspective on what it means to flourish together. My goal is to help employees develop to their fullest potential.[10]

I guess we can all start by being our own CEO – in this case the **Chief Eudaimonia Officer**.

Endnotes

1. CIPD (2019) Organization design. Available from: www.cipd.co.uk/knowledge/strategy/organisational-development/design-factsheet (archived at https://perma.cc/832E-M9AJ)
2. www.socialcapitalresearch.com/literature/definition/ (archived at https://perma.cc/TA8W-UKFA)
3. quora.com/What-is-a-product-story-and-how-to-develop-a-convincing-one (archived at https://perma.cc/2G7X-9AKN)
4. https://techterms.com/definition/stack (archived at https://perma.cc/VH4B-DFSV)
5. Bofarull, I (2019) Merit Summit, *YouTube*. Available from: www.youtube.com/watch?v=t7ahPxX9Oog (archived at https://perma.cc/U9VK-3XHX)
6. www.pthr.co.uk/ (archived at https://perma.cc/FUM6-47P5)
7. https://bridge-partnership.com/ (archived at https://perma.cc/QF3H-Z5M9)
8. https://rebellion.earth/ (archived at https://perma.cc/3GJD-GWVH)
9. www.widen.com/ (archived at https://perma.cc/Y8PB-6LDM)
10. Fox, M (2018) Why This CEO leads with eudaimonia: a commitment to happiness, health and prosperity for all, *Forbes*. Available from: www.forbes.com/sites/meimeifox/2018/01/10/why-this-ceo-leads-with-eudaimonia-a-commitment-to-happiness-health-and-prosperity-for-all/#4055b9fb65bd (archived at https://perma.cc/Q448-VFVV)

INDEX

absence management 5, 57, 85, 137, 145, 162
abundance 16, 91, 179
adjustment 33–34
age of enlightenment 17
ageing population 77–80
agencies 82, *199*
Agile methodology 29–30, 34, 65, 143, 182, *196*, 198
AI (artificial intelligence) 6, 16, 55, 56
ajna 114
'Ain't No Mountain High Enough' (Gaye & Terrell) 45
Alexander, Delisa 158
alternative medicine 95, 99
 see also Qi; Qigong
altruism 16, 19
Alzheimer's 78
anahata 113
anchoring 33–34, 108
Anderson, Ray 142, 162
annual leave (vacation) 65–66, 153
antidepressants 99, 119
Apple 3, 128
Ardern, Jacinda 49–50, 87, 122
Aristotle 84
artificial intelligence (AI) 6, 16, 55, 56
artificial stimulants 99, 119
athletes 117
authenticity 43, 142
automation 6, 12, 27, 32, 36, 67, 69, 97–98, 181, 201
 see also machines; robots (robotic process automation)
autonomy 15–16, 30, 162, 184
availability 16, 33
awareness 100, 114, 174, 179, 181
'Awesomeness reports' 160

'bad me' personification 175
balanced life (work-life balance) 97–102, 119, 143, 174, 205
bandwagon jumpers 141

banking sector 12, 17, 41, 50–51, 128, 135, 143
Barrett, Richard 120, 205
Barrett Values Centre (Barrett Model) 31, 50–51, 120
Barry-Wehmiller 142
Benson, Obie 46
Berners-Lee, Tim 17, 129
Best Companies to Work For 160, 163
Best Workplaces for Parents 158
better work and working lives (CIPD) 56, 118
bioengineering 15
biotechnology 15, 79–80
black swan events 34
blockchain 16
blood supply 62
Bofarull, Professor Ivan 199
boring work 41–42
bottom line 17, 68
brain energy 39, 58, 62, 63–64, 72, 143, 174, 205
Branson, Sir Richard 65, 129, 130
breaks, work 65, 66–67, 72, 172
Bregman, Rutger 16
BrewDog 156–57
Bridge Partnership 203
British Airways 61
British Medical Association 97
brutal openness 133–34
burnout 56, 57–63, 70, 171
Business Model You 170
Business Roundtable 86, 87, 88, 206
bystander effect 184

call centres (call handling) 4, 35
Calment, Jeanne 79
cancer survival rates 5, 77–78
capitalist models 3, 16, 91, 171
Capra, Fritjof 105–06
car industry 14, 192
 see also Tesla

career structures 13, 48, 79, 80, 169
  see also freelancing; gig working; portfolio careers
centralization 183–84
CEOs 70, 137, 154, 157, 195–96, 207
Chakras 95, 96, 109–20, 205
change 101, 144, 190
Chapman, Bob 142
charity sector 40
childhood 80
China 78
Chinese body clock 107
Chouinard, Yvon 142
Cicerone training 156
CIPD 27, 56–57, 82, 118, 139, 190
clean energy 17–18, 91
Climate Change strikes 14
climate emergency 39, 69, 90, 171, 207
cloud technology 191–92
Cluetrain Manifesto 30
coaching 16, 42, 96, 102, 103, 117
cognitive work 97–98
collaboration 17, 137, 157, 182, 184, 193, 205, 206
colleague letters of understanding 178
collective unconscious 104–05
Columbia University 98
comfort breaks 173
communication 113–14
computers 12, 61
conditioned mindset 24–25
conflation 140, 141
Connecting HR 31
connectivity 17–18, 59, 98
consciousness model 120–21
consumerism 57, 91, 100
Cooke, Sam 44
corporate social responsibility (CSR) 17, 171
creativity 32, 35, 46–47, 68, 112, 143, 158, 180
crime analysis 40
criminal rehabilitation 15
crown Chakra 114
Csikszentmihalyi, Professor Mihaly 178–79
cult 130
cult workplaces 128–34, 146
culture 137, 161
  long-hours 3–4, 57, 58, 66, 119
current organization mapping 195, 197, 204
customers 86, 153, 171
Cyberclick 153–54

de Grey, Aubrey 79
deal, the 177–78
decentralization 15, 17, 152, 158
decision making 30, 35, 145, 152, 183, 202, 203
deep work 67, 72, 179–80, 181
defined phenomena 40
deliberately developmental organizations (DDOs) 144–45
Descartes 168
design 46–47
development programmes 161
digital Taylorism 82, 134
digitalization (digital signage) 17–18, 144
dirty energy 99, 119
discovery 184
disengagement 5, 6, 18, 25, 36, 48–49
  see also engagement
dog years 156
doughnut economics theory 17, 88–89
Douglas, Michael 26
Dozier, Lamont 45
drains 185
dress codes 143

Earth Overshoot Day 89
Eastern mysticism 95, 99–100, 105–06, 120, 121–22
ecological environment 1, 3, 17, 89, 207
  see also environmental impact; nature; regenerative economic model
economic models 1, 3, 14, 17, 88–90, 91–92
economic performance 49–51
Edelman Trust Barometer 69–70
Edge, The 183–85, 186
Edmondson, Professor Amy 68, 70
education 12–13, 17, 80, 159–60
ego construct 175
80/20 rule 39–54
Eitel, Maria 142
electrification 14
electro-magnetic impulses 116
electrophotonic imaging device (EPI) 115, 116–21
'Emergent Cyclic Levels of Existence Theory' (Graves) 22
emotional quotient 167
emotional tagging 62
empiricism 43
employee experience 35, 139, 163
employee perks (benefits) 59, 96, 99, 156–57, 160, 161
  see also pension funds; sabbaticals

employee value proposition 177–78
employees 70, 82, 86, 160, 161, 177–78
  see also burnout; disengagement;
    employee experience; employee
    perks (benefits); empowerment;
    engagement; temporary staff
employer brand 133, 138, 140
employer-employee contract (promise) 70,
  177–78
employers of choice 139
empowerment 30, 31, 70, 152–53, 155, 158,
  196
energy, five layers of 102, 122
energy depletion 58–63, 64, 66, 71
energy drains 72, 133, 172, *173*, 185
'Energy Field, Chakras and neuroscience
  experiment' (Torp) 115–21
energy management 66–67, 100
energy mapping 173, 201–02, 204
energy regeneration 61, 171, 206
energy requirements 58
energy sources (planet) 14, 16, 17–18, 91
energy sustainability 59
engagement 39, 40–41, 53, 65, 84–85, 131,
  142, 177
  see also disengagement
enterprise 17
environmental impact 86, 90, 91, 162, 171,
  192, 207
  see also ecological environment; nature;
    regenerative economic model
EPI (electrophotonic imaging device) 115,
  116–21
epidemics 78
EQ 167
eudaimonia 20, 39, 84–87, 89, 90, 92,
  201–02, 207
European Working Time Directive 97
EVP 177–78
EX (employee experience) 35, 139, 163
exhaustion 58–63, 64, 206
existentialism 43
explorer stage 81
Exponential Organizations (Ismail, Malone
  & Van Geest) 135
externalizing 174
Extinction Rebellion 207
extroversion 104
eyebrow Chakra 114

Facebook 128, 129, 135
failures 61–62, 68
fatigue (tiredness) 61–62, 64

faux trendy 138–42, 146
fear 4, 22, 29, 62–63, 98, 112
feeling 104, 105
feminine principle 96
five layers of energy 102, 122
five stage model of working life 81–87
flat organizational structures 195–96
flexible scheduling (working) 160, 161, 203
flow 178–81, 184
'For the Love of Money' (O'Jays) 46
Four Tops, The 46
freedom 21, 31, 50, 108, 152, 154, 159
freelancing 5, 31–32, 48
Freud, Sigmund 175
FTSE 39, 85
fun 119, 140, 155–56, 161, 168
Fuqua, Harvey 44

GAFA 3
  see also Apple; Facebook; Google
    (Google Bus)
Gallup surveys 18, 40, 85
Gates, Bill 134
Gay, Marvin Senior 44
Gaye, Marvin Pentz Junior 44–47, 48, 53,
  176
GDP 39, 49–50, 52, 87
Gekko, Gordon 26
genetics 15
Gibran, Khalil 21
gig working 3, 82–83
Glassdoor 128–29, 138, 139, 141, 151, 156,
  157, 158, 163
goal setting 59, 153
Gonnering, Matthew 207
'good me' personification 175
Good Work 82, 118
Google (Google Bus) 3, 128, 129–30
Gordy, Berry Jr 44–45, 46
government 6, 15, 69, 194–96
graduate trainees 4–5
Graves, Professor Clare 22–23, 90,
  120, 205
Grey, Aubrey de 79
growth 88–89
growth mindsets 158

H&H Comms 2019 survey 1
hacks 184
Handy, Charles 81
Happy Ltd 99, 162
Harvard Business Review 26, 62
Harvard Medical School 61

healing 113, 171
    see also meditation; mindfulness
Health & Safety Executive 5, 85
Health and Well-being Champions 118
healthcare sector 1, 4, 5, 72, 77–78, 110, 193
    see also medical professionals; nursing profession
heart Chakra 113, 117
heuristics 32–36
hierarchy of needs 26, 105
hiring 139, 160
    see also recruitment
history of work 25–26
Holland, Brian 45
Holland, Eddie 45
Hoover, Martha 142
HR (Human Resources) 27, 36, 56, 57, 86, 100, 115, 116, 120, 191
human capital 15–16
human energy crisis 59
human energy profile 115
human evolution 21–23
humility 108, 153
Hyperloop 14

IBM 158
Iceland 50–51, 52–53, 120
ideas schemes 161
Ideas Worth Spreading (TED) 139
'If There's a Hell Below' (Mayfield) 46
ikigai 168–70, 176
illness 57, 60, 66, 71, 85, 100
Impact 142
inclusion (inclusivity) 13, 31, 50, 86, 139, 154, 157–58, 177, 192, 206
independent producers 81, 82
indoctrination 133
ING Bank 143
Ingham, Jon 31
injuries 85, 117
innovation 50, 135, 144, 157–58, 162, 184–85, 195
inside (inner) world 101, 174
intelligence quotient (IQ) 167
interests 42–43
Interface 162
internalizing 174
Internet of Things 13
introspective energy 174–75
introversion 104
intuition 104, 105, 106, 107, 189

Jaguar 14
job design (work design) 2–4, 5–7, 12, 21–32
jobless class 98
Jobs, Steve 95, 130, 134
Jones, Gareth 31
Jung, Carl Gustav 104–05, 114
juvenescence 81

Kantian philosophy 108
karoshi 3
Kelleher, Herb 142
Kelly, Kevin 18
Kets de Vries, Manfried 130–31, 134
Keynesian model 87
Kim, Professor Stuart 79
King, Dr Martin Luther Junior 7, 45
Kipchoge, Eliud 119
knowing 46–47, 48
knowledge workers 2, 32, 67

leadership 57, 70, 85–86, 130, 142, 158, 161, 193, 203, 204
lean production 26, 35, 67, 138
learning 13, 59, 153, 159, 160, 184
Learning and Development 27–28
learning organization 159
legislation 61, 67, 82, 97
leisure 64–65, 154
life expectancy 15, 77–79, 98
life skills 13
LinkedIn 138
'Living for the City' (Wonder) 46
living museums 142–46
local communities 15, 70, 86, 161
Lombardi, Vince 43
long-hours culture 3–4, 57, 58, 66, 119
love 113, 119, *131*

machines 6, 12, 16, 17, 18, 61, 117, 118, 120
Malcolm X 45
management 34–35, 57, 160–61
manipura 112–13
manual work 2, 97–98
masculine principle 96–97
Maslow, Abraham 26, 39, 48, 105, 114
Matt Black Systems 162
Maverick (Semler) 28–29
Mayfield, Curtis 46
mechanics 32–33
media 69
medical professionals 13, 97
meditation 61, 95, 96, 171, *173*, 174–75

Menlo Innovations 182
mental energy (health) 5, 56–57, 72, 95–96, 167
mentoring 45
merchants 2
mindfulness 109–11, 171, 174
mindsets 24–25, 158
Mindvalley 159–60
minimum viable practice (MVP) 186
mission 168–70
mood hoovers 185
Moody's 78
Moonglows, The 44
Morning Star 30–31, 178
Motortown Revue 45
Motown Records 46
muladhara 111–12
Musk, Elon 130, 134, 184

Nan Huai-Chin 5
nature 101–02, 140
neuroendocrine system 103
New Economics Foundation 99
New Zealand 49–50
 see also Ardern, Jacinda
Newport, Cal 67, 179
NGOs (not-for-profit organizations) 69
NHS 26, 109–10
Nike Foundation 142
nirvana 23, 39
NQ (eNergy Quotient) 167, 168–86
nursing profession 64
nutrition 171

OECD (Organization for Economic Co-operation and Development) 3
offices 2, 157
O'Jays, The 46
'old age' point 79
open value organizations 157–58
openness 68, 72, 108, 112, 133–34, 154, 157–58
organization design (OD) 28–29, 36–37, 84, 87, 91, 100, 189–208
organization development 26–28, 190–91
organization mapping 194–204
organization modelling 200–01, 204
organization restructures 29–30, 37, 101, 191
organization structure 3, 195–96, 202–03, 204
outside (outer) world 101, 104
over-attachment 128, 130, 133
over-glamourizing 141, 151

over-identification with brand 133
ownership 16, 30, 35, 36
oxytocin 62–63

Pareto, Vilfredo 40
Pareto's rule 39–54
passion 168–70
Patachou Foundation 142
Patagonia 16, 140, 142
pattern recognition 62
Pavlovian conditioning 24
pawternity leave 157
peak work 1, 3–6
pension funds 77, 78
people development (talent development) 20, 45, 47, 53, 81, 136, 139, 144–45, 160
performance
 economic 49–51
 employee 117, 190
performance enhancers 119
personal growth-focused organizations 159–61
personal robotic concierges 12
philanthropy 16–17, 19, 88, 134, 161
physical activity 98, 103, 143
physical body 102
physics 105–06
Pixar 68
planning 138
political environment 1, 6, 12
Pomodoro technique 66–67
portfolio careers 13, 81–83
post-materialism 100–01
power 112–13
presence *see* awareness
presenteeism 56, 66, 72
process of individualization 105
process tsars 144
processes 144
Product Story (Agile) 198
production costs 14, 16, 28
productivity (tools) 3, 5, 26, 41, 47–48, 49, 180
professional services sector 3, 65
professions 168–70
profits 28, 49, 60, 88, 160, 206
promotions 145
protopia 18
prototypes 34
psychological detachment 65–66, 72
psychological energy 63–66
psychological safety 67–71, 72, 177
'Psychological Types' (Jung) 104

psychology 22–23
PTHR business model 199–200
purpose 176–77
purpose washing 140, 141, 176

Qi 106–07
QiGong 95, 121, 205
quality standards 203

R&B (rhythm & blues) 45
radiators 185
Raichle, Dr. Marcus 64
rationalism 43, 105, 106
Raworth, Kate 17, 88–89
re-contracting exercises 178
realignment 19, 20
recalibration 19, 20, 49, 178
recessions 59
recruitment 6, 132, 136–37, 139, 177, 199
 see also hiring
Red Hat 157–58
#RedHatOpenStudio 158
reflective journals (tools) 172, 177–78
regenerative economic model 14, 17, 88–90, 91–92
regressive adaptation 22
REI 162–63
reinvention 19, 20, 160
rejuvenation therapies 79
relationships 59, 185
remote working (telecommuting) 158, 161, 193
repetition 4, 32, 35, 60, 97–98, 181
representativeness 33
resources 161
respect 86, 131, 153, 175
restructuring 29–30, 37, 101, 191
retirement 77, 79, 80
rewarding organizations 154–57, 161
rhythm & blues (R&B) 45
Ringelmann, Professor Max 145
Robinson, Smokey 45
robots (robotic process automation) 6, 12–13, 15, 36, 55, 97
role expansion 137, 138
root Chakra 111–12
RSA 82
Rushkoff, Douglas 129

S&P 39, 85
sabbaticals 84, 156
sacral Chakra 112

safety 67–71
sages 2
sahasrara 114
Sanskrit 103, 111, 112, 113, 114
scaling up 135–38, 146
scare-ups 134–38
second jobs 83
sedentary living 98–99
self-actualization 39, 48, 105, 114, 159
self-care 167–88
self-employment 82, 83
self-managed organizations 30–31, 152–54, 162
self-motivation 19
self-system (self-dynamism) 175–76
senolytic therapy 79
sensing 104, 121
serfdom (serfs) 2, 3, 122
service sector 59
seven levels of national consciousness 51
sexuality 112
shallow work 67, 72, 180
shareholders 68, 85, 87, 88, 138, 171
Silicon Valley 24, 65, 129
Singularity University 135
skills 13, 192–93
Skoda 14
slash economy *see* gig economy
sleep 61, 95, 103, 141, 172
sleep deprivation 61
sleep pods 61, 141
smart devices 12, 135
smartphones 12, 121, 135
social loafing 145
social media 30, 127–28, 132, 138–39, 159
 see also Facebook; Twitter; WhatsApp
socialization 30, 98, 154
society 14–15, 57, 70, 80, 85, 89, 205
solar Chakra 112–13
soldiers 2
SomeOne 155–56
#SomeSummerParty 19, 155
soulfulness 107–08
Sounds of Young America 45
sources 170–73, 176
Southwest Airlines 142
spiral dynamics 90
spirituality 107–09, 114, 167–86
stacks 193, 199–200, 202
staff *see* employees
stakeholders 86, 87, 192, 203
 see also employees; shareholders
start-ups 5, 61, 128, 135, 138

stimulation 2 0, 35, 42, 140, 143, 155, 168, 181
straplines 139
strategy 138, *199*
stress 5, 56–57, 62–63, 171
    see also burnout
super-aged countries 78
supermarkets 151–52, 160–61, 181
suppliers 86, 192, 195, 200
surveys 1, 4, 5, 40, 69, 85, 142, 153, 160–61
sustainable energy 59, 170–73
swadisthana 112

taijitu 96–97
take back your time movement 180
talent development (people development) 20, 45, 47, 53, 81, 136, 139, 144–45, 160
Tamla Motown 44
Tao 96–97, 120
Tao of Physics (Capra) 105–06
taxation 16, 17
Taylor, F W (Taylorism) 2, 26, 32, 60–61, 71, 82, 134, 163, 181
Taylor, Matthew 82
teams 28, 30, 33–34, 159, 178, 193, 195, 201, 202–03
technology 26, 80, 191–92
    see also artificial intelligence (AI); automation; bioengineering; biotechnology; blockchain; cloud technology; computers; digitalization (digital signage); electrification; Internet of Things; robots (robotic automation process); smart devices; smartphones; tracking devices
technology sector 65
telecommunications sector 4
telecommuting (remote working) 158, 161, 193
temporary staff 82
Terrell, Tammi 45
Tesla 14, 130, 135, 184
thinking (thought) 104, 105
Three Mile Island disaster 61
three-stage model 80
3E model 17
throat Chakra 113–14
Thurman, Howard 19
timeboxing 181–83
Times Best Companies to Work For 163
tiredness (fatigue) 61–62, 64

titans of technology 3
    see also Apple; Facebook; Google (Google Bus)
'to be' organizational structure 198–200, 204
Top Employers Institute 163
Torp, Dr Andronicus 115–21
total concentration 179
toxic working conditions 127–49
Toyota 14
tracking devices 134
training 59, 70, 86, 117, 118, 156, 161
transcendence 100, 108, 114, 168
triple bottom line 17
'trivial many' 41
trust 69–70, 72, 111–12
tuition assistance 161
Twitter 130, 158

Uber 82, 135
Unconferences 31
unconscious mind 104–05
Unicorn fund 156
unicorn start-ups 128
United Nations 39, 77
United States (US) 32, 45, 61, 78, 79, 85, 97
    see also Business Roundtable
Universal Basic Income 15

vacation (annual leave) 65–66, 153
value creation 89, 158, 203
value propositions 138, 177
values 50–53, 133, 137, 139–40, 154, 205
vampires 185
variety 181–83
Vedas 103
Vedic wisdom 111
vibrations 103, 108, 115–16
Virgin Group 65, 128–29
vishuddi 113–14
vital few 41

Wall Street 26
War for Talent (McKinsey) 139
warehousing 2, 4, 82, 98
Wegmans 160–61
well-being 49–50, 56, 87, 96, 117–19, 122, 162–63
Wells, Mary 45
Western science 105–06
Weston, Kim 45
WeWork 132
'What's Going On' (Gaye) 46

WhatsApp 135, 138
Whitehurst, Jim 157, 158
Whitfield, Norman 45
'who are we' 43–47, 48, 103
Williams, Professor Chris 109
wisdom 112–13
woke behaviour 100
Wonder, Stevie 46
work 18–19
work breaks 65, 66–67, 72, 172
work design (job design) 2–4, 5–7, 12, 21–32
work improvement 117
work-life balance (balanced life) 97–102, 119, 143, 174, 205
work stacks 193, 199–200, 202
working conditions (atmosphere) 4, 24, 67, 85, 118–19, 122, 127–49, 172
working hours (weeks) 4–5, 13–14, 98, 99, 153, 160, 193

working life 77, 78, 80
World Economic Forum 16, 32, 87
World Health Organization (WHO) 57, 58, 70
world wide web 17, 30, 129
WorldBlu 31, 50, 154, 159
World's Best Employers (Forbes) 158
writing on the wall technique 195–204

yin yang 96–97
yoga 95, 96, 103, 121
young employees 160
'You're All I Need To Get By' (Gaye & Terrell) 45
YouTube 143

Zen 95
zero-hours contracts 82
Zuckerberg, Mark 130, 134